Social Psychology
and
Political Behavior

Merrill Political Science Series

Under the General Editorship of

John C. Wahlke

Department of Political Science

State University of New York at Stony Brook

Edited by

Gilbert Abcarian

and

John W. Soule

Florida State University

Social Psychology
and
Political Behavior:
Problems and Prospects

Charles E. Merrill Publishing Company
A Bell & Howell Company
Columbus, Ohio

ISBN: 0-675-09261-2

Library of Congress Catalog Card Number: 79-138967

1 2 3 4 5 6 7 8 9 10 — 76 75 74 73 72 71

Printed in the United States of America

Preface

THE CONTRIBUTORS TO THIS VOLUME, ALL DISTINGUISHED SCHOLARS IN their respective fields, appeared on the Florida State University campus during the 1968-69 academic year to participate in the Department of Government's lecture series on "Social Psychology and Political Behavior." We express our sincere appreciation to each lecturer for contributing to a stimulating and well-received program.

Contemporary efforts to develop a viable science of political behavior center on research models that stress the importance of establishing linkages between social-psychological variables and political outcomes. The lecture series provided an opportunity for assessment of the possibilities and limitations of such linkages by subjecting several salient variables (attitudes, values, socialization and communications) to scholarly exploration. The general topic hence served as an umbrella under which a group of scholars assessed, by reference to their recent research and reflection, the specific ways in which society, culture and personality constitute indispensable perspectives through which understanding of collective patterns of political behavior may be advanced.

We are grateful to Professor John Wahlke for his valuable editorial advice in the preparation of the manuscript. Special thanks are due our faculty and student colleagues for their support and intellectual nourishment of the lecture series. In the end, the typing and technical labors of Carol Fitzpatrick, Frances Jones, Agnes Raker, and Lora Abcarian meant a great deal to us.

G. A.

J. W. S.

v

Contents

POLITICAL THERAPEUTICS

John W. Soule

Gilbert Abcarian

Political Attitudes, Socialization, Communication, and Therapeutics: Prospects and Perspectives

Professors Abcarian and Soule are on the faculty of the Department of Government of Florida State University.

CURIOSITY ABOUT FIELDS OF MAJOR INTEREST EXPRESSED BY YOUNGER political scientists recently led Heinz Eulau (1969) to some interesting data in the American Political Science Association's *Biographical Directory*.

Dividing APSA members into three age cohorts, Eulau learned that such areas of political science as personnel administration, administrative law, and regulation of business are decidedly in a state of decline. For the group born since 1930 the "swinging field" is political psychology, closely followed by political socialization. Indeed, 87% of those declaring political psychology as first-choice field of specialization were born in 1930 and later (the comparable figure for political socialization is 84%). Very roughly speaking, this group of professionals expresses its preference for cognitive data drawn from analysis of the individual as the focal point in a social psychological setting. Such data were scorned as "soul stuff" by Arthur Bentley, a view now confined to a minority of political scientists suspicious of cognitive psychology.

Today, social psychology serves for many political scientists as a salient frame of reference. From it are drawn a large number of analytical models, concepts, methodologies, and research insights. Social psychology places primary emphasis on the formulation and testing of concepts that treat society as a system of interactions between persons and collective entities. It is notable that because social psychology has progressed without the development of any single paradigm, it is best understood in terms of levels or foci of research emphasis. In practice, two levels of research emphasis may be distinguished: first, social structure (institutions, ideology, class, status, mobility, etc.), and second, individual structure (attitudes, motivation, personality, learning, perception, values, etc.) (Sampson, 1965, p. 2).

Political scientists of the behavioral persuasion have drawn upon both levels in their research. More importantly, however, they have inclined to the view that every aspect of individual life should be explored for clues to the understanding of political behavior. The reduction of the individual into "political," "economic," and other roles has been largely rejected. With social psychologists, the behavioral political scientist tends to view the individual as the focus of inquiry and to treat interpersonal behavioral events as the basic units of analysis. Increasingly, such study takes place in field and laboratory research settings. There has developed a heavy concentration of work devoted to probing the interaction between stimuli and personal values in a wide variety of behavior situations.

The contributions to this volume lean heavily on psychological variables and are characterized by diverse approaches. Consistent with the original plan of the Florida State University lecture series, four

1

subject areas are explored: political attitudes, communication, socialization, and therapeutics. As will readily be recognized, each area is very much on the cutting edge of contemporary American political science. A brief discussion of each area follows in order to provide a larger framework within which the eight studies may be critically assessed.

I. Political Attitudes

As students from many academic disciplines search the literature for definitions of the term "attitude," it becomes apparent that there is little agreement on its meaning. Other terms are frequently employed, such as belief, value, predisposition, or cognition. But these render the original concept even more ambiguous. The problem of clarification is also complicated by recent attempts to distinguish specific attitudes on the basis of multidimensional scaling techniques, factor analysis, and latent structure analysis. These methods have been utilized despite the fact that scholars do not yet know how to *count* the number of attitudes involved in a single analysis or hypothesized to determine a particular behavior. For present purposes we employ the definition of attitude as a relatively enduring organization of beliefs around an object predisposing one to respond in some preferential manner (Rokeach, 1968, p. 112).

Political scientists have, of course, heartily welcomed the concept of attitude in their own research in order to predict political behavior. Most political scientists have been reluctant to move into rigorous experimental research designs because they fail to deal with "real" behavior and hence seem to preclude the study of most ongoing political activity. Political learning, political institutions, and politicians themselves are topics shrouded in subtlety and complexity. Experimental laboratory behavior is so remote from actual political activity as to invalidate most inferences beyond the immediate situation. As a consequence, political scientists depend heavily upon survey research in relatively uncontrolled field or real-life situations. Attitude, or similar cognitive concept, understandably becomes indispensable to the establishment of an explanatory link between subjects' responses to various survey instruments and some antecedent or subsequent behavior. Most political scientists are interested in substantive aspects of politics and are not satisfied to think purely in stimulus-response terms; when observing correlations between responses on survey instruments and political behaviors, they are quick to infer reasons for such correlations and, customarily, to explain them in cognitive terms. Most survey designs reflect the assumption that responses to interviews or questionnaires are indicative of something the respondent carries around inside his head that will predispose him to behave similarly in other situations. Even when correlations between verbal behavior (attitudes) and some other behavior are low, as they frequently are, this assumption is seldom questioned. The normal recourse is to remain a loyal cognitive theorist and to hypothesize that the behavior is determined by other attitudes untapped by the survey instrument.

Some cognitively-oriented researchers seek to escape the definitional problems involved in cognitive concepts by resorting to an analogy frequently used by social scientists. They argue that these concepts are just as scientific as those in the physical sciences, such as genes and electrons. Like attitudes, electrons cannot be observed directly; it is only through a process that *infers* certain effects that their existence can be posited. Several flaws mar this comparison, however. Too facile and oversimplified, it consequently leads researchers away from areas where basic work is needed. With respect to precision, the way in which physical scientists can measure the effects of electrons and the way in which social scientists measure the effects of attitudes represents a quantum difference, one which puts the latter in an extremely poor position to draw inferences from data.

The qualities one may wish to impute to attitudes through definitions are concerned not only with number or positive and negative effect, but also with complex social content, the degree of effect, the structure in relation to hundreds of other attitudes, the functions attitudes serve for individual personalities, and the behavioral consequences of the attitudes.

Now, the above is certainly not intended to condemn the cognitive orientation of contemporary political science research. An alternative approach, the strict stimulus-response paradigm in which no cognitive states are assumed, is hardly suitable. It is clear that for the near future, political scientists will and should be heavily involved in cognitive explanations of behavior. What is needed is awareness of the limits inherent in such explanations and the difficulties posed by the assumptions underlying them. What are the most important recent developments in cognitive theories which appear particularly relevant to the study of political attitudes?

Despite the proliferation of studies by scholars in many disciplines, the "attitude" concept remains highly ambiguous. Doob (1947) has argued that attitude has no systematic status as a scientific construct and therefore should be replaced with classical learning theory constructs such as afferent- and efferent-habit strength, drive, anticipatory, and implicit or mediating responses. Blumer (1955) urges abandonment of the concept owing in part to its lack of empirical reference beyond responses to the immediate operational stimuli presented to a respondent. Rokeach has recommended a shift of attention away from attitudes in favor of focusing more generally upon values and value structures (his paper in the present volume stresses the development of a reliable and valid instrument with which to measure individuals' value hierarchies).

Rokeach (1968) has probably done more than any other single scholar to distinguish conceptually beliefs, attitudes, and values. Beliefs and attitudes are held to have cognitive, affective, and behavioral components, although most researchers have been empirically unable to isolate and manipulate individual components (Harding, Kutner, Prozhansky, and Chein, 1954; Rosenberg, 1960). These components form the basis for much of the research done on balance, harmony, strain toward symmetry, dissonance and congruity (Fishbein, 1967, Part III). The common assumption in this research is that man strives to maintain consistency among cognitive, affective, and behavioral components within a single attitude or among two or more related attitudes. Research revolves around experimental efforts to induce imbalance or dissonance and to measure the ways individuals respond to continuing inconsistency.

The study of attitude components has been ignored by political scientists, probably owing to their inability to adapt precise survey instruments to field situations. The price for this neglect may be a high one. Correlations between attitude scale scores of respondents and some behavioral index (e.g., voting, roll-call behavior, group membership and political participation) may be depressed since only cognitive or affective components of attitudes are tapped despite central concern with making inferences about the behavioral components. If the three components were in perfect harmony, behavioral prediction would not require individual distinctions. Political scientists are discovering, however, that consistency does not obtain for many political attitudes. Research reported by Converse (1964) indicates a lack of constraint among the political beliefs of many citizens, suggesting the difficulty of predicting one political attitude from another.

A further and related difficulty with the correlational approach to the study of attitudes and political behavior is that researchers typically survey attitudes in a setting situationally and temporally distinct from the behavior they wish to predict. Rokeach (1968, Ch. 6) has argued cogently that attitudes are focused both on objects (i.e., the content of survey questions) and situations (i.e., the total configuration of stimuli present). These he has called A_o and A_s. The resulting behavior is treated as a function of the interaction between *both* types of attitudes. Rokeach as well as Osgood and Tannenbaum (1955) have urged that while social behavior is a function of two types of attitudes, it is essential to assess the relative importance of each to the other. This dual conception of attitudes is particularly important because observed attitude change may occur in either or both the A_s or A_o. Thus a Congressman's attitude may indicate unwavering opposition to the Viet Nam war (A_o), but his roll-call behavior at two points in time may lead to the inference that his attitude toward the war has changed. An equally valid inference would be that his attitudes toward each roll-call situation (A_s) are different.

Political scientists have been particularly sensitive to this issue in the area of race relations. There is a general notion that something systematic happens to the attitudes of Negroes when they are interviewed by blacks rather than whites. By and large, however, the problem of situational bias has been neglected. Political scientists do not know what systematic effects mailed questionnaires as opposed to personal interviews have upon responses. They do not know what effect student and non-student interviews have upon responses of politicians and have no idea what effect the interview environment has upon the subject's responses (Goffman, 1963). In short, there has been neglect of A_s and, as a consequence, inferences about relationships between attitudes (A_o) and other behaviors suffer from defective or unrecognized assumptions.

Only recently have political scientists built into their survey designs techniques for measuring independent but related attitudes that interact to produce a particular behavior. William Gamson has written in this volume on the importance of "trust" *and* "efficacy" for the prediction of riot behavior, civil rights activity, and voting. Intuitively, one might expect to find a linear relationship between trust in the political system and riot participation. Yet, only when this attitudinal variable is combined with efficacy does trust become important in predicting riot participation. The study of the interaction effects of cognitive variables should continue to enlarge our capacity for predicting political behavior.

II. Political Socialization

Study of children's acquisition of political attitudes has experienced meteoric popularity within the past few years. Several summaries of findings have been published (Dawson, 1966; Hyman, 1959; Dawson and Prewitt, 1969). Here, the purpose is to highlight some of the difficulties present in contemporary research.

At its narrowest, political socialization has been conceived as the inculcation of political information and values by instructional agents formally charged by society with this responsibility. A broader conception encompasses all learning relevant to political events, issues, and personalities whether formally or informally transmitted (Greenstein, 1965). For the most part, efforts have been directed at accounting for the acquisition of nominally political attitudes, e.g., attitudes toward the President, Supreme Court, mayors, police, political parties.

Although there has been no agreement on a definition by students of political socialization, Mitchell (1962) has summed up the process by asking: (a) Who (b) learns what (c) from whom (d) under what conditions (e) with what effects? Rather than recapitulate discussions of each of these points (Greenstein, 1965), it will be useful to comment on the concept of "learning."

Learning theories have a long history in psychology which has been ignored by most research on political learning. Studies of political socialization have emphasized political maturation or development among young people rather than learning as a dynamic process. Political scientists have concentrated their energies on describing the political attitudes of children and have shirked the more difficult task of explaining *how* these attitudes are acquired.

Undoubtedly, political scientists have made important strides in describing the content of individual's political attitudes. Greenstein (1960) has documented the existence of positive feelings toward the American Presidency among very young children. Easton and Hess (1962) have provided data on children's orientations toward government, regime, and political community. Almond and Verba's (1963) classification of the content of political attitudes is aimed at determining whether they are directed toward (1) specific roles and structures, (2) incumbents of roles, or (3) particular public policies, decisions, or enforcements of decisions. Jennings and Niemi (1968) have explored parent-child correlations in party identification, political cynicism, and attitudes toward salient social issues.

As stated earlier, however, political scientists have not been as diligent in investigating empirically the separate question of how such attitudes are learned. Almond and Verba suggest the importance of latent as contrasted with manifest learning. Jennings and Niemi refer to the "transmission" (or lack of transmission) of attitudes from parents to their children in observing correlations between attitudes from parents and students (twelfth graders). Hyman notes that "Foremost among agencies of socialization into politics is the family" (1959, p. 69). Hess and Torney conclude that "the public school is the most important and effective instrument of political socialization in the United States" (1965, p. 93). Assesment of how effective various socialization agents have been in inculcating political attitudes is ambiguous, to say the least. It is likely that this question will continue to generate conflicting answers until various types of political attitudes are distinguished and then measured in conjunction with established learning theory concepts. The popular idea of "agents" of socialization as used does not shed much light on the learning process. Measurement of the effectiveness of various agents will involve determination of the relative influence of each; since it is highly probable that for most individuals the agents of socialization reinforce each other, one cannot expect a single agent to influence the acquisition of all political attitudes. Furthermore, the influence of socialization should be expected to vary longitudinally, i.e., different agents will be influential at different points in the individual's life.

A second difficulty regarding agents of socialization involves the actual mechanisms which operate to form political attitudes. Granted that many children tend to reflect their parents' party identification (Jennings and Niemi, 1968; Greenstein, 1960; Hess and Easton, 1960), does this occur because they imitate or model adult behavior (Bandura and Walters, 1963), because specific reinforcements are meted out for approximations of preferred behavior, or both? If *political socialization* is regarded as identical to *political learning,* attention must be given to such learning theory principles as imitation, reinforcement, identification, and modeling with regard to each of the various agents of political socialization. Criticism of past socialization research for failure to explicate the concept of "learning" does not mean that critics are setting up a straw man. "Learning" appears frequently in the socialization literature (Froman, 1962, entitles his article, "Learning Political Attitudes"), but the concept has yet to be explicated in terms of existing learning theory principles.

In his study here, Hess makes the point that a careful conceptualization of political learning would aid in explaining change in political attitudes from generation to generation. He suggests that the learning of attitudes which do not support the existing system can occur via the same mechanisms as attitudes that do support the system. Earlier conceptions of socialization which focused on content rather than the learning process largely ignore the acquisition of attitudes whose intent is to change the system in constructive or violent ways.

Reflecting his interest in developing societies, Pye also addresses himself to the problem of attitude change. He comments on the obstacles faced by newer nations in developing viable political cultures and the problems they must confront in re-socializing their citizens. Efforts to explain current behavior by tracing it back to some analogous pattern, Pye argues, are not flexible enough to account for the dynamics of change. Thus, findings that many children reflect their parents' political values do not get at the reasons behind this sharing of values nor do they convincingly explain those cases where children reject parental values. Hopefully, a more direct focus on the transmission process will produce better explanations of changes in attitudes of citizens and changes in political systems themselves.

III. Political Communication

Political communication provides the context for a growing body of empirical research and theorizing. Defined in narrow terms, political communication refers to the activity of specialized institutions that disseminate information, ideas, and attitudes about the political system. A broader definition portrays political communication as the transmission of signs, signals, or symbols between persons or institutions (Pool, 1965). It is useful to identify certain points where communications research in psychology has converged with that in political science and to explore various factors inhibiting further convergence.

Utilizing the narrower definition of political communication, political scientists typically have focused on studies of psychological warfare or inter-state communications (Lasswell, 1938; Daugherty and Lerner, et al., 1958), political campaigns (Herring, 1940; Childs, 1965), letters to Congress, committee documents, and floor speeches (Schattschneider, 1935), intra-office memoranda and letters (Simon, 1961, Ch. 8), and mass media broadcasting (Klapper, 1960). More recently, however, the call has gone out to extend the study of political communications to environs other than those of specialized communications institutions (Pool, 1965; Berelson, Lazarsfeld and McPhee, 1959; Schramm, 1964). In this connection, Deutsch (1966) has provided a comprehensive review of the literature on political communication.

As viewed by social psychologists, the communication process refers to a fairly simple functional system. A communicator wishes to convey certain attitudes or information to someone else. The transmission is commonly achieved through a shared linguistic code whereby the communicator symbolizes that which he wishes to convey to others. The recipient decodes this message by transforming it into a set of inferences about the attitudes or information that the sender seeks to convey. The recipient's inferences are made on the basis of variables independent of the content of the message, as well as those deriving from the message itself.

Political scientists can accept this paradigm if the focus on individuals is complemented by analyses of institutions. The paradigm is deceptively simple. When it is explicated more fully, a number of factors relevant to political communication become evident. One may concentrate his efforts on deciphering Aesopian meanings from political messages (Strauss, 1958; 1963). Hidden or obscured meanings frequently become important when a political group simultaneously feels obligated to communicate and yet constrained to communicate less than frankly (Pool, 1965). In this connection, the content of information has been systematically scrutinized by various scholars to produce cross-national comparisons of political symbols (Pool and Lasswell, *et al.,* 1951).

Osgood's present contribution develops a somewhat different line of attack on the problem of studying messages. He and other semanticists have begun to document the effects that smaller units (words and sentences) in a message have upon the reception of the message as a whole. Words and sentences, as building blocks of messages, often provide independent cues to which the recipient responds. Osgood and his colleagues have concentrated their research on the semantics of Cold War messages. They have explored the static nature of words over time, a quality which does much to obscure or confine the meanings of these messages. Osgood observes that key words reappearing in Cold War messages cause people to think about new problems in ways characteristic of older, different problems. The same words are assigned to changing events and issues. These words convey affective and cognitive connotations that stimulate stereotyped thinking and oversimplified conceptions of complex situations.

Heavy emphasis on the content of political communications frequently underscores the lack of access of political scientists to communicators and recipients. Psychologists, on the other hand, have not been hampered in this respect. They have studied informal social communication in experimental settings from a variety of viewpoints. Carl Hovland and his associates (1964) have experienced some success, under laboratory conditions, in predicting circumstances under which messages do persuade. Individuals vary in their informational support and ego commitment to various attitude objects; the presentation of persuasive messages has been found to have systematic effects on the receiver's attitudes, depending on the above variables. Other studies have experimentally manipulated the recipient's immunization to persuasive messages (Manis, 1965).

Ithiel de Sola Pool (1965) has pointed out, however, that persuasion as such is only a small part of political communications. Most communications merely seek to modify the data base on which people act, given their particular attitudes and values. The inferential process in which the communication recipient engages becomes crucial to assessment of the success or failure of the communicator's intent and efforts. There is mounting evidence from experimental studies that communication is not uniformly successful. In his present study, Manis explores the effects of the recipient's attitudes on his decoding behavior, and the impact of contextual variables on the communication process. The various interpretations that recipients give to a common message are distorted in systematic, replicable ways. These can be characterized as *assimilation* or *contrast* effects. In the former case the message is distorted by the recipient in a direction consistent with the recipient's preferred stand, while in the case of contrast effects the message is displaced away from the recipient's preferred stand. Important contextual variables affecting this decoding process include the recipient's relationship with the communicators, and the visual stimuli that accompany the message. Manis has shown that these variables affect the communicator's behavior in important ways just as it may the recipient's. He has extrapolated his data into the political realm for the development of several intriguing hypotheses.

IV. Political Therapeutics

Introducing an essay by Dahl, Pool notes that the intense descriptivism of political scientists has resulted in a withdrawal from the task of evaluating political systems. This has become a source of regret to such writers as Dahl and Pye, whose concern for the normative dimensions of their work, says Pool, seems to evidence "a striking change of trend" (1967, p. 166). Leaving evaluation of this "trend" to others, we turn to brief consideration of one of its aspects, namely, the case for a linkage of normative and empirical concerns in political science (Golembiewski, 1969). It is precisely this linkage, or lack of it, that is troubling many students and a growing number of professional political scientists today. The recent demands that political scientists are experiencing from students and granting agencies for "relevance" appear to boil down essentially to a desire to make research bear more directly on the controversies of today. Viewed from this perspective, it is not a novelty to find two of the papers that follow addressing themselves to highly visible problems possessing strong normative overtones.

The classical tradition of normative theory was largely devoted to defining and actualizing the "best" political order. In a related and yet somewhat altered sense, a contemporary normative theorist is apt to seek those definitions of research relevance and methodology that are most appropriate to the goal of producing a humane political and social world. Classicists asked: what kind of knowledge will ensure the attainment of a universally valid political order? The modern normative political theorist tends to ask: which political systems are or are not the most likely to encourage the production and utilization of scientific knowledge essential to political freedom and individual welfare.

The papers by Bay and Rogow are "normative" in the sense that they posit an urgent need for sensitivity to empirical-valuational linkages among political and social scientists. Each author casts his normative concerns in the context of political therapeutics—literally, the application of scientific knowledge to the treatment and invigoration of presumably sick polities and sub-systems.

Why the need for a therapeutic dimension in American political science? Dahl (1967) has observed that the explosion of empirical data and measures on national political systems has created an urgent need for "a new breed of political scientist, equipped with new methods for vanquishing the rising tide of data on political systems" in order to "resume an ancient [normative] obligation for our craft" (p. 179). Political psychology has helped in assessing the consequences of individual political behavior for the functioning of political systems (Cantril, 1968; Eulau, 1968). That assessment includes normative concerns over ultimate goals and values as well as purely descriptive concerns with data, efficiency, function, or utility. Conversely, political psychology with its primary unit of analysis being the individual, is in a position to assess the consequences of government action for individuals.

The normative-therapeutic aspect of political psychology focuses, then, on such traditional questions as value hierarchies (Lane, 1962; Maslow, 1943, 1954), individual needs and wants (Bay, 1965), political priorities (Rothenberg, 1961), and the presence or absence of a sense of political community (Christensen, 1959; Fromm, 1941; Pranger, 1968).

Formal empirical studies are a case in point. While often remaining implicit in such studies and commentaries, as in the illustrative literature cited next, the normative-therapeutic aspect is much in evidence in a number of key concepts central to contemporary political psychology and sociology, such as: *political culture* (Almond and Verba, 1965; Almond and Powell, 1966); *participation* (Levinson, 1955; Millbrath, 1965), *trust* (Gamson, 1968), *personality* (Frenkel-Brunswik, 1952; Greenstein, 1967; Keniston, 1965; Rokeach, 1960), *conflict resolution* (Naess, 1958), *alienation* (Janda; Levin, 1960), *efficacy* (Prewitt, 1968), and *cynicism/apathy* (Agger, 1961; Campbell, 1962; Litt, 1963).

Two observations about these concepts are in order. First, they have been empirically operationalized. Second, they are drawn from, and have serious consequences for, normative-therapeutic concerns about the political arena. They hold promise, in short, for providing normative-empirical linkages. But why speak of the need for linkage at all? Bay and Rogow address themselves to this question.

In a previously published paper, Bay (1965) admonished political behavioralists to eschew "pseudopolitics" (the study of personal neuroses or selfish group interests) and embrace authentic politics (the satisfaction of basic human needs), defined as scientific preoccupation with problems of human welfare. He suggests a need to transcend ideological cliches about democracy, to move "toward research-based knowledge on what [aspects of] democratic institutions have what kinds of values for human development" (p. 49). In his present paper he elaborates this theme by combining an empirical with a normative approach in an endeavor to support the proposition that some political orientations are, in a meaningful sense, better than others.

Rogow (1968) has made his therapeutic concerns explicit in urging political scientists to draw upon psychiatry. This should be done, he says, in order to achieve a "merger of methods and insights" that will point the way toward the establishment of "a therapeutic community," one that makes it possible for the individual to develop the potential for "neurosis-free behavior." His specific prescriptions include careful attention by political scientists to free association interviews, the study of dreams and fantasies, and utilization of the "insight" literature of psychiatry for a better understanding of the antecedents of political behavior. His contribution to the present volume continues that interest by exploring some compelling reasons why a psychiatric approach to politics is urgently needed and suggesting how that approach might assist in generating hypotheses and research studies that will contribute to a productive relationship between empirical science and normative-therapeutic goals.

V. Summary

We have attempted to tie the basic theoretical and methodological problems confronting four basic research areas that link social psychology and political science. These areas are attitude theory and measurement, political socialization, political communication, and normative or policy research. Emphasis has fallen on the problems posed by recent research in each of the areas.

In the remainder of the book, eight scholars report on their recent research. The authors have been paired in such a way that two perspectives are provided for each subject area. Several of the authors have brought empirical data to bear on problems in their respective domains, while others write in a mood of critical reflection and normative exhortation.

References

Agger, Robert E., *et al.* "Political Cynicism: Measurement and Meaning," *Journal of Politics,* 23 (1961), 477-506.

Almond, G. and S. Verba. *The Civic Culture.* Boston: Little, Brown & Co., 1965.

Almond, G. and G. B. Powell. *Comparative Politics.* Boston: Little, Brown & Co., 1966.

Bandura, A. and R. H. Walters. *Social Learning and Personality Development.* New York: Holt, Rinehart & Winston, 1963.

Bay, Christian. "Politics and Pseudopolitics: A Critical Evaluation of Some Behavioral Literature," *American Political Science Review,* LIX (March, 1965), 39-51.

Berelson, B., P. F. Lazarsfeld, and W. N. McPhee. *Voting: A Study of Opinion Formation in a Presidential Campaign.* Chicago: University of Chicago Press, 1959.

Blumer, H. "Attitudes and the Social Act," *Social Problems,* 3 (1955), 59-64.

Brown, Roger W. *Social Psychology.* Glencoe: The Free Press, 1965.

Campbell, Angus. "The Passive Citizen," *Acta Sociologica,* 6 (1962), 9-21.

Cantril, Hadley. "Some Requirements For a Political Psychology," in M. B. Parsons, ed., *Perspectives in the Study of Politics.* Chicago: Rand McNally & Co., 1968, pp. 124-145.

Childs, H. L. *Public Opinion.* Princeton: D. Van Nostrand, 1965.

Christiansen, Bjørn. *Attitudes Toward Foreign Affairs as a Function of Personality.* Oslo: Oslo University Press, 1959.

Connolly, William E. *Political Science and Ideology.* New York: Atherton, 1967.

Converse, P. E. "The Nature of Belief Systems in Mass Publics," in D. Apter, ed., *Ideology and Discontent.* New York: Macmillan, 1964.

Dahl, Robert A. "The Evaluation of Political Systems," in I. S. Pool, ed., *Contemporary Political Science.* New York: McGraw-Hill, 1967, pp. 166-181.

Dahl, Robert A. *Modern Political Analysis.* Englewood Cliffs, N.J.: Prentice-Hall, 1964.

Daugherty, W. E., D. Lerner, *et al. A Psychological Warfare Casebook.* Baltimore: The Johns Hopkins Press, 1958.

Dawson, R. E. "Political Socialization," in J. A. Robinson, ed., *Political Science Annual 1966.* New York: Bobbs-Merrill, 1966.

Doob, L. W. "The Behavior of Attitudes," *Psychological Review,* 54 (1947), 135-156.

Easton, D. and R. D. Hess. "The Child's Political World," *Mid West Journal of Politics,* 1 (1962), 229-246.

Eulau, Heinz. "Political Behavior," *International Encyclopedia of the Social Sciences,* vol. 12 (1968).

Eulau, Heinz. "Quo Vadimus?" *Political Science,* II (Winter, 1969), 12-13.

Eysenck, H. J. *The Psychology of Politics.* New York: Humanities Press, 1963.

Fishbein, M. *Readings in Attitude Theory and Measurement.* New York: John Wiley and Sons, 1967.

Frenkel-Brunswik, Else. "Interaction of Psychological and Sociological Factors in Political Behavior," *American Political Science Review,* 46 (1952), 44-65.

Froman, L. A. "Learning Political Attitudes," *Western Political Quarterly,* XV (1962), 304-313.

Fromm, Erich, *Escape From Freedom.* New York: Rinehart, 1941.

Gamson, William A. *Power and Discontent.* Homewood, Illinois: Dorsey Press, 1968.

Goffman, E. *Behavior in Public Places.* New York: Free Press, 1963.

Golembiewski, R. T., W. A. Welch, and W. J. Crotty. *A Methodological Primer for Political Scientists*. Chicago: Rand McNally, 1969.

Greenstein, F. I. "The Benevolent Leader: Children's Image of Political Authority," *American Political Science Review,* LVI (1960), 934-945.

Greenstein, F. I. "Personality and Politics: Problems of Evidence, Inference, and Conceptualization," *American Behavioral Scientist,* (November-December, 1967), pp. 38-51.

Greenstein, F. I. "Political Socialization," in *International Encyclopedia of the Social Sciences*. New York: Macmillan and Free Press, 1965.

Harding, J., *et al.* "Prejudice and Ethnic Relations," in G. Lindsey, ed., *Handbook of Social Psychology*. Reading, Mass.: Addison-Wesley, 1954, pp. 1021-1061.

Heider, Fritz. *The Psychology of Interpersonal Relations*. New York: John Wiley and Sons, 1958.

Herring, P. *The Politics of Democracy*. New York: Norton Co., 1940.

Hess, R. D. and J. V. Torney. *The Development of Political Attitudes in Children*. Chicago: Aldine Press, 1967.

Hoffer, Eric. *The True Believer*. New York: New American Library. 1958.

Hovland, C. I., *et al. Communication and Persuasion: Psychological Studies of Opinion Change*. New Haven: Yale University Press, 1954.

Hyman H. *Political Socialization*. Glencoe: Free Press, 1959.

Janda, Kenneth. "A Comparative Study of Political Alienation and Voting Behavior in Three Suburban Communities," in *Studies in History and the Social Sciences: Studies in Honor of John A. Kinneman*. Normal: Illinois State University Press.

Jennings, M. K. and R. G. Niemi. "The Transmission of Political Values from Parent to Child," *American Political Science Review,* LXII (1968), 169-185.

Johnston, T. *Freud and Political Thought*. New York: Citadel Publishers, 1965.

Kariel, Henry S. "The Political Relevance of Behavioral and Existential Psychology," *American Political Science Review,* 61 (June, 1967).

Keniston, Kenneth. *The Uncommitted*. New York: Harcourt, Brace & World, 1965.

Lane, Robert E. *Political Ideology*. Glencoe: The Free Press, 1962.

Lasswell, H. D. *Propaganda Techniques in the World War*. New York: P. Smith, 1938.

Lasswell, H. D. "What Psychiatrists and Political Scientists Can Learn From One Another," *Psychiatry,* I (1938), 33-39.

Lerner, D. *Propaganda in War and Crisis: Materials for American Policy.* New York: S. W. Stewart, 1951.

Levin, Murray B. *The Alienated Voter.* New York: Holt, Rinehart & Winston, 1960.

Levinson, Daniel J. "The Relevance of Personality for Political Participation," *Public Opinion Quarterly,* 22 (1955), 3-10.

Litt, Edgar. "Political Cynicism and Political Futility," *Journal of Politics,* 25 (1963), 312-323.

Manis, Melvin. "Immunization, Delay, and the Interpretation of Persuasive Messages," *Journal of Personality and Social Psychology,* 1 (1965), 541-550.

Maslow, A. H. "A Theory of Human Motivation," *Psychological Review,* 50 (1943).

Maslow, A. H. *Motivation and Personality.* New York: Harper, 1954.

Millbrath, L. W. *Political Participation.* Chicago: Rand McNally, 1965.

Money-Kyrle, R. *Psychoanalysis and Politics.* Englewood Cliffs: Prentice-Hall, 1963.

Naess, Arne. "A Systematization of Gandhian Ethics of Conflict Resolution," *Journal of Conflict Resolution,* 2 (1958).

Osgood, C. E. and P. H. Tannenbaum. "The Principle of Congruity in the Prediction of Attitude Change," *Psychological Review,* (1955), pp. 42-55.

Pool, I. S., ed. *Contemporary Political Science.* New York: McGraw-Hill, 1967.

Pool, I., *et al. Symbols of Internationalism.* Stanford: Stanford University Press, 1951.

Pool, I. "Political Communications," *International Encyclopedia of the Social Sciences.* New York: Macmillan and Free Press, 1968.

Pranger, Robert J. *The Eclipse of Citizenship.* New York: Holt, Rinehart & Winston, 1968.

Prewitt, Kenneth. "Political Efficacy," *International Encyclopedia of the Social Sciences,* vol. 12. New York: Macmillan & Free Press, 1968.

Rieselbach, L. N. and C. I. Balch. *Psychology and Politics.* New York: Holt, Rinehart & Winston, 1969.

Roazen, Paul. *Freud: Political and Social Thought.* New York: Alfred A. Knopf, 1968.

Rogow, Arnold A. "Psychiatry, History, and Political Science: Notes on An Emergent Synthesis," in J. Marmor, ed., *Modern Psychoanalysis.* New York: Basic Books, 1968, pp. 663-691.

Rokeach, M. *Beliefs, Attitudes and Values.* San Francisco: Jossez-Bass, 1968.

Rokeach, M. *The Open and Closed Mind.* New York: Basic Books, 1960.

Rosenberg, M. J., *et al.,* eds. *Attitude Organization and Change.* New Haven: Yale University Press, 1960.

Rothenberg, Jerome. *The Measurement of Social Welfare.* Englewood Cliffs: Prentice-Hall, 1961.

Sampson E. E. *Approaches, Contexts, and Problems of Social Psychology.* Englewood Cliffs: Prentice-Hall, 1965.

Schattschneider, E. E. *Politics, Pressures, and the Tariff.* Englewood Cliffs: Prentice-Hall, 1935.

Schramm, W. *Mass Media and National Development: The Role of Mass Media in Developing Countries.* Stanford: Stanford University Press, 1964.

Strauss, L. *On Tyranny.* Glencoe: Free Press, 1963.

Strauss, L. *Thoughts on Machiavelli.* Glencoe: Free Press, 1958.

Verba, S. "Comparative Political Socialization," Paper prepared for the Sixtieth Meeting of the American Political Science Association, Chicago, 1963.

Political
Attitudes

Milton Rokeach

The Measurement of Values
and Value Systems

Professor Rokeach is on the faculty of the Department of Psychology at Michigan State University. Preparation of this paper as well as the research reported herein was supported by a grant from the National Science Foundation on organization and change in values, attitudes and behavior.

OVER THE PAST 50 YEARS EMPIRICALLY-ORIENTED SOCIAL SCIENTISTS have paid considerably more attention to the theory and measurement of attitudes than to the theory and measurement of values. This greater emphasis on attitudes has not, in my opinion, arisen out of any deep conviction that man's attitudes are more important determinants of social behavior than man's values. Rather, it has been forced upon us, or has evolved out of the more rapid development of methods for measuring attitudes, combined, perhaps, with a certain vagueness of understanding about the conceptual difference between values and attitudes and about the relation between values and attitudes. This over-emphasis on attitude, I have argued elsewhere (Rokeach 1968a, 1968b), is conceptually indefensible given the widely-accepted view that values, however difficult to define or to measure, play a more central and more dynamic role than attitudes within a person's cognitive-affective system.

It is difficult to conceive of a human problem that would not be better illuminated if relevant and reliable value data concerning it were available. Differences, for example, in culture, social class, occupation, sex, religion, or politics are all equally translatable into questions concerning differences in underlying values and value systems; differences, for example, in deviant versus non-deviant behavior, competitive versus cooperative behavior are also amenable to analysis in terms of value differences; similarly, studies of change as a result of maturation, education, or therapy are all reducible to questions concerning development and change in values and value systems.

In order to enable us to pose and to answer a wide variety of questions such as those just mentioned we have devoted considerable attention over the past few years to the development and standardization of a simple method for measuring values and value systems in the hope that it would have a wide variety of applications to problems in psychology and psychiatry, sociology and anthropology, political science and education. My main purpose in this paper is to describe our approach to the measurement of values and value systems, to report some of the statistical properties of our value scales, and to report a few illustrative substantive findings that would be especially relevant to students of political behavior. The reader is referred elsewhere (Rokeach, 1968a, 1968b, 1968-69) for discussions of the conceptual differences between values and attitudes, of the manner in which they are conceived to be organized with respect to one another, of the manner in which values and attitudes are conceived to determine behavior, and of the conditions under which change may be induced in values, attitudes, and behavior.

Our approach to the measurement of values was a phenomenological one. We assumed that every person who has undergone a process of socialization has learned a set of beliefs about *modes of behavior* and about *end-states of existence* that he considers to be personally and socially desirable. The former kind of values we call instrumental values, the latter, terminal values. We have also assumed that every person differs from every other person not so much in whether or not he possesses such values but rather in the way he arranges them into value systems, a hierarchy or rank-ordering of terminal or instrumental values along a continuum of perceived importance.

From a phenomenological standpoint, everything that a person does and all that he believes is capable of being justified, defended, explained, and rationalized in value terms, that is, justified in terms of modes of behavior and end-states of existence that are personally and socially worth striving for. Hence, a phenomenological approach commits us to elicit from a person the conceptions he has of his own values, conceptions he is willing or even eager to admit possessing, to others as well as to himself. Such admissions cannot, of course, be couched in socially undesirable terms (e.g., cowardice, irresponsibility, dishonesty) or in terms so positive as to give the impression of immodesty or boastfulness (e.g., brilliance, cleverness, charm).

The Value Scales

Table I shows two lists of 18 alphabetically-arranged instrumental and terminal values that we have ended up with after several years of research. Each value is presented to the respondent along with a brief definition in parentheses. The instructions to the respondent direct him to "arrange them in order of importance to YOU, as guiding principles in YOUR life." In committing ourselves to the ranking method of measuring values we have assumed that it is not the absolute presence or absence of a value that is crucial but rather the relative ordering of values with respect to one another. In Form E, one of two forms we are now using, the subject is presented with two mimeographed pages of values, the first containing the 18 terminal values and the second containing the 18 instrumental values. For each set of values, the subject is asked to rank them from 1 to 18, from most to least important. In Form D, the form we are now using most extensively, each value is printed on a gummed label and the subject is instructed to "Study the list carefully and pick out the value which is the most important for you. Peel it off and paste it in Box 1 on the left. Then pick out the value which is second most important for you. Peel it off and paste it in Box 2. Then do the same for each of the remaining values. The value which is least important goes in Box 18. Work slowly and think carefully. If you change your mind, feel free to change your answers. The labels peel off easily and can be moved from place to place."

Since all the terminal and instrumental values are socially desirable ones it is no wonder that the great majority of the subjects report that the ranking task is a very difficult one, a task they have little confidence in having completed in a reliable manner. The rank ordering imposed on the two sets of 18 values comes primarily from within the respondent and is not inherent in the structure of the stimulus material. The respondent has only or primarily his own internalized system of values to guide him in organizing each set of 18 values. In this sense, the two value scales are highly projective in nature, much like the Rorschach or the Thematic Apperception Test. At the same time the stimulus materials are far more structured than the ambiguous materials ordinarily employed in projective tests, yielding responses that are readily described in quantitative terms.

A few words are in order about how the particular values shown in Table 2 were selected. First of all, they evolved from earlier versions of value scales containing 12 terminal and 12 instrumental values. These sets of 12 were increased to 18 when it became evident that too many important values had been omitted. A ceiling of 18 was imposed because it was felt to be too burdensome for respondents to rank order more than 18.[1]

The list of 18 terminal values is considered to be a reasonably comprehensive list of such values. They are a distillation of a rather large list of values, several hundreds, obtained from various sources: a review of the literature, my own terminal values, those obtained from 25 or 30 graduate students in psychology, and those obtained by interviewing a representative sample of almost 100 adults in metropolitan Lansing. Many of these values were eliminated because they were judged to be more or less synonymous with one another (e.g., freedom and liberty, brotherhood of man and equality, salvation and unity with God,[2] peace of mind and inner harmony), others were eliminated because they overlapped (e.g., religion and salvation), yet others were eliminated because they were not general enough (e.g., spousehood is more specific than family security), and yet others were eliminated because they did not represent end-states of existence (e.g., wisdom is an end-state of existence but education is not).

A somewhat different procedure was employed in selecting the 18 instrumental values. Our point of departure was a list of 555 personality-trait words for which positive and negative evaluative ratings have been made available by Anderson (1968). This list was taken from a larger list of about 18,000 trait-names originally compiled by Allport and

Odbert (1936). Since we were interested only in values that were, generally speaking, positively evaluated, so that they would be suitable for self-descriptive purposes, we were immediately able to reduce Anderson's list to about 200 positively-evaluated trait-names. The 18 instrumental values were selected from this smaller list according to a number of criteria: by retaining only one value from a group of synonyms or near-synonyms (e.g., helpful, kind, kind-hearted, thoughtful, considerate, friendly, unselfish), by retaining values judged to be minimally intercorrelated,[3] by retaining values judged to be important across culture, status, and sex, by retaining values one would readily admit to without appearing to be immodest or boastful (e.g., thus eliminating such words as brilliant, clever, ingenious, and charming).

Value Measures

A variety of measures may be obtained with our rank ordering procedure. Some of these are parameters of value systems considered as a whole, while others are parameters of values taken one at a time.

1. *Value system stability*

We may obtain an index of value system stability or reliability by correlating the rank orders given by a respondent on one occasion with those he gives on a later occasion (Penner, Homant, and Rokeach, 1968). Table 2 shows the frequency distribution of such reliabilities for Forms D and E of the terminal and instrumental value scales. The subjects were all students in introductory psychology courses, mostly freshmen and sophomores, and the interval from test to retest was anywhere from three to seven weeks. It will be noted that the frequency distributions of reliabilities are highly skewed. Form D (gummed labels) reliabilities range from the −.30's to the high .90's for the terminal value systems and from the .10's to the high .90's for the instrumental value systems. The median reliabilities are from .78 to .80 for the terminal values and are from .70 to .72 for the instrumental values. For Form E, which employs the more traditional method of ranking (the subject writes in numbers from 1 to 18 in the blanks provided), the reliabilities range from about .10 to the high .90's for the terminal values and from about −.20 to the high .90's for the instrumental values. The Form E median reliabilities are somewhat lower than those for Form D, .74 and .65, respectively, for the terminal and instrumental values.

Despite the fact that respondents generally consider the rank ordering task to be a very difficult one, it is clear from Table 1 that

TABLE 1

RELIABILITIES OF INDIVIDUAL TERMINAL AND
INSTRUMENTAL VALUES, FORM D

(N=250)

Terminal Value	r	Instrumental Value	r
A comfortable life (a prosperous life)	.70	Ambitious (hard-working, aspiring)	.70
An exciting life (a stimulating, active life)	.73	Broadminded (open-minded)	.57
A sense of accomplishment (lasting contribution)	.51	Capable (competent, effective)	.51
A world at peace (free of war and conflict)	.67	Cheerful (lighthearted, joyful)	.65
A world of beauty (beauty of nature and the arts)	.66	Clean (neat, tidy)	.66
Equality (brotherhood, equal opportunity for all)	.71	Courageous (standing up for your beliefs)	.52
Family security (taking care of loved ones)	.64	Forgiving (willing to pardon others)	.62
Freedom (independence, free choice)	.61	Helpful (working for the welfare of others)	.66
Happiness (contentedness)	.62	Honest (sincere, truthful)	.62
Inner harmony (freedom from inner conflict)	.65	Imaginative (daring, creative)	.69
Mature love (sexual and spiritual intimacy)	.68	Independent (self-reliant, self-sufficient)	.60
National security (protection from attack)	.67	Intellectual (intelligent, reflective)	.67
Pleasure (an enjoyable, leisurely life)	.57	Logical (consistent, rational)	.57
Salvation (saved, eternal life)	.88	Loving (affectionate, tender)	.65
Self-respect (self-esteem)	.58	Obedient (dutiful, respectful)	.53
Social recognition (respect, admiration)	.65	Polite (courteous, well-mannered)	.53
True friendship (close companionship)	.59	Responsible (dependable, reliable)	.45
Wisdom (a mature understanding of life)	.60	Self-controlled (restrained, self-disciplined)	.52

the overall reliabilities are on the whole satisfactory for research purposes. Form D is consistently found to be more reliable than Form E for college students and I would anticipate (although data are not yet available on this point) that this difference in reliability will be even greater for respondents having lesser education. We also find consistently higher reliabilities for terminal as compared with instrumental values.

Individual differences in value system stability. The fact that individuals differ widely in value system stability led us to wonder about the correlates or determinants of such individual differences. We consistently find small, significant relationships in the .20's to .30's between stability of terminal value systems and stability of instrumental value systems. Moreover, we find that women have significantly (or near-significantly) more stable terminal and instrumental value systems than men. More stable terminal and instrumental value systems are also found in younger college students as compared with older college students, among those with a favorable attitude toward civil rights as compared with those having less favorable attitudes toward civil rights, and among those who are intellectually-oriented as compared with those who are socially-oriented.

Political party identification shows a significant relationship with terminal value system stability but not with instrumental value system stability. Those who identify themselves as conservative Democrats have the least stable terminal value systems and those reporting no political identification have the most stable systems.

We find quite a few variables to be significantly related to instrumental (but not terminal) value system stability. More stable instrumental value systems are found among honors students as compared with non-honor students, among those planning to go on for higher degrees as compared with those not planning to go on for a higher degree and among social science and communication majors as compared with home economics majors. We find that freshmen have the most stable instrumental value systems and that sophomores and juniors have the least stable systems, suggesting that a college experience leads to significant changes in value systems. More stable instrumental value systems are found among those who identify themselves as liberals rather than conservatives, and among those favoring China's admission into the United Nations as compared with those less favorable. Finally, we find that college students who aspire to extremely low or extremely high future incomes have significantly less stable instrumental value systems than those who aspire to moderate future incomes.

Hollen (1967) found no relationship between value system stability and dogmatism, or with independently-obtained ratings of commitment, importance, vagueness, difficulty, or uncertainty about one's value system. Other variables that have been found to be insignificantly related to stability of value systems, terminal or instrumental, are attitude toward public welfare, membership in fraternities or sororities, hours spent studying, having or not having aspirations to surpass parents' income, authoritarian versus equalitarian relationship with parents, attitude toward American presence in Viet Nam, frequency of church attendance, rural versus urban background, and religious preference.

We are at this stage of research not altogether clear about the fundamental determinants of individual differences in value system stability. All we are prepared to say at this moment is that sex, intelligence and liberalism seem to be clearly implicated as determinants. The problem of individual differences deserves continued attention.

2. *Value system change*

The correlation between the rank orders obtained on two separate occasions is useful not only as a measure of value stability but also of value system change—as a function of socialization, or therapy, or as a function of the experimental induction of change in target values (Rokeach, 1968a or 1968b). In this case, the smaller the correlation between the rank orderings obtained on test and retest the greater the change in value system.

3. *Value system similarity between two persons*

The correlation (rho) between the rank orderings obtained from any two persons is an index of similarity between their value systems. Beech (1966) employed such a measure in his study of the relationship between value system similarity and interpersonal attraction. Such a measure would be useful in studies of the acquaintance process (Newcomb, 1961), in studies of similarity in value systems between parents and children, spouses, peers, etc.

4. *Value system similarity in more than two persons*

The coefficient of concordance can be employed as an index of value system similarity or homogeneity in more than two persons. Thus, in a national area probability sample obtained through the National Opinion Research Center the terminal value system concordance coefficient obtained for Jews, Catholics, Protestants and for those professing no religion are .37, .28, .28, and .24, respectively, suggesting that Jews are the most homogeneous and that the non-religious are the least homogeneous in this respect. The concordance coefficients for the same four groups are much lower for instrumental value systems, .21, .16, .21, and .20, respectively, and apparently not substantially different from one another.

5. *Reliability of single values*

Our rank ordering method permits us to obtain reliability measures for each value separately as well as for value systems as a whole. Hollen

(1967) has reported on the reliabilities of individual values for Forms A and B of the value scales, which are uniformly good. Comparable results for Form D reliabilities (product-moment) are shown in Table 2.

TABLE 2

FREQUENCY DISTRIBUTIONS OF VALUE SYSTEM RELIABILITIES
OBTAINED FOR FORMS D AND E

Reliability	Terminal Value Scale		Instrumental Value Scale	
	Form D	Form E	Form D	Form E
.90- .99	21	11	15	5
.80- .89	84	54	46	26
.70- .79	77	45	73	49
.60- .69	29	35	43	31
.50- .59	23	27	32	28
.40- .49	8	9	20	20
.30- .39	5	3	16	10
.20- .29	—	2	4	7
.10- .19	—	3	1	6
.00- .09	2			2
−.10-−.01	—			4
−.20-−.11	—			1
−.30-−.21	—			
−.40-−.31	1			
N=	250	189	250	189

For the terminal values the reliabilities range from .51 for *a sense of accomplishment* to .88 for *salvation*. Three of the values have reliabilities in the .70's, ten have reliabilities in the .60's, and four in the .50's. The average reliability of the individual terminal values is around .65. The reliabilities of the individual instrumental values are generally a bit lower, averaging around .60. They range from .45 for *responsible* to .70 for *ambitious*. Nine of the reliabilities are in the .60's and seven are in the .50's. It is thus seen that the 36 terminal and instrumental value reliabilities are generally quite impressive, especially when we consider the fact that they are based on subject responses to one-item tests that are one-word or one-phrase long.

6. *Change in single values*

To round out our reliability studies, we have measured the extent to which the test-retest change in a given value is a function of its initial ranking. Figure 1 shows the results obtained for Form D, which is typical of the results we have obtained with the other versions of the value scales (Hollen, 1967). It is immediately obvious that terminal and instrumental values that are initially ranked high and low change the least from test to retest (three weeks later), and that those ranked in the middle change the most. The relationship is clearly U-shaped. It should also be noted that the terminal values are typically more stable than the instrumental values.

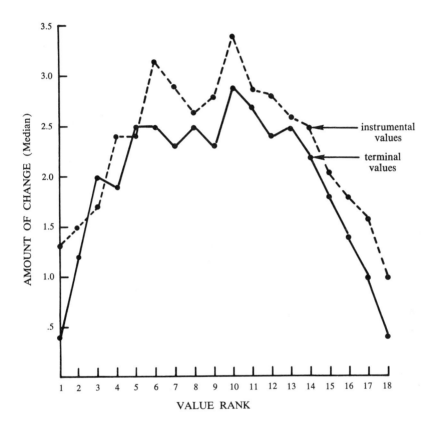

FIGURE 1

MEDIAN AMOUNT OF CHANGE FOR TERMINAL AND INSTRUMENTAL VALUES RANKED FIRST TO LAST (N-115)

The measurement of change in single values is also useful for a variety of other research purposes—in experimental studies of value change (Rokeach, 1968a or 1968b), in studies of value change as a function of development, education, therapy, etc.

Some Illustrative Findings
Concerning Values and Politics

We have collected a large body of data relating our value scales to demographic, attitudinal, and behavioral variables. To illustrate how we analyze our data I will present here some results collected during the presidential campaign of 1968 that were designed to determine whether a particular presidential candidate attracted supporters having a particular system of values, or, conversely, whether a particular voter had a system of values predisposing him to prefer one presidential candidate over others. We were also interested in ascertaining whether certain values were more predictive than others of candidate preference.

In late April, 1968, field interviewers of the National Opinion Research Center of the University of Chicago administered Form D of the Value Survey to an area probability sample of about 1400 Americans over 21. Many other kinds of data were obtained from the respondents, including responses to the following question: "As it stands now, which *one* of these possible candidates would you personally like to see elected president next November?" Their selections were limited to Lyndon Johnson, Robert Kennedy, Eugene McCarthy, Richard Nixon, Ronald Reagan, Nelson Rockefeller and George Wallace. At the time of testing Kennedy was still alive, Humphrey had not yet announced his candidacy, and while Johnson had already removed himself from the presidential race, it was too late to remove his name from the printed survey forms.

Tables 3 and 4 show the median rankings for the terminal and instrumental values and also the rank order of these medians (composite rank order) for the seven groups. Because of the non-parametric nature of the data, statistical significance of the differences was determined for each value separately by the median test (Siegel, 1956). Of the 18 terminal values 8 show significant differences among the seven groups beyond the .05 level; of the 18 instrumental values 6 show comparable levels of significance.

Foreign policy differences. Two terminal values seem to underlie differences on foreign policy. The ranking for *a world at peace* significantly differentiates Democrats on the one hand from Republican and Wallace supporters on the other ($p < .005$); Johnson, Kennedy and McCarthy supporters all rank *a world at peace* first on the average while Republican and Wallace supporters rank it second.

These differences in rankings are, however, rather subtle ones and do not throw a light on the bitter differences that had developed by the

TABLE 3

TERMINAL VALUE MEDIANS AND COMPOSITE RANK ORDERS FOR SUPPORTERS OF SEVEN PRESIDENTIAL CANDIDATES IN 1968

(N=1233)

N =	Kennedy 273 Med	Rnk	Johnson 221 Med	Rnk	McCarthy 149 Med	Rnk	Rockefeller 129 Med	Rnk	Nixon 291 Med	Rnk	Reagan 52 Med	Rnk	Wallace 118 Med	Rnk	Median Test X²=	P=
A comfortable life	8.1	7	8.5	9	10.6	11	10.5	12	9.5	11	11.1	13	7.0	5	31.96	.001
An exciting life	15.3	18	15.7	18	15.0	17	14.6	16	15.2	18	14.7	17	14.4	17	8.80	.185
A sense of accomp.	9.5	10	9.3	10	8.4	8	7.8	6	8.6	8	8.2	8	8.9	10	12.13	.059
A world at peace	3.4	1	2.7	1	3.3	1	4.1	2	3.7	2	3.8	2	3.6	2	14.67	.023
A world of beauty	14.2	16	13.6	15	13.2	15	12.6	14	13.5	15	13.0	15	14.0	15	14.11	.028
Equality	6.2	4	7.0	4	7.3	6	8.6	9	9.8	12	10.3	10	13.0	14	72.86	.001
Family security	4.0	2	3.8	2	3.9	2	4.0	1	3.6	1	3.3	1	3.4	1	4.08	.666
Freedom	5.5	3	5.3	3	5.1	3	5.4	3	6.4	3	4.8	3	5.8	3	12.10	.060
Happiness	7.6	5	7.3	5	8.0	7	8.4	8	7.7	6	7.3	5	8.3	8	5.83	.443
Inner harmony	10.9	13	10.9	13	10.0	10	10.1	11	10.4	13	9.5	9	11.3	13	7.90	.245
Mature love	13.1	14	13.2	14	11.9	14	12.7	15	12.0	14	10.5	12	10.6	12	17.06	.009
National security	9.9	12	8.4	8	11.1	13	9.0	10	8.9	10	10.3	11	9.3	11	6.75	.345
Pleasure	14.6	17	14.2	16	15.1	18	14.8	18	15.0	17	13.4	16	14.3	16	7.06	.315
Salvation	9.3	9	8.1	7	10.7	12	11.3	13	7.6	5	7.3	6	6.5	4	18.90	.004
Self-respect	7.7	6	7.8	6	7.2	5	7.7	5	7.9	7	6.5	4	8.1	6	3.49	.745
Social recognition	13.6	15	14.3	17	15.0	16	14.8	17	14.7	16	15.5	18	14.6	18	11.79	.067
True friendship	9.9	11	9.8	12	9.4	9	8.2	7	8.8	9	11.7	14	8.1	7	19.44	.003
Wisdom	8.8	8	9.6	11	6.9	4	7.2	4	7.2	4	7.8	7	8.5	9	25.80	.001

31

131232

TABLE 4
INSTRUMENTAL VALUE MEDIANS AND COMPOSITE RANK ORDERS FOR SUPPORTERS OF SEVEN PRESIDENTIAL CANDIDATES IN 1968
(N=1233)

N =	Kennedy 273 Med	Rnk	Johnson 221 Med	Rnk	McCarthy 149 Med	Rnk	Rockefeller 129 Med	Rnk	Nixon 291 Med	Rnk	Reagan 52 Med	Rnk	Wallace 118 Med	Rnk	Median X²=	Test P=
Ambitious	6.1	2	6.2	2	6.9	3	7.1	4	6.5	3	7.5	4	5.8	3	2.94	.816
Broadminded	7.6	6	7.5	6	6.6	2	6.8	3	7.8	6	10.0	13	7.7	6	5.14	.526
Capable	10.1	10	8.9	9	9.8	12	9.7	10	9.6	9	8.8	7	10.9	14	12.93	.044
Cheerful	8.9	9	10.1	11	9.7	11	9.9	12	10.2	12	10.2	14	9.8	11	1.89	.929
Clean	7.2	3	7.0	3	10.1	13	9.5	9	9.8	10	9.7	11	7.7	5	30.70	.001
Courageous	7.8	7	8.9	8	7.5	6	7.8	5	7.3	5	6.5	3	7.5	4	8.19	.224
Forgiving	7.3	4	7.3	5	6.9	4	8.0	6	6.9	4	8.5	5	5.7	2	7.29	.295
Helpful	8.0	8	8.2	7	7.7	7	8.1	7	8.5	7	9.6	10	9.3	10	7.98	.239
Honest	3.5	1	3.4	1	3.7	1	2.8	1	3.1	1	3.1	1	3.6	1	4.63	.592
Imaginative	15.4	18	15.7	18	14.5	17	14.7	18	15.7	18	14.8	18	15.8	18	10.18	.117
Independent	10.6	13	10.3	14	9.7	10	11.6	14	11.0	13	8.8	6	10.1	12	7.30	.294
Intellectual	13.0	16	13.6	16	11.7	14	12.5	15	12.7	15	13.8	16	13.7	16	8.38	.212
Logical	14.8	17	14.7	17	13.6	16	12.9	16	13.8	16	13.5	15	14.7	17	11.85	.065
Loving	10.5	12	10.2	13	9.6	9	9.8	11	8.6	8	9.5	9	8.6	9	7.35	.290
Obedient	12.2	15	12.9	15	14.9	18	14.4	17	14.2	17	14.0	17	12.8	15	30.61	.001
Polite	10.6	14	10.1	12	12.4	15	10.9	13	11.1	14	9.9	12	10.7	13	22.54	.001
Responsible	7.6	5	7.2	4	6.9	5	6.0	2	6.0	2	6.0	2	7.7	7	19.52	.003
Self-controlled	10.4	11	9.3	10	9.1	8	9.2	8	10.1	11	9.5	8	8.3	8	12.69	.048

spring of 1968 over the American presence in Viet Nam, particularly between Johnson supporters on the one hand and McCarthy and Kennedy supporters on the other. The key value that seems to help account for such differences is *national security*. Even though the overall median test turned out to be insignificant we found that Johnson supporters value *national security* more highly than did any of the other groups, ranking it eighth in importance. McCarthy supporters diverged most sharply from Johnson supporters in this respect, ranking *national security* thirteenth in importance. And close behind the McCarthy supporters were the Kennedy supporters who ranked it twelfth. The rankings by McCarthy supporters are significantly different from those obtained for the Johnson supporters (p $<$.05). And falling inbetween the Johnson and McCarthy-Kennedy rankings are those obtained for Rockefeller, Nixon, Reagan and Wallace supporters. These findings would suggest that support for Johnson's Viet Nam position came more from Republicans and Wallace supporters with similar concerns for *national security* than from those supporting other Democratic candidates.

Civil rights and economic security. The seven groups did not differ from one another in their value for *freedom*. All groups uniformly ranked it third in importance. But the seven groups diverged most sharply from one another in their ranking of *equality*. Kennedy, Johnson and McCarthy supporters ranked it among the top six values; Rockefeller, Nixon and Reagan supporters ranked it among the middle six; and Wallace supporters ranked it among the bottom six. Among the three Republican groups the Reagan supporters have the lowest median on *equality*, coming closest to the Wallace supporters in their low regard for it. Each of the Republican groups (as well as each of the Democratic groups) differ significantly from the Wallace group, but not from one another in their value for *equality*.

More than any of the other 36 values, the *equality* rankings order the seven groups most clearly along a liberalism-conservatism dimension. This difference with respect to *equality* contrasts sharply with the absence of differences among the seven groups on *freedom*. When considered together, these findings on *equality* and *freedom* can best be understood by relating them to a broader set of findings obtained from a content analysis of writings by Goldwater, Lenin, Hitler and socialist ideologists. A straightforward count of the values found in *Conscience of a Conservative* revealed that Goldwater mentioned *freedom* most frequently and *equality* least frequently among 17 terminal values. A similar count of Lenin's *Collected Works,* employing the same 17 terminal values, showed the opposite: *equality* was mentioned most frequently and *freedom* least frequently. For the socialists, *freedom* ranked first and *equality* second among the 17 values, and for Hitler's *Mein Kampf* content analysis revealed that *freedom* and *equality* were at the bottom of his list of values (Rokeach, 1968a or 1968b).

It would thus appear that partisan politics in the United States does not produce all the variations possible concerning the value placed on *freedom* and *equality*. Wallace supporters, at least those tested in April, 1968, looked most like Goldwater conservatives; McCarthy, Kennedy and Johnson supporters looked most like social democrats, humanists, or socialists. Supporters of Rockefeller, Nixon and Reagan were inbetween Wallace supporters on the one side and Democratic supporters on the other, having ranked *freedom* relatively high but having ranked *equality* in the middle of their scale of values. As would be expected, none of the seven political groups manifested fascist or communist patterns for *freedom* and *equality*.

Consider next the differential appeal that *a comfortable life* had for the seven groups. Now it is the liberal Kennedy supporters and the conservative Wallace supporters who valued *a comfortable life* most. These relatively high rankings are probably due to the fact that there were many poor minority group members within the Kennedy camp and many poor whites within the Wallace camp. This socio-economic interpretation is supported by an analysis of the relationship between rankings for *a comfortable life* and *income*, as shown in Table 5. The linear relationship between the two variables is obvious; those in the lowest income bracket, under $2,000, valued *a comfortable life* sixth on the average while those in the highest income bracket valued it fifteenth.

TABLE 5

MEDIAN RANKINGS AND COMPOSITE RANK ORDERS FOR A COMFORTABLE LIFE, CLEAN, AND OBEDIENT FOR GROUPS VARYING IN INCOME*

		A Comfortable Life		Clean		Obedient	
Income Level	N	Median Rank	Composite Rank Order	Median Rank	Composite Rank Order	Median Rank	Composite Rank Order
Under $2,000	139	7.2	6	6.4	2	12.0	15
2,000- 3,999	239	8.5	7	7.3	5	12.4	15
4,000- 5,999	217	8.4	7	8.0	7	13.3	15
6,000- 7,999	249	8.1	6	8.6	8	13.2	15
8,000- 9,999	178	10.0	11	9.3	10	14.2	17
10,000-14,999	208	11.0	13	10.4	12	14.3	17
15,000 or more	95	13.4	15	14.4	17	15.3	18

*The results shown are all significant beyond the .001 level by the Median Test (X^2=41.8, 72.4, and 27.1 for *a comfortable life, clean,* and *obedient,* respectively.

Religious differences. Table 3 shows that supporters of the seven presidential candidates also differed significantly in their value for *salvation.* Wallace, Reagan and Nixon supporters, all on the conservative side of the continuum, ranked it relatively high while Kennedy, McCarthy and Johnson supporters ranked it lower. But lowest of all were the Rockefeller supporters who, on the average, ranked *salvation* thirteenth. It would thus seem that the value for *salvation* produced the sharpest split within the three Republican camps, between the Rockefeller supporters on the one hand and the Nixon and Reagan supporters on the other. These findings suggest that Rockefeller's appeal among Republicans would have been considerably greater had he been able to project a more "reverent" image. That Rockefeller did not appeal more to those who valued *salvation* highly is possibly due to the fact that many Republicans had not altogether forgotten his divorce of several years ago.

Among the three Democratic groups, Johnson supporters valued *salvation* most and McCarthy supporters least highly. It would thus seem that it is the Rockefeller supporters among the Republicans and the McCarthy supporters among the Democrats who were the least religious-minded of the seven groups.

Other value differences. A number of other values, terminal and instrumental, were found to differentiate significantly among the seven groups. These include *a world of beauty, true friendship, wisdom, capable, clean, obedient, polite, responsible,* and *self-controlled.* To conserve space I will not discuss them all here. The interested reader can readily ascertain the nature and direction of these differences by inspecting Tables 3 and 4. While it would have been difficult to predict all these differences in advance they nevertheless seem to be consistent with what is generally known about the various groups of presidential supporters. We note, for example, that it is the generally young, middle class McCarthy supporters who ranked *clean, obedient* and *polite* lowest among the instrumental values, findings that can be attributed to social class (see Table 5) and age differences. Wallace supporters, who were most worried about racial integration and the law-and-order issue ranked *self-controlled* higher than did any of the other groups but, paradoxically, they also ranked *responsible* lower than did any of the remaining groups.

The two instrumental values that differentiated most reliably among the seven political groups were *clean* and *obedient.* Kennedy, Johnson and Wallace supporters ranked *clean* and *obedient* relatively highly, the Republicans ranked them lower, and the McCarthy supporters ranked them lowest in importance. To a large extent these findings would again seem to reflect social class differences among the seven groups, as shown in Table 5. *Clean* ranked second on the average for those in the lowest income bracket and seventeenth for those in the highest income bracket. *Obedient* shows significant differences that are similar in direction even though the differences are not as marked as those found for *clean*.

Some general observations on American value systems. Despite the differences discussed here, the seven American groups are on the whole remarkably alike in their systems of values. Sharper value differences would probably have been obtained had we compared French or Italian rather than American political groupings from extreme left to right. The major differences observed among the seven American groups seem to be primarily differences in the judged importance of a relatively few values, above all, differences in the terminal values, *equality* and *a comfortable life*, and differences in the instrumental values, *clean* and *obedient*. It would seem reasonable to suggest that the differential appeal that the seven presidential candidates of 1968 had for the American public arose primarily from the different images they projected concerning the relatively small number of values that have been identified here. This hypothesis can be empirically tested by doing a content analysis of the values found in the political writings of the seven candidates.

The Meaning
of Values

A question is often raised as to whether the values we have employed in our research mean the same thing to all the respondents. Several answers are possible to this question. First, regardless of differences in the meaning of a given value, it represents a specific stimulus, which when presented to our respondents, yields reliable and replicable responses that are often predictable on the basis of one or another theoretical consideration.

Second, if by "the meaning of values" we mean connotative meaning, it is possible to measure such meaning with Osgood's semantic differential technique (Osgood, Suci, and Tannenbaum, 1957). Homant (1967) measured the semantic meaning of each terminal and instrumental value and correlated these indices of meaning with the rank ordering of values obtained for each subject. The median correlations found between the evaluative factor of the semantic differential and the rank ordering of 18 terminal and 18 instrumental values were .68 and

.63, respectively. For the potency factor, the correlations were .37 and .47, respectively, and for the activity factor the correlations were .45 and .33, respectively. When we take the reliabilities of the terminal and instrumental scales into account it is obvious that the correlations between the value rankings and Osgood's evaluative factor (which is of greatest interest here) are very high indeed. These findings indicate that the simple rankings from 1 to 18 give us essentially the same kind of information about a person as that obtained with the more complex semantic differential technique, and also that our value scales measure essentially the same kind of meaning as that measured by Osgood's evaluative factor.

A third kind of answer that can be given is the following: Over and above the question of semantic meaning, the *psychological significance* that a particular value has for a particular person can best be understood by noting the manner in which the respondent relates it to other relevant values. Let us assume, for example, that Persons A and B both rank *salvation* first on the terminal value scale, but that Person A ranks *forgiveness* first and Person B ranks *forgiveness* last on the instrumental value scale. It could then be suggested that even though *salvation* had the same semantic meaning for A and B it does not necessarily have the same psychological significance for both. Similarly, we have found that both Hitler and Lenin ranked *freedom* low on their scale of values. Does *freedom* mean the same thing to Hitler and Lenin? Notice that Hitler also ranks *equality* low while Lenin ranks *equality* high in his scale of values. These *freedom-equality* findings suggest that in Hitler's case the denial of freedom by the state is understood to be a weapon to coerce inequality; in Lenin's case it is understood to be a weapon to coerce equality. Thus, the psychological significance of *freedom,* or its denial, is obviously different for Hitler and Lenin, even though both rank *freedom* equally low, and even though *freedom* may mean the same thing semantically to both. Similarly, both Goldwater and the socialists ranked *freedom* high in their scale of values. But we would again be reluctant to conclude from this finding that *freedom* has the same psychological significance for both. The high regard for *freedom* is to be understood, in Goldwater's case, by relating it to a low regard for *equality,* and in the socialist case, to a high regard for *equality.*

Concluding Comments

I have pointed out elsewhere (Rokeach, 1968-69) that an analysis of recent textbooks in social psychology and of citations in recent issues of the *Psychological Abstracts* reveals that attitudes occupy about five or six times more of our combined attention than values. And, as I have already suggested in my opening remarks, a major reason why we have paid more attention to the attitude than value concept is that more sophisticated methods have been available for measuring attitudes. This greater availability of methods for measuring attitudes brings to mind Abraham Kaplan's *law of the instrument*: "Give a small boy a hammer, and he will find that everything he encounters needs pounding." (1964, p. 28).

The value instrument described here is in many ways an ideal instrument. In a matter of 10 to 20 minutes it yields up reasonably reliable measures of a respondent's 36 values; it is simple in design, easy to administer to individuals or groups, easy to understand regardless of educational level, and interesting enough to prompt many respondents to ask for an extra copy to take home to a friend or spouse.

The danger of this instrument is not only that it will exhibit the properties of Kaplan's hammer but also those of an all-purpose patent medicine: "everything needs pounding"; moreover, "it is good for everything." Ironically enough, we are all the more in jeopardy—in double jeopardy, one might say—because the measurement of values *is* relevant to virtually any human problem one might be able to think of.

Notes

[1] Form D, which employs the gummed label technique, was devised to facilitate the rank ordering of the 18 terminal and 18 instrumental values. It has several advantages over the traditional method of rank ordering. First of all, it has a game-like quality. The respondent is doing something with his hands; it does not require pen or pencil; it is fun to be able to paste, remove, and repaste objects without becoming "messy." More important, with every value that is rank ordered, the original list of values becomes smaller. As the respondent proceeds with the rank ordering task, he does not have to hunt through the original list of all 18 values to find the next most important value. For example, after the respondent has rank ordered twelve values he has only 6 remaining values to search through. Thus, the *average* length of the list of values that the respondent works with is not 18 but 9.5.

[2] Since we were not sure whether *salvation* and *unity with God* were synonymous, we presented these two along with 10 other terminal values to a group of undergraduate students for rank ordering. The correlation between rankings of *salvation* and *unity with God* was over .80 and we therefore eliminated the latter as redundant.

[3] The maximum correlation found within the correlation matrix of 18 instrumental values for a national area probability sample of about 1400 adults tested by the National Opinion Research Center was —.32 between *clean* and *logical*; for the 18 terminal values the maximum correlation was +.35 between *a comfortable life* and *pleasure*.

References

Allport, G. W. and H. S. Odbert. "Trait-Names: A Psycho-Lexical Study," *Psychological Monographs,* Vol. 70, No. 211 (1936).

Anderson, N. H. "Likableness Ratings of 555 Personality-Trait Words," *Journal of Personality and Social Psychology,* 9 (1968), 272-279.

Beech, R. P. "Value Systems, Attitudes, and Interpersonal Attraction." Unpublished Ph.D. dissertation, Michigan State University, 1966.

Hollen, C. C. "The Stability of Values and Value Systems." Unpublished Master's thesis, Michigan State University, 1967.

Homant, R. "The Meaning and Ranking of Values." Unpublished Master's thesis, Michigan State University, 1967.

Kaplan, A. *The Conduct of Inquiry.* San Francisco: Chandler, 1964.

Newcomb, T. M. *The Acquaintance Process.* New York: Holt, Rinehart, and Winston, 1961.

Osgood, C. E., G. J. Suci, and P. H. Tannenbaum. *The Measurement of Meaning.* Urbana: University of Illinois Press, 1957.

Penner, L., R. Homant, and M. Rokeach. "Comparison of Rank-Order and Paired-Comparison Methods for Measuring Value Systems." *Perceptual and Motor Skills,* 27 (1968), 417-418.

Rokeach, M. "A Theory of Organization and Change within Value-Attitude Systems," *Journal of Social Issues,* 24 (1968), 13-33 (a)

Rokeach, M. *Beliefs, Attitudes, and Values.* San Francisco: Jossey-Bass, 1968. (b)

Rokeach, M. "The Role of Values in Public Opinion Research," *Public Opinion Quarterly,* 1968-69.

Siegel, S. *Nonparametric Statistics for the Behavioral Sciences.* New York: McGraw-Hill, 1956.

William A. Gamson

Political Trust and Its Ramifications

Professor Gamson is on the faculty of the Department of Political Science of the University of Michigan.

TRUST, LIKE LOVE, RECEIVES A CONSISTENTLY FAVORABLE PRESS. IT IS tempting to find some way to debunk such an exalted state of mind and I will find a few strictures but mostly I intend to add my approbation. However, my argument has little to do with such general sentiments as "If only people trusted each other, we could solve all our problems." In addition to denying the existence of real conflicts among people and organizations, such a suggestion tells us little about how trust operates. Is it merely a symptom or by-product of certain happy situations or does it help to create solutions where they would otherwise be difficult if not impossible? What specific phenomena can it help us to understand?

The phenomena I am interested in understanding are political and the trust has a political focus.[1] A wide array of relevant terms testifies to the importance of this dimension for understanding political life. We describe citizens as loyal, confident, supportive, allegiant, enthusiastic, satisfied, or negatively as alienated, discontented, disaffected, apathetic, rebellious. Clearly, we ascribe important consequences for the political system to these different states of mind that we may find among the citizenry. My task is to analyse some of these consequences.

What is Trust?

Trust in the government is a political attitude. Like any attitude, it is a predisposition to act for or against some object—it has an evaluative component. It is distinguished from other attitudes in having the government as its target. Political attitudes, like other attitudes, may be held with varying degrees of intensity, may be tightly or loosely related to other attitudes, and may be directed toward broad or narrow objects.

Trust is a special kind of attitude. The term "political attitude" typically connotes an opinion on some specific public issue or public figure—for example, an attitude toward Medicare or toward Richard Nixon. Trust, however, refers to a different and more basic type of political orientation. It refers to the general expectations people have about the quality of the product that the political system produces. It is more generalized, cumulative, and stable than attitudes on specific public issues.

It is important to distinguish trust from a closely related attitude—political efficacy. Efficacy refers to the *ability to* influence; trust refers to the *necessity for* influence. Of course, if one feels he cannot contribute significant inputs to the political system, he is also likely to feel unhappy with the outputs but this is an empirical hypothesis which might prove false under some conditions. A benevolent paternalism, for example, might provide an exception. In any event, trust will be used here to refer to an attitude toward the product or outputs of the political system.

41

The Objects of
Political Trust

As the object of a general attitude, the political system is a variegated one. It is perfectly possible for an individual to feel great confidence in his local government while feeling alienated from the federal government, or vice versa. Furthermore, a man may be confident in political institutions while feeling alienated from the incumbents who man them. Political trust is best regarded as a differentiated attitude toward different levels of the political system—toward the public philosophy which justifies a regime, its political institutions, or the authorities who hold office at a particular time.

There is probably a hierarchical relationship among different objects of political trust. An unpleasant outcome on a specific issue may not have any appreciable effect on more general attitudes of trust. However, if such unpleasant outcomes are repeated frequently or if one of them is especially important, the dissatisfied recipients may conclude that the authorities are biased against them. And if such experiences extend over several sets of authorities, they may conclude that the institutions themselves are a source of bias and that throwing the rascals out will have little effect. The seeds of revolution are contained in such generalization of political trust.

The Dual Importance
of Trust

It happens that trust is critically important in understanding two very different but related kinds of political phenomena. It is important in helping us to understand the capacity of leaders to solve problems on behalf of their constituency; and it is equally important to an understanding of the process by which members of a political system mobilize and attempt to influence political leaders. We will examine each of these in turn.

Trust as the Creator of Collective Power

"In wartime, if you desire service, you must give loyalty" Winston Churchill told his parliamentary critics during a censure debate (1962, Vol. 4, p. 352). But the same argument applies to peacetime as well. Parsons has articulated it most fully. Any group of leaders must make many decisions under conditions of great uncertainty. Many of these decisions require the commitment of resources which the leader must draw from his followers. And frequently leaders commit their followers without prior consent. Indeed, prior consent is typically impossible because of the uncertainties which the future holds. As Parsons puts it, "Effectiveness . . . necessitates the capacity to make decisions and to commit resources, *independently of specific conditions prescribed in advance* . . . by some kind of prior agreement" (1961, p. 52). The freedom which leaders have to invest or spend the resources they have 'borrowed' from their followers, allows leaders to generate additional resources. Thus, if they provide effective leadership, they provide their constituency with a generous return on its loan in the form of public goods or increased resources.

To quote Parsons again, "Like economic firms, units specializing in political function are dependent on the return of the power they have 'spent' or 'invested' through their decisions about the allocation of resources. This return, analogous to that from consumers' spending, takes the form of the constituency's satisfaction or dissatisfaction with these decisions, and it thus directly affects the leadership's capacity to make further commitments" (1961, p. 53).

The effectiveness of political leadership, then, depends on the ability of authorities to claim the loyal cooperation of members of the system without having to specify in advance what such cooperation will entail. Within certain limits, effectiveness depends on a blank check. The importance of trust becomes apparent: *the loss of trust is the loss of system power,* the loss of a generalized capacity for authorities to commit resources to attain collective goals.

Now we all know that authorities sometimes use their power selfishly or stupidly. As a result, they experience a loss of credit which reduces their power. Witness the collapse of power in the Johnson Administration from 1964 to 1968. In the summer of 1964 when the President's credit rating was high, he asked and received from Congress a generalized grant of authority in the form of the "Bay of Tonkin" resolution. Following a highly ambiguous incident off the coast of North Vietnam, a trusting Congress agreed to give the President a wide latitude in making military commitments in Southeast Asia. An overwhelming election victory in November, 1964, increased such latitude even further.

In early 1965, President Johnson had a virtually unlimited capacity to make commitments. This itself is a neutral fact which is given meaning only by the trust one had in his leadership. He might have used the power wisely. For example, he might have extricated the United States from its involvement in Vietnam at that time. To do so would have involved some risks including the possibility that events would occur which would have made the President vulnerable to opposition charges of 'appeasement' or 'softness.' However, the high trust he enjoyed gave him a vital margin with which to take such risks had he wished to do so. It also gave him the ability to make a full-scale commitment of United States military forces and prestige to the prosecution of the war, a course with its own risks which he chose. By the end of March, 1968, on the eve of the Wisconsin presidential primary, President Johnson had become a casualty of his own decision.

The ebb and flow of trust is a dynamic process which feeds back upon itself. As confidence in the President eroded, his capacity to take actions to restore confidence was simultaneously eroded. Less trust means less power and less power means less freedom to remove past errors and thus halt or reverse the process of power collapse. Failure breeds distrust and in thus reducing power creates the conditions for further failure.

Parsons has pointed to this 'deflationary spiral' as an essential part of the dynamics of revolution. A well-functioning government is, like a well-functioning bank, " 'insolvent' at any given moment with respect to its formal obligations if there is insistence on their fulfillment too rapidly" (Parsons, 1964, p. 60). A bank, of course, does not keep its depositors' money in a vault but lends and invests it on the secure knowledge that all its depositors will not appear for their funds on the same day. Furthermore, it lends to others money beyond what its depositors have lent it and thereby creates new money. A well-functioning government has similarly undertaken a series of obligations beyond its capacity to fulfill them instantaneously.

The decline of trust has the effect of encouraging groups to demand explicit fulfillment of the government's obligations to them. These demands may be fully legitimate ones which the government does not in any way deny. But if its ability to meet them is called into question, this encourages other groups to press their demands. Thus, it is possible for the loss of trust to encourage what amounts to a run on the bank. The beleaguered Lindsay administration in New York City experienced something very much like this process in the autumn of 1968.

Finally, there is an additional factor which may accelerate this process. As discontent rises, various portions of the population become increasingly mobilized and may resort to actions which generate additional problems for the government. Thus, it becomes necessary for the government to turn its attention from the problems which cause the discontent to the control of the discontented group. This requires a diversion of resources at a moment when they are already overextended. Its general capacity to meet existing commitments is reduced further and the whole deflationary process is given an additional boost.

In sum, political trust is a kind of "diffuse support" which "forms a reservoir of favorable attitudes or good will that helps members to accept or tolerate outputs to which they are opposed or the effect of which they see as damaging to their wants" (Easton, 1965, p. 273). When the supply in the reservoir is high, leaders are able to make new commitments on the basis of it and, if successful, increase support even more. When it is low and declining, leaders may find it difficult to meet existing commitments and to govern effectively.

The argument that loss of trust leads to the loss of system power has many empirical implications. It provides an interpretation for a variety of political events. For example, it helps us to understand why President Johnson could get a broad grant of authority from Congress in 1964 and was refused a similar grant in 1967 prior to his attendance at a meeting of the Organization of American States. It helps us to understand the process by which the authority of a government collapses in the course of a successful revolution. It helps us to understand the political "honeymoon" which newly elected leaders enjoy and why this honeymoon period is generally regarded as the most opportune time for innovation.

But can this interpretation be tested more systematically? Some of the implications certainly can. For example, if the argument is correct, we ought to find that decision latitude varies systematically and directly with trust. We can measure trust in a variety of ways, most simply by asking people how likely they think it is that a given set of authorities will do a good job. The traditional Gallup Poll question, asking respondents their evaluation of the President's performance, provides a rough and ready measure of trust in the White House.

The measurement of decision latitude is more formidable but still manageable. One operationalization might involve self-ratings by incumbents. They could be asked to report at which periods in their incumbency they felt freest to innovate and, conversely, most inhibited or constrained. Such judgments are frequently implicit or even explicit in the memoirs of particular periods and might be culled from a content analysis of such accounts. The ratings of a panel of outside observers might also be used to determine the times at which decision latitudes were highest and lowest. Finally, one could look at such behavioral measures as the rate of introduction of legislation, issuance of executive orders, and so forth. In the latter case, one would have to control for seasonal factors and other possible artifacts. Ultimately, with independent measures of trust and decision-latitude over the same time period, it would be possible to see if these measures covaried in the manner predicted above.

Trust as the Source of Inactivity

Interpreting inactivity is at least as difficult as reading tea leaves. It may reflect very different amounts of trust and taken by iself it tells us little about the underlying attitudes of the inactive. First, it can be an expression of low trust or alienation. The military dictatorship in Greece, for example, was anxious to produce a high percentage of "Yes" votes in a plebescite for the constitution it intended to impose; inactivity in such a situation was taken by the regime to indicate non-support. But even in the United States, with genuinely competitive elections, inactivity or failure to vote is interpreted as non-support for the political system. This is why local newspapers urge a citizen to vote for any candidate as long as he votes. Non-voting as a means of with-holding support from the system has never been better expressed than in comedian Mort Sahl's advice to voters during the 1960 Presidential election campaign to "Vote 'No' and keep the White House empty for another four years."

Ironically, inactivity can also be an expression of high trust. For example, there is evidence that participation in the political system increases in times of crisis. "In Germany and Austria," Lipset points out (1960, p. 189), "the normally high turnout reached its greatest heights in 1932-33, in the last elections before the destruction of the democratic system itself." This fact suggests that some people were not participating because they were reasonably satisfied or at least uncon-cerned and began participating when they really became upset about the political system. Inactivity can be a sign of confidence or high trust; it may express the feeling that any of those gentlemen would do a fine job as President so why bother to choose. Or, inactivity may simply be a sign of the irrelevance of politics and government for many people much of the time.

Inactivity or apathy and its counterparts of arousal or mobilization are rich in complexity, and the key to understanding them is the con-cept of political trust. High trust in the political system is double-edged. For authorities, it is beneficial since it increases their capacity; for the leaders of disadvantaged groups in the system, it is an obstacle to change since it leads to apathy among their followers. High trust in the authorities who man the political system implies some lack of necessity for influencing them. From the standpoint of partisan group leaders who very much believe that influence is necessary, the loss of trust in authorities by their potential membership means that their followers may become more politically active, join organizations, and contribute increasing time and money to influencing authorities.

High trust in the political system, then, can be a problem for groups interested in change. Interest groups face two simultaneous tasks and must consider their tactics in the light of both. On the one hand, they are concerned with influencing authorities and producing favorable policies. On the other hand, they must maintain, or in many cases, create the support of a constituency. If trust in the system is sufficiently high, interest groups may appear to be unnecessary mediators of solidary group interests. Why put time, energy, and money into an organization aimed at influencing authorities if these men can already be counted on to be responsive to the group's needs? A loss of trust in authorities may have the consequence of increasing the resources of interest groups by making the necessity of using them to influence authorities more apparent to their constituency.

The trust variable makes the relation between successful influence and building the support of a constituency an extremely delicate one. In some cases, the two goals of interest groups are complementary, successful influence stimulating member support and increased support stimulating more effective influence. However, with a relatively unorganized constituency, the problem of mobilizing support is likely to dominate the concerns of the interest group and short-run influence may be willingly sacrificed to this goal. In some cases, apparent defeats may even be preferred to victories if they occur in ways that diminish trust in authorities and increase group solidarity and personal investment in interest groups.

Organizers frequently seem to be aware of this point but the same cannot be said of their targets. Targets of influence typically speak of being firm and of "not rewarding disruptive tactics" without realizing that their rigidity may be a critical input to the mobilization of the partisan group they are confronting. Flexibility, on the other hand, may undercut the mobilization process and satisfy the more marginally discontented members of the partisan group's constituency, thus creating internal divisions and problems of integration in the partisan group. Organizers concerned with mobilization frequently regard the Bull Connors and Mayor Daleys as their most precious assets.

My moral here is not that "nothing succeeds like failure." Failure and frustration are frequently debilitating and demoralizing and increases in discontent can have an effect that is the opposite from mobilizing people. More specifically, I would hypothesize that a combination of a high sense of political efficacy and low political trust is the optimum combination for mobilization—a belief that influence is both possible and necessary. But, as noted above, a sense of efficacy and trust do not vary independently and any group strategy must be judged in terms of its effects on both variables.

Some Suggestive Data

These thoughts on trust and efficacy have a good many empirical implications. In the remainder of this paper, I will examine some data which suggests their relevance, most of it collected and analysed by Jeffery M. Paige.[2] Paige's concern was with the more general problem of the meaning of collective violence, particularly as it was manifested in the urban disorders of the 1960's. My focus here is on one aspect of this more general issue.

I argued above that a combination of high efficacy and low trust is a potent combination, leading to high mobilization for political action. But trust also is related to the means of political action chosen and, as we we will see in a moment, this is likely to make the combination even more explosive.

The argument connecting means of influence with political trust is a complicated one. Since I have made it in detail elsewhere,[3] I will merely restate the conclusion here. Means of influence can be categorized as constraints, inducements, or persuasion. *Constraints* are the addition of new disadvantages to the situation or the threat to do so, regardless of the particular resources used. *Inducements* are the addition of new advantages to the situation or the promise to do so, regardless of the particular resources used. Finally, *persuasion* involves some change in the minds of the target of influence without admitting anything new to their situation.

How are these means of influence related to political trust? This latter concept can be defined as the probability of obtaining preferred outcomes from the political system even when this system is left untended. A preferred outcome is one that is regarded as most favorable to one's interests when they conflict with those of others, *or* as the most efficient for the system as a whole.

The probability of receiving preferred outcomes without doing anything to bring them about—let me call this P_b—can range from 0 to 1.0. Although the trust variable is continuous, it is convenient to describe three pure points on the dimension for the purposes of discussion. *Confidence* is the belief that for any given decision, $P_b = 1.0$. For a group to have confidence in authorities means that it perceives them as its agents, that the group members identify with them. *Neutrality* is the belief that for any given decision, $P_b = .5$. Neutrality toward authorities means that a group believes that such authorities are moderately competent and efficient in achieving collective goals but that they offer no special leadership skills. On questions of conflict, a group with a neutral attitude regards the authorities as indifferent and disinterested. Finally, *alienation* is the belief that for any given decision, $P_b = 0$. Alienation from authorites means that they are regarded as incompetent and stupid in achieving collective goals and biased against the group in handling conflicts of interest. They are anti-agents of the group, the agents of groups with conflicting goals.

A plausible theoretical argument can be made that the means of influence that a partisan group directs against a set of authorities will tend to emphasize a dominant means. More specifically, a confident group will tend to rely on persuasion as a means of influence; a neutral group will tend to rely on inducements; and an alienated group will tend to rely on constraints.

Now there is some evidence that the explosive combination of high efficacy and low trust may be present among many Negroes in the urban ghettos of the North. At least this is what political party workers in the ghetto seem to feel about the attitudes of their constituents according to Rossi *et al.* (1968). These party workers "saw their constituents," Rossi *et al.* (p. 75) suggest, "as rejecting the present set of politicians, having little faith in their elected representatives but at the same time being politically agitated and active."

Paige (1968) has data which allows us to pursue this line of argument more closely. The data consists of interviews, conducted by Negro interviewers, of a probability sample of 236 males between the ages of 15 and 35 years, living in the core riot area of Newark, New Jersey. The interviews were conducted in the winter of 1967-68, about six months after the major disturbance in the summer of 1967. The questionnaire included a wide range of items including those aimed at assessing riot participation. Respondents were classified as riot participants if they admitted to being active on a general question or said that they had engaged in one of a series of specific riot-related actions that they were asked about later in the interview. Paige has a thorough discussion of the validity problems involved in using this kind of self report. In spite of what one might expect in the way of reluctance to admit participation, 46% of the Newark respondents emerged as riot participants by this criterion.

To test the hypotheses about the interaction of trust and efficacy, one needs independent measures of these two variables. It is no simple task to measure efficacy uncontaminated by trust. As Paige puts it, "No matter how interested or active an individual is, he is unlikely to say that he can influence political affairs if he regards the government as essentially unresponsive" (1968, p. 125). Paige's strategy was to use a measure that is uncontaminated by trust but quite highly related to efficacy—namely, a measure of political information. Information may be regarded as a necessary but not a sufficient condition for influence. Not all of those who are informed will feel that they can influence the outcomes of the political system but it is hard to see how those who lack knowledge will feel that they can select the appropriate targets and tactics for influence.

Political information was measured by asking respondents to identify the race of nine Negro and white political figures. Those who identified six or fewer names were placed in the low information group; those who identified seven or more, in the high information group. If this measure is accepted as an admittedly rough approximation of efficacy, we may be able to shed some light on the hypotheses.

Political trust was measured directly by asking respondents, "How much do you think you can trust the government in Newark to do what is right—just about always, most of the time, some of the time, or almost never?" It turns out that in Newark, Paige reports, only 2% felt that they could trust the government "just about always" and another 10% felt that the government can be trusted "most of the time." These two groups are combined in the analysis. In contrast, 38% felt that they could almost never trust the government.

Now it was important to obtain reasonably independent measures of efficacy and trust and apparently Paige was quite successful in doing this in Newark. Ordinarily, one would expect the better informed or more efficacious to have higher trust; this relationship is implicit in arguments that link lack of social integration with extremist political views. But in Newark, the correlation between political information and political trust was actually slightly negative ($-.19$)! As Paige (1968, p. 127) remarks wryly, "It seems that the more that is known about the government, the less it is trusted."

Trust, Efficacy, and Riot Participation

It may be that riot behavior has little or no political component—that it is merely an expression of unfocused personal frustration or of personal acquisitiveness. If this is so, then we should find no relationship with political trust (except for spurious relationships produced by some third variable related to both rioting and trust). Thus, in examining the variables we are interested in here, we are implicitly testing an interpretation of riot participation as a form of political activity.

From previous studies, we should expect to find that information or efficacy increases monotonically with political activity—including both the conventional sort and more dramatic forms such as riot participation. However, I have argued here that trust interacts with efficacy to produce important differences among high efficacy respondents. Specifically, the combination of high efficacy with low trust should produce a high percentage of riot participants but the same degree of efficacy with high trust should not.

Paige tested this hypothesis and found the results indicated in Figure 1 below. This figure, he concludes, "demonstrates a striking confirmation of the predicted interaction between information and trust. The high-information, low-trust cell is clearly the highest on riot participation. In fact, there is a 38 percentage-point spread between the low and high information cells in the low-trust condition . . . Those low on information and low on trust are actually the lowest cell on riot participation." In sum, there is no independent linear relationship between political trust and riot participation—the alienated are no more likely to have participated in riots than are the confident. But when this variable is combined with efficacy, trust is extremely important in explaining the behavior of those who are high in efficacy.

Paige also asked his respondents about participation in more conventional political acts such as voting and civil rights activity. With a little stretching, it is possible to interpret these different types of activities as reflecting different means of influence and, thus, to explore the earlier hypotheses relating trust to choice of a means of influence. Paige suggests that since civil rights groups use the threat of demonstrations or legal action to influence white authorities, their activity may be viewed as a form of mild constraint. Thus, the political activities reported upon run from voting (a form of inducement) to civil rights activity (a mild constraint) to rioting (a severe constraint). Since the mean level of participation differs for each activity, we should not necessarily expect that different kinds will be absolutely higher at different trust levels. Instead, Paige argues, the hypothesis suggests that the relative occurrence of each type of activity will reach a maximum at a different trust level. Specifically, "voting should be highest among those who feel the government can be trusted most of the time, rioting among those who feel it can almost never be trusted, and civil rights activity should peak among those intermediate on trust. These predictions hold only for the high-information subjects, since those low on information would be unlikely to show any consistent pattern in their reactions to government activities with which they are only peripherally concerned" (Paige, 1968, pp. 130-31).

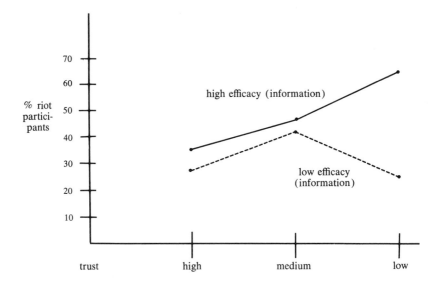

FIGURE 1[a]

RIOT PARTICIPATION, TRUST, AND EFFICACY IN NEWARK

[a] Adapted from Paige (1968, p. 128).

The data to test these predictions are presented in Figure 2. This figure includes only those who are high in efficacy or information and once again the predictions are nicely confirmed. Voting falls sharply and linearly as trust decreases; rioting, on the other hand, is lowest among those high in trust and increases linearly as trust decreases. Civil rights activity is in between the others—rising as trust declines from high to medium but falling again sharply as trust declines from medium to low. Paige concludes that "In general, there is evidence that rioting can profitably be considered a form of revolutionary political protest engaged in by those who have become highly distrustful of existing political institutions" (1968, p. 134).

Conclusion

By now, I hope, you are convinced of the efficacy of the concept of trust and have learned to trust the concept of efficacy. Let me now

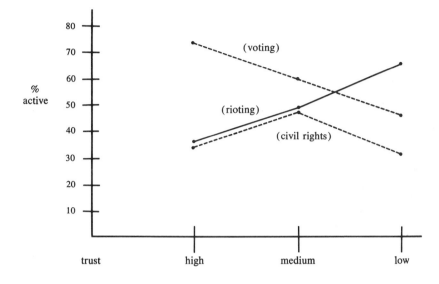

FIGURE 2ᵃ

VOTING, CIVIL RIGHTS ACTIVITY, AND RIOTING BY TRUST FOR
HIGH EFFICACY RESPONDENTS IN NEWARK

ᵃ Adapted from Paige (1968, p. 131).

return to some final implications of the points argued above, implications for the present state in which we find our political system. Of all the attitude combinations a citizenry may have, the combination of high efficacy and low trust is the least stable.

Paige suggests a fourfold typology between efficacy and trust linking the orientation of citizens with different types of political systems. A high trust-high efficacy orientation he calls *allegiant* and suggests that it is characteristic of *democratic* political systems. A high trust-low efficacy system describes a subordinate orientation and is characteristic of *traditional* or paternalistic political systems. A low trust-low efficacy orientation describes an *alienated* population and is characteristic of *totalitarian* political systems which may be quite stable with the use of coercion. The high efficacy-low trust orientation he calls *dissident* and suggests that it describes an *unstable* political system with a high potential for radical action or revolution.

The degree of instability depends, of course, on the size of the group with this dissident orientation. The instability can be resolved in one of two ways—through responsiveness or repression. If repression is successful, trust will be unaffected but efficacy will be reduced so that it falls into line with low trust. This involves a movement toward a police state and the acceptance of an alienated but cowed population. The other alternative, responsiveness, attempts to remove the instability by raising trust rather than lowering efficacy. Presumably this is what is meant by such phrases as ruling with the "consent of the governed."

One might be tempted to conclude from the foregoing discussion that a political system can't have too much trust for its own good. However, if every group in a political system were completely confident, there would be something amiss. Since groups have different preferred outcomes on many issues, some would have to be either ignorant or deluded. In a relatively open system, such overconfidence in the government may be a potential source of instability in its own right. With such a fragile foundation for trust, there is always a danger of a sudden collapse of credit. Such a collapse may come at a time when the government has heavy commitments and can ill afford it. The more accurate the perceptions of the political process by different groups, the greater is the likelihood that highly confident groups will have alienated counterparts. On issues which involve conflict of interest, there is a more stable foundation if different groups perceive the system as neutral—that is, as unbiased.

This stricture is not true with respect to the efficiency of the political system. The existence of high confidence for one part of the population need not imply less confidence for any other part. Here, the rule of "the more trust, the better" applies. This suggests that one might get some reading on the success of a political system by looking at both the *mean* level of trust among different groups in the society and the *variance* in trust between groups. Thus, the political system in a society in which average trust is relatively high but variance in trust between different groups is also substantial is doing well in the achievement of collective goals but has problems of equity in distribution. One in which average trust is relatively low but more or less equal between groups is like the man in the New Yorker cartoon who announces that he hates everyone regardless of race, creed, or national origin: in such a system, every group gets its fair share of misery. Finally, the ideal political system should have a comfortably high level of overall trust and a low variance in trust between groups. Such a system would have achieved efficiency without sacrificing equity.

Notes

[1] The discussion in the first part of this paper draws heavily on Gamson (1968), especially Ch. 3.

[2] The part of this study referred to here is reported most fully in Paige (1968). Accounts of other parts of this research have appeared in the report of the National Advisory Commission on Civil Disorders (1968) and in Caplan and Paige (1968).

[3] See Gamson (1968), especially Ch. 8.

References

Caplan, Nathan and Paige, Jeffery M. "A Study of Ghetto Rioters," *Scientific American* (August, 1968), pp. 15-21.

Churchill, Winston. *The Second World War,* Vol. 4. New York: Bantam Books, 1962.

Easton, David. *A Systems Analysis of Political Life.* New York: John Wiley and Sons, 1965.

Gamson, William A. *Power and Discontent.* Homewood, Illinois: The Dorsey Press, 1968.

Lipset, Seymour Martin. *Political Man.* Garden City, N.Y.: Doubleday, 1960.

National Advisory Commission on Civil Disorders, Report of the Commission. New York: Bantam, 1968.

Paige, Jeffery M. "Collective Violence and the Culture of Subordination." Ph.D. Dissertation, University of Michigan, 1968.

Parsons, Talcott. "Some Reflections on the Place of Force in Social Process" in Harry Eckstein, ed., *Internal War.* New York: The Free Press, 1964, pp. 33-70.

Parsons, Talcott, Edward Shils, Kaspar D. Naegele, and Jesse R. Pitts. *Theories of Society.* New York: The Free Press, 1961.

Rossi, Peter H. *et al.* "Between White and Black: The Faces of American Institutions in the Ghetto," in Supplemental Studies for the National Advisory Commission on Civil Disorders. U.S. Government Printing Office, 1968.

Political
Socialization

Robert D. Hess

The Acquisition of Feelings of
Political Efficacy in Pre-Adults

Professor Hess is on the faculty of the School of Education of
Stanford University. He wishes to acknowledge the aid of Miss
Karen Fox in the preparation of this paper.

POLITICAL ACTIVITY IN THE YOUNG IS A SOCIAL PHENOMENON AND, like other social features of a complex society, it is constantly changing. It confronts the observer with a moving facade—a series of transitional events behind which it is difficult to discern basic, enduring patterns. The range of political activities and the intensity of political involvement of youth in this country have changed dramatically in the past few years, and any single study of political socialization can only reveal, at best, a level or kind of activity as stable, characteristic of the time at which the study was conducted. Studies of political attitudes and behavior in the young can then be viewed less as attempts to identify basic principles with long-term validity than as a series of specific observations. From them eventually may emerge a comprehensive description of the processes by which political behavior in pre-adults is acquired, but at present the study of those processes is at a very early stage. Researchers are attempting to define boundaries, to select methods and concepts, and to gain the perspective needed to interpret data in ways that will contribute to an orderly, cumulative growth in this new field of inquiry.

The purpose of this paper is to examine the usefulness of the concept of political socialization as a way of explaining the development of political behavior in children using political efficacy as an example of a significant area of activity. The term "political socialization" was brought into prominence by Hyman in 1959 in a book bearing that title, and it has been a central concept in much of the early research by Greenstein and by Easton and Hess and their associates in their major study, Torney and Dennis. When these projects began, in the late fifties, one feature of the political life of pre-adults was a general lack of fervor and conflict over political issues and problems. This apparent lack of political consciousness, which we addressed in an early paper (Easton and Hess, 1961), suggested that the young in this country were over-socialized—that they accepted the political norms and orientations of the nation so completely that there was little motivation for conflict, debate and protest. In that relatively tranquil atmosphere, the concept of political socialization seemed singularly apt.

Since then, the political life of the youth of this country has changed in dramatic ways. College, high school and even junior high school students have been drawn into and helped create major conflicts and confrontations between generations, between the poor and the affluent, and between students and school authorities over issues of racial discrimination, poverty, the war in Vietnam, the draft, the quality of education, population growth, and abuse of the environment. As the first generation to grow up in an era when the coupling of technology and overpopulation has made it necessary to protect the physical environment from man, it has become deeply involved in political discussion and action.

The concept of political socialization is no longer adequate as a tool for understanding the political behavior of the young or for studying the processes through which it is acquired. At best, it helps explain only a part of the phenomena with which we are now concerned.

Political socialization, as a theoretical or conceptual construct, is an outgrowth from the concept of socialization—a term that has been knocking about in literature, both lay and professional, for a long time. In its early usage it had strong connotations of domestication—of pressure by the social institutions of society to compel conformity to normative standards of conduct and behavior. There was little humanism in these early conceptions; the demands and asserted needs of the social unit were primary and the notion that the initiate should be indoctrinated into adult norms was apparently not challenged.

There is a considerable confusion in the field about the definition and conceptualization of political socialization, deriving in part from confusion over the term "socialization" itself.[1] In the psychological literature socialization (or childrearing as it was more frequently called) applied primarily to toilet training, weaning, and the training of physiologically based behavior or impulses in the small child (Child, 1954). The term still has this connotation. It is derived in part from the Freudian concept of personality that must be shaped and modified into socially acceptable forms. In the sociological literature, on the other hand, socialization means the transmission of group values, norms, and role-relevant behavior. When this concept is applied to the emergence of political behavior in pre-adults, it thus draws from different lines of theory, none of which is comprehensive. As used in recent discussions, however, there is a tendency to conceptualize the process as one of transmission of adult political norms, knowledge, beliefs, and orientations to pre-adults (Hyman, 1959; Greenstein, 1965; Dawson & Prewitt, 1969).

The General Model
of Socialization

In order to examine the usefulness of this traditional conceptualization it may be useful to summarize the components of a general socialization model. Such a model would include these seven distinct conceptual elements:

1. An environmental structure of some sort—political, social, educational, and religious institutions, for example—which has formal responsibility for the young of a society.
2. A body of beliefs, attitudes, values, skills, laws, rules and customs which are integral to the operation of institutional structures.
3. Designated agents, both individual and institutional, who act in behalf of the society in dealing with pre-adults.
4. Objects of socialization—children and adolescents or, more generally, initiates into social units or institutions.
5. A process of teaching and learning, in which content (norms, beliefs, values, etc.) is transmitted by socializing agents to the young. The general principles of learning apply (imitation, reinforcement, identification, modeling, and the like). Since socialization is merely a particular type of learning that takes place under certain conditions.
6. A behavioral outcome in the form of expressed attitudes and acceptance of norms and conformity with the values of the social systems.
7. System-sustaining behavior, including support of the goals of the system and attempts to persuade others to accept its norms.

This general model describes the operation of a system that includes the structural elements as well as the impact of this structure through socializing agents upon the individual pre-adult member, bringing him to the level of the adult matrix of behavior and thus assisting in maintaining the system. From a functional point of view, the purpose of socialization is to maintain the systems. Thus, a completely successful socializing process would tend to prevent or at least resist social change.

Although socialization is a process which links social structure to individual behavior, different disciplines in behavioral science have been concerned with different components of the socialization model. Child psychologists, for example, have studied the link between the socializing agent, especially parents, and the object of socialization, usually the young child. They have been less concerned with the relation between parental behavior and larger social structures. Sociologists, on the other hand, have devoted less attention to the acquisition process and to the internal states of socializing agent and socializee and more to the relation between behavioral outcomes and social structure and between social structures and the behavior of the socializing agents. Inkeles (1960) and Kohn (1963) have both dealt extensively with the relationship between occupational structures and the working conditions of industrial society and the value outcomes for workers, which presumably are transmitted to their children. Education, as a discipline, has tended to avoid the notion that the education is a socializing process and has dealt with the interaction between school and child primarily in terms of learning and teaching—only one component of the total process. This definition of the school as a teaching (rather than as a socializing) institution and thus primarily responsible for pupil performance has also invited attack on the schools which might have been somewhat redirected if the school's role as one of several agents of the society had been more clearly emphasized. The responsibility of other social institutions and of the community at large for the quality of education would perhaps be more readily recognized.

The general model of socialization is more useful, in my opinion, for understanding the *teaching* activities of institutions than it is to explain the acquisition of behavior by the young. A number of objections may be raised to this model. These qualifications and criticisms apply particularly to the usefulness of this model in the study of the acquisition of political behavior.

Perhaps the most significant defect of this model is that it assumes that the learner is passive and receptive. The system affects the individual, but the individual appears to bring virtually nothing to the socializing process himself. Thus the model discounts not only the potential contribution of the learner but the possibility of autonomy, in such matters as choosing what is to be learned and interpreting what is being taught. The extent to which this conception errs as a description of the political "socialization" of college, high school, and even (in some areas) junior high school youth in the United States at present is so obvious as to need little comment. In the area of political behavior, a concept of a passive learner accepting political norms from the establishment is no longer adequate.

The general model also ignores relevant learning from non-normative sources—that is, the political behavior that a person may acquire either directly, as from personal experience, or from nonstandard socializing agents such as peers. A distinction should be made between political learning and political socialization. In the distinction being made here, *political learning* applies to the acquisition of political information from non-institutional sources. The radicalization of students on a college campus as a result of an attack by police on campus protestors would be an instance of political learning—that is, the acquisition of political attitudes or information. This suggests that political attitudes or information learned from peers would be included in a definition of political learning but not in political socialization, except in instances in which it reinforces the norms of the system. Other behavior that could be called political learning—acquired through observation and experience—would thus be included in this conceptualization of political learning.

The traditional concept of socialization also ignores the acquisition of attitudes and behavior whose intent is to change the system in constructive ways. Strategies of legal protest and demonstration, while not necessarily new in principle, have emerged during the past few years in the civil rights and anti-war movements in forms that are clearly not the result of attitudes and behavior transmitted by the society's socializing agents. Socialization theory assumes a relatively static society in which drastic methods designed to force basic social change are not necessary. This assumption is obviously not shared by a good many young people and adults today.

Perhaps one of the most troublesome features of socialization theory is that it assumes a homogeneous society. This point is particularly relevant to issues that concern public school policy. Teaching values or attitudes within the public schools assumes a consensus in the community about the attitudes and values to be taught. Socialization practices in the school draw from content areas in which consensus is evident but in a highly differentiated society, particularly when there are confrontations between groups, there is a striking lack of consensus on many matters. Thus certain programs with political relevance (ethnic studies, for example) are curtailed or not permitted at all in the public schools of many communities, because there is enough division within the community to force the school to avoid the issues in question.

Although the traditional model of socialization is a valid way to organize certain kinds of learning, it is less helpful in understanding the political beliefs and political behavior of high school and college students. We seem to need a more complex, more individualized schematization of the process through which young people acquire political behavior. The pattern should certainly include the more "classic" forms of political indoctrination and socialization. However, it should also accommodate such things as attitudes of protest and rebellion against major institutions of the society, perhaps learned from peers; the ingenuity and creativity required to devise new forms of action directed at social change; and the attitudes and conclusions a young person may reach on his own through observing and reflecting upon events.

Reformulating the Concept
of Efficacy

Against this background a consideration of the recent research on political efficacy may serve to indicate the limitations of this traditional model of socialization. Political efficacy illustrates the difficulties of the model particularly well; it is also a crucial topic, since many segments of the population are expressing strong feelings of powerlessness in various ways, on high school and college campuses and in the larger society.

Studies of voting behavior carried out by Campbell and his associates at the Survey Research Center of the University of Michigan since the early 1950's have shaped much of the subsequent inquiry into political efficacy and its correlates. They established the theoretical definition of efficacy that is most frequently employed: a "sense of political efficacy" is "the feeling that individual political action does have, or can have, an impact upon the political process, i.e., that it is worth while to perform one's civic duties" (Campbell, 1954, p. 187). It includes the feeling that change, both political and social, is possible and that the individual citizen can participate in accomplishing this change.

Political efficacy was measured by Campbell through responses to four questions:

1. I don't think public officials care much what people like me think.
2. Voting is the only way that people like me can have any say about how the government runs things.
3. People like me don't have any say about what the government does.
4. Sometimes politics and government seem so complicated that a person like me can't really understand what's going on.

Campbell found that political efficacy was greater for individuals with more education, higher income, and higher occupational status. Men felt more able to influence government than did women, and blacks felt less efficacious than whites. The studies also provided empirical support for the hypothesis that political participation and a sense of political efficacy tend to go together.

A sense of political efficacy is related to or overlaps with a sense of personal effectiveness or personal competence. Douvan and Walker (1956) found that feelings of political effectiveness and personal

competence were positively correlated. Personal competence was measured by an index of questions about life satisfaction, anticipation of
future satisfactions such as job security, and control over one's future.
Political effectiveness was measured by asking, "How much influence
do you think the average citizen can have on decisions" concerning two
national problems, the threat of atomic war and inflation.

To test the hypothesis that personal effectiveness was directly and
positively related to political efficacy, Campbell *et al.* (1960) used a
set of eight items that measured personal effectiveness but had no
manifest political content. The responses indicate a trend—that those
high in sense of personal effectiveness were also high in sense of political
efficacy. However, those who were lowest in personal effectiveness were
spread rather evenly over the low, medium, and high categories on
political efficacy. The authors argue that a sense of political efficacy is
more than a specific expression of a general sense of efficacy, but that it
results in part from "the interplay between education and ego strength."
They refer to studies which suggest that education heightens ego strength
and also that adolescents with a strong sense of personal competence
are more likely to pursue their education, since their social aspirations
are higher than those with a lower sense of personal competence.

Education and ego strength seem to contribute to political efficacy
independently as well, according to Campbell. If sense of personal
competence is held constant, those with more education are likely to
rate higher on political efficacy, and if level of education is held constant, there is a similar positive relationship between personal competence and political efficacy. Furthermore, education and ego strength
each have a higher correlation with political efficacy than they do with
each other.

Almond and Verba, in an extensive study of five nations reported
in *The Civic Culture* (1965), asked respondents about their childhood
participation in family and school decision-making in order to examine
the relation between childhood experiences (socialization) and their
sense of civic competence during adulthood. They distinguish two levels
of competence. The first seems to correspond to Campbell's "sense of
political efficacy": the person who *believes* he can influence a political
decision is "subjectively competent." The second applies to the person
who can in fact exert such influence; he is considered by Almond and
Verba to *be* "politically competent."

The data show a significant correlation between participation in
family and school decisions and a sense of subjective competence but
little correlation between either type of competence and education

through or beyond the 12th grade. Subjective and objective competence were estimated on the basis of interviews in which each respondent was asked what he thought he could do if a national or local governing body was considering a law that he thought very unjust and harmful, and then how likely it was that he actually *would* do something. Although the interview procedure offered certain advantages, it may be that the self-reports of actual behavior were inaccurate.

In recent studies of political efficacy, the focus has tended to shift from adults and the demographic correlates of political efficacy to the socialization of efficacy in children and adolescents. Children's feelings of efficacy are customarily measured by asking a child what feelings he thinks an adult citizen might have, and the questions (often adapted from Campbell's S.R.C. items) are usually phrased so that the child responds with how he thinks the adults in his family feel.

Extensive data on political efficacy in elementary school children have been collected in recent years (Easton and Dennis, 1967; Hess and Torney, 1968). Adapting the S.R.C. items and adding others, they investigated four related ideas: The extent to which government officials and other authorities are responsive to the desires of individual citizens; the amount of power the individual feels he has to influence the political process; the existence of means of influencing the political process; and the extent to which the political process is open to influence by citizens (or, alternatively predestined and intractable). The relevant items were:

1. Voting is the only way that people like my mother and father can have any say about how the government runs things.
2. Sometimes I can't understand what goes on in the government.
3. What happens in the government will happen no matter what people do. It is like the weather—there is nothing people can do about it.
4. There are some big, powerful men in the government who are running the whole thing and they do not care about us ordinary people.
5. My family doesn't have any say about what the government does.
6. I don't think people in the government care much what people like my family think.
7. Citizens don't have a chance to say what they think about running the government.
8. How much do each of these people help decide which laws are made for our country? (People and groups listed were rich people, unions, President, newspapers, churches, average per-

son, policeman, and big companies; choices were very much, some, very little, not at all, and don't know.)

The children's responses showed a marked increase in feelings of efficacy from the third to the eighth grade, with sharpest increase between grades four and five. By the end of the eighth grade the students expressed feelings of efficacy that approximated those of the teachers in the classes in which testing took place.

As measured by these items, efficacy was significantly related to both the child's IQ and his social status, but more closely related to IQ. The effects of IQ and social status seemed to increase with age: the older the children, the larger difference between low-IQ, low-SES children and high-IQ, high SES children. In grades 7 and 8, the average level of efficacy in the low-IQ, low-status group still had not reached the level found in the high-IQ, high-status group at grades 3 and 4.

Although it is not clear precisely how IQ contributes to feelings of efficacy, there are several possibilities. For example, high-IQ children in the public schools probably feel confident in relation to their peers, satisfied that they have an impact upon the teacher, and effective within the school system, and they may generalize these feelings to the political world. Children in low-prestige, low-power cultural and social situations within the United States may be caught in an opposite cycle, in which a general, culturally based sense of powerlessness is reflected not only in feelings of little political efficacy but in low IQ scores and low achievement at school.

The items measured subjective competence, in Almond and Verba's terminology—attitudes and feelings rather than actual effectiveness. The relation between feelings of effectiveness and ability to have an impact on the system remains unknown. A high level of feelings of effectiveness among adults may as Prewitt suggests, imply that citizens feel they have a "reserve of influence" whether they attempt to use it or not. Feeling that they have the potential to exert influence if they should wish to do so, people in general are satisfied to support governmental authorities (Prewitt, 1969, p. 227).

In a study of secondary school students in Jamaica, Langton (1967) was also interested in the effect of the social-class climate in peer groups and schools on political attitudes and behavior. His results suggest that homogeneous working class peer groups and schools reinforce the political attitudes and behavior of the working-class students, while working-class students in heterogeneous peer groups and schools tend to move toward the political norms held by students from higher

classes. Langton's study, while not dealing explicitly with political efficacy, does strongly suggest that any manipulation of school social-class
environment should be carefully considered for the effects of such
manipulation upon political attitudes.

Langton and Jennings (1968) investigated the impact of civics
instruction on a national probability sample of 1669 high school seniors,
using the following items:

1. Sometimes politics and government seem so complicated that
   a person like me can't really understand what's going on.
2. Voting is the only way that people like my mother and father
   can have any say about how the government runs things.

There was a slight tendency for students who had taken civics to express
less agreement with the two items than those who had not, but the relationships were extremely weak. The authors say that, on the whole,
their results "do not support the thinking of those who look to the civics
curriculum in American high schools as even a minor source of political
socialization." As a possible explanation, they suggest "information
redundancy": civics courses may repeat information gained from other
courses, from television and other media, or from formal organizations
and primary groups.

They tested this hypothesis by examining a small Negro subsample,
assuming that information redundancy would be less likely for blacks
than for whites. Almost twice as many students in the Negro subsample
scored low on political efficacy than did whites, and the racial differences remained when the effect of parental education was partialed out.
As for the effect of civics courses, they did moderately strengthen the
sense of efficacy for Negro students, particularly those from less educated families.

In these studies of the development of political efficacy, the conceptualization of the term, the items used in measuring efficacy, and
the interpretation of the data gathered assume an acceptance on the
part of the child of the political system and its processes. It is based on
the view that feelings of political efficacy are socialized in traditional
patterns of adult-to-child transmission processes and cannot accommodate activities which challenge the legitimacy of the political establishment. The relationship of the child and adolescent to the political world
is much more complex than the classic model of socialization suggests.

Any reconsideration of the modes and patterns of interaction between the child and an authority system of which he is a part would
also involve a reformulation of the concept of efficacy. The conclusions
that may be drawn from recent research in political attitudes of children

suggest that there are several different components of this concept which may be distinguished in studies of the development of political behavior in pre-adults. There are several different rationales on which children's feelings of efficacy may be based. The first of these is *naive trust*. It is typical of children, and of some adults, that feelings of effectiveness within the political system are largely on trust in the benevolence and the responsiveness of the system itself. It has overtones of religious faith and a belief that a powerful authority does care for and protect the individual.

Second, feelings of efficacy may be based on the belief that efficacy is guaranteed by the system itself. The system is obligated to respond, and it assures the individual of the right to be heard and the right to protection and justice. This belief comes from the individual's perception of or knowledge about the system, and thus it could conceivably be based on misinformation. It is best thought of as the individual's feeling that he has a right to invoke the rules of the system in order to get it to respond to him. According to this belief, the responsiveness of the system derives from its regulations and procedures rather than from the ability of the individual to persuade officials to decide in his favor. The government is awarded reciprocal rights: its right to collect income tax is as valid as the citizen's right to receive a tax refund if he is entitled to one. This view of responsiveness may have its roots in early experiences within the family, as when the young child expects his parents to keep promises they have made. It is an indication of confidence in the operation of the political system and does not represent a feeling of effectiveness in relation to bringing about some kind of political or social change.

A third source of feelings of efficacy could be called *system efficiency*. In this view, the responsiveness of the system is based primarily on its characteristics as an efficient governmental network. The things one is entitled to will indeed be forthcoming; they will not be lost in the red tape of a bureaucratic structure. For example, a businessman may believe that the post office delivers mail quickly and accurately, and a welfare mother may believe that her check will be on time in the right amount. The businessman and the mother may extend these beliefs to cover the system as a whole. Thus responsiveness and caring by the government is indicated by its efficiency in serving the individual citizen, and administrative inefficiencies would not be permitted to interfere with governmental response to individual needs. This process can also work in reverse, of course, leading to a lack of faith in system efficiency.

A fourth source of feelings of efficacy is a sense of identity with a powerful and influential group, such as a labor union, or large professional association. In group-based efficacy, the individual derives his sense of personal skill or competence from membership in a larger group. The basis of the group's power may be its size, or it may be related to prestige or political connections in local, state, or national legislatures.

A fifth type of efficacy is also more traditional, based on individual power or wealth, which are seen as offering access to those in power in ways that can force a response from governmental and political authority.

A sixth type of efficacy is based on perhaps more traditional assumptions about the meaning of the word "efficacy." It is the feeling of efficacy that grows out of a sense of individual competence, a confidence in one's ability to manipulate the environment, to effect change, to get things done through some kind of action. There are two clear differences between this kind of efficacy and those described above. In this instance, the responsibility for initiating action and carrying it through lies more with the individual citizen than with the system.

The exercise of individual competence or skill implies the ability to change the decision-making of people within the government or to replace governmental officials who are regarded as incompetent or insensitive. It may be that a sense of efficacy based on confidence in one's ability to influence the system is qualitatively different from a sense of efficacy built on trust as described above. It is feelings of efficacy based on the ability to effect change, perhaps, that are most susceptible to modification as a result of direct experience or attempts to have an impact on the political scene. The feeling that the government cares about the individual citizen is a much easier feeling to maintain than the feeling that one can alter in a significant way the government or its operations. It is perhaps on this point that there is the greatest likelihood of confusion in interpreting feelings of efficacy in children. In most cases a child has very little opportunity to develop efficacious feelings of the kind described here; thus, his feelings are usually based upon confidence in the system and trust in the benign intent of government. If the child tries later on—in high school or college, say—to act on his assumption that the system does indeed care about his needs and interests, he runs the risk of disappointment and disillusionment.

More recently there has developed within both the civil rights and college campus areas a sense of effectiveness based on the ability to organize public protest to disrupt or destroy. These protests, both violent and nonviolent, have often been rewarded by responses that are intended to deal in some way with the grievances that gave rise to the protest. Although public outcry and protest demonstrations may in some cases be part of a long-term strategy to achieve goals, they also seem to indicate a belief by many of the participating individuals that extreme action can force an immediate response from institutional and political authorities.

There are three components which underlie feelings of efficacy. One is trust in the system and its representatives. The system is set up to operate responsively, and concrete instances of responsiveness are testimony to its effectiveness and efficiency. A second component is a confidence that one can manipulate the system and deal with it in various ways to maximize the probability that one's own actions will effect change or at least have an impact. A third component is the belief that one can coerce the system to some degree and force a complete or a partial response.

If it is true that political socialization as a model for understanding the acquisition of political behavior in pre-adults is no longer adequate, a number of considerations are relevant for a reconceptualization of the process through which feelings of efficacy are acquired and maintained.

A major neglected point in writings about the emergence of political involvement in the young is the extent to which feelings of political efficacy are specific to particular political objects and situations. It seems likely both from empirical evidence and from common sense that efficacy is a global feeling and operates over a wide range of interpersonal, personal, and institutional contacts. The diffuse nature of the feeling, however, is almost certainly modified quickly and sharply in individual encounters with various representatives of institutions and of government. That is, it is entirely possible for an individual who feels efficacious in relation to a broad entity such as the government—to feel completely helpless and powerless in verbal encounter with a traffic policeman. A sense of efficacy can sustain some negative instances, presumably, but the impact of such experiences are scarcely studied or understood. Also neglected has been the relationship between a sense of efficacy (even a general one) toward political objects and a sense of efficacy toward other objects, such as school, family and religious authorities. A study of the emergence of political efficacy in children would need to take into account the degree to which global attitudes toward the political system are differentiated from attitudes toward other major features of the social environment.

There are of course additional variations on this theme. A black man may feel much less efficacious in a southern state than he would in a small northern community; an urbanite with competence and sophistication in dealing with the complexities of urban government may find that his techniques are not very effective in a small rural western town. Other variations by sex, religion, and the like could easily be cited.

Relationships Between
Environment and Efficacy

Given such variations, then a sense of efficacy is one expression by the individual of his relation to his environment. The relationship is reciprocal in the sense that it depends on both the individual and the system; it is more fluid than the traditional image of efficacy as a set of inherent properties or attitudes that a citizen carries around with him makes it appear. This line of argument suggests that a person's sense of efficacy varies from one social or political context to another, and there is considerable reason to think this is true. The individual's perceptions of the particular environment in which he is operating (especially his reception of its responsiveness or susceptibility to influence) are crucial.

In this context the psychological concept *locus of control* has particular relevance. As used in the literature, locus of control refers to an individual's belief in his ability to control the rewards that he desires. If he believes that his own actions and efforts determine whether he achieves a goal or obtains a reward, he has a sense of internal control. If he believes that rewards are controlled by fate or that whether he will reach a goal depends not on him but on others, his orientation is external control. The essential element is the degree to which the person feels that he has and can maintain some kind of control over his destiny. Thus the relationship between an individual and his environment can be examined for locus of control: does the individual think he or some other force has control over what happens? And are there *contingencies* or effective functional links between the individual's behavior and the degree to which he thinks the environment is responsive to him. (This point is central to the type of efficacy based on the individual's ability to alter, change, modify or have some other impact upon his political environment; it is less closely related to types of efficacy based on trust and confidence in the system.)

Studies of locus of control (e.g., Rotter, 1966) have indicated that a person's belief in his control of a situation and his efforts to control it are related to whether he thinks the factors that control his rewards operate essentially without reference to his own behavior or sees functional linkages that make it possible for him to exert some influence upon it. For example, subjects who are given a task and told that their success depends mainly on chance work much less hard and have different attitudes toward their own responses and success than subjects who are told that the task is difficult but can be figured out. The subjects who believe that there is a discoverable solution expend much more time and energy looking for it. The relevance of this finding to alienation and isolation from the social system, as found with great frequency among the poor and especially the ethnic poor, is obvious.

Belief in internal control in an experimental situation seems to depend on two event patterns. First, a person can develop a belief in internal control, in his own control of rewards, by direct experience. That is, if he can do better than chance in a game, for example, or is able to predict the reward or response that follows from his actions, his feelings of internal control tend to grow. The second source of feelings of internal control is a definition by an authority of the conditions of the task. That is, if the experimenter states that a task is difficult but can be done by people with skill and practice, then the subject not only works harder but also tends to raise his estimate of his chances of success.

Feelings of political efficacy in children may have similar origins. Children have little direct experience to support feelings of efficacy in relation to the political system, although such feelings can be generated through experience with other systems, such as the family and the school. For a child (and, indeed, for an adult) the relationship between an individual political act and an outcome is often very obscure. If there is a discernible response at all, it may be long delayed, and it may occur through a distant mechanism or agency. In many cases the behavior of the individual in relation to a political authority gets no response; at best, the effect is likely to be diffuse.

These circumstances would lead, according to most theories of behavior acquisition, to the extinguishing of the behavior. However, it sometimes persists. Part of the reason lies in the social and cultural antecedents of efficacy—in the way an "authority" has defined the "task." For instance, there is reason to believe that the behavior of socializing adults in the family or at school explains some of the variation in a sense of efficacy by socio-economic status. Recent studies of mother-child interaction indicate that mothers in middle-class homes tend to make it clearer to their children that there is a connection between the child's behavior and what the mother does to or for him. They tend to monitor his behavior (that is, to respond to it) much more frequently than working-class mothers.

In working-class families there is likely to be less direct interaction between mother and child and a greater tendency for the mother to ignore the child's activities, his signals to her, and the impact that a situation is likely to have upon him (Kamii and Radin, 1967; Walters, et al., 1964). This picture is congruent with the results of quasi-experimental situations in which mothers were asked to teach their children simple tasks. Working-class urban mothers tended to overlook critical bits of information and directions that the child would need to solve the problem (Hess, *et al.,* 1969). The mediating instructions and orientation that a child needs in order to feel that he can cope with the environment and have some impact on it are more frequently given in middle-class homes and more frequently set up by socializing adults who are aware of the needs of the child and alert to the limitations of his own perspective of the environment.

The tendency of the lower-class mother to be less concerned with the links between her own behavior and the actions of her children and to show her children fewer connections between their own actions and what happens in the environment probably reflects what the mother herself has learned from the social situation in which the family lives. Adults in poor neighborhoods tend to see little logical connection between their own behavior and what happens to them. The treatment that a lower-class family (especially if it is on welfare) gets from governmental agencies tends to support the belief that the system's requirements are not easily understood, that changes occur without warning, and outcomes are unpredictable. In the community as at work, lower-class adults rarely have a voice in policy decisions and are more likely to be assigned tasks than to assign them; in general they are more acted upon than acting.

Thus the mother's behavior toward her child reflects the place of the working-class family in the larger community. The state of uncertainty about relation between one's own behavior and what happens to one seems to be transmitted to children through fairly specific types of mother-child interactions and to have a noticeable effect on the child's educational and cognitive development (Hess, 1968, 1969).

Thus the child's experience, through his parents, with the social environment seems to offer a partial explanation of the connections he comes to see between his own actions and the course of events. Another source of feelings of efficacy is what the child learns at school. How does that authority define the political relation between individual and environment, and with what effect on the child's expectation of responsiveness and predictability in the social and political system?

The schools traditionally present a view of the government as responsive and concerned, as a benign and interested network of officials ready to assist the citizen and work for the benefit of all. Our data indicate that the initial trust of young children in the President and the country are translated during the elementary grades into confidence in the government institutions and political processes. Is this perhaps analogous to a locus-of-control study in which subjects were told that effort and skill will result in a higher score when the task is a game of chance (Rotter, 1966)? These expressions of trust in the responsiveness of government, which may be primarily the result of a mis-definition of the true state of affairs by teachers and other socializing adults have been regarded nonetheless as indicating feelings of efficacy in relation to the political system. Such feelings of efficacy are not based primarily on direct learning experiences in which a form of behavior is rewarded, strengthening the behavior. Rather, they result from instruction—indoctrination—and a desire to believe that there is indeed a connection between individual action and the action of larger institutions, whether schools, city governments, or larger political units.

Why is it that, in the absence of the rewards usually associated with learning, pre-adults will persist in behavior aimed at political change? I know of children in junior high and elementary school who refuse to salute the flag. They will stand in class when the National Anthem is being played, but they will not salute. In some instances the decision not to salute is an individual one, not a joint effort by a group. Many of these protests result in punishment of one kind or another—withdrawal of approval, dismissal from school, letters to parents, criticism by the press. Positive reinforcement for these activities clearly does not come from adult socializing agents. Much "protest" behavior also runs counter to a model of political socialization; that is, it is political behavior that has not been socialized. Nonetheless, it is exceedingly persistent, maintained in the face of opposition and discouragement of various kinds, and clearly very highly motivated. It covers a wide age range and includes some adults.

I would suggest that political behavior is a special case of learning and reflects the transfer of socialization from other areas of behavior. Much political behavior in pre-adults, including protests against the establishment, is not learned as political behavior but transferred from other areas. It seems to be the application to political objects of behavior that originated in non-political areas of experience and perhaps continues to be reinforced in those areas. These processes involve moral judgments, emotion, gross display of anger, love, and hostility, direct action, and commitment to a group. It may be in these non-political areas that an understanding may be found of some of the contemporary political behavior of pre-adults.

Notes

[1] See Clausen (1968) for a comprehensive discussion of the concept of socialization and its usage in different disciplines of social science.

References

Almond, Gabriel, and Sidney Verba. *The Civic Culture.* Princeton, N.J.: Princeton University Press, 1963.

Battle, Esther and J. B. Rotter. "Children's Feelings of Personal Control as Related to Social Class and Ethnic Groups," *Journal of Personality,* 31 (1963), 482-490.

Bay, Christian. *The Structure of Freedom.* New York: Athenum, 1968.

Campbell, Angus, Philip Converse, Warren Miller, and Donald Stokes. *The American Voter.* New York: John Wiley and Sons, 1960.

Campbell, Angus, Gerald Gurin, and Warren Miller. *The Voter Decides.* Evanston, Illinois: Row, Peterson, 1954.

Child, I., "Socialization," in G. Lindzey, ed., *Handbook of Social Psychology,* Vol. 2, Chap. 18. Cambridge, Massachusetts: Addison-Wesley, 1954, pp. 655-692.

Clausen, John A., ed. *Socialization and Society.* Boston: Little, Brown, & Co., 1968.

Coleman, James. *Equality of Educational Opportunity,* Washington, D.C.: U.S. Government Printing Office, 1966.

Dawson, Richard E. and Kenneth Prewitt. *Political Socialization.* Boston: Little, Brown, 1969.

Douvan, Elizabeth, and Allan Walker. "The Sense of Effectiveness in Public Affairs," *Psychological Monographs,* Vol. 70, No. 22 (1956).

Easton, David, and Jack Dennis. "The Child's Acquisition of Regime Norms: Political Efficacy," *American Political Science Review,* 61 (March, 1967), No. 1, pp. 25-39.

Easton, David, and Robert D. Hess. "Youth and the Political System," in Seymour Martin Lipset, and Leo Lowenthal, eds., *Culture and Social Character.* Glencoe, Illinois: Free Press, 1961, pp. 226-251.

Greenstein, F. I. *Children and Politics.* New Haven: Yale University Press, 1965.

Haggstrom, Warren. "The Power of the Poor," in L. Ferman *et al.,* eds., *Poverty in America.* Ann Arbor: University of Michigan Press, 1965.

Hess, Robert D. and Judith V. Torney. *The Development of Political Attitudes in Children.* Chicago: Aldine, 1967.

Hess, Robert D. "Political Attitudes in Children," *Psychology Today,* 2 (January, 1969) No. 8, 24-28.

Hess, Robert D. "Political Attitudes in Children," in *Readings in Psychology Today.* Del Mar, California: CRM Books, 1969, pp. 204-208.

Hess, Robert D. (with Virginia Shipman, Jere Brophy, Roberta Bear). *The Cognitive Environments of Urban Preschool Children.* Chicago: The Graduate School of Education, University of Chicago, 1968.

Hess, Robert D. (with Virginia Shipman, Jere Brophy, Roberta Bear). *The Cognitive Environments of Urban Preschool Children: Follow-up Phase.* Chicago: The Graduate School of Education, University of Chicago, 1969.

Hess, Robert D. "Parental Behavior and Children's School Achievement: Implications for Head Start." Paper presented at the fifth Head Start Research Seminar, Washington, D.C., January, 1969.

Hess, Robert D. "Political Socialization in the Schools," *Harvard Educational Review,* Vol. 38 (Summer 1968), No. 3, pp. 528-536.

Hyman, H. H. *Political Socialization: A Study in the Psychology of Political Behavior.* Glencoe, Illinois: Free Press, 1959.

Inkeles, A. "Industrial Man: the Relation of Status to Experience, Perception, and Value," *The American Journal of Sociology,* Vol. 66 (1960), 1-31.

Kamii, C. and N. Radin. "Class Differences in the Socialization Practices of Negro mothers," *Journal of Marriage and the Family,* 29 (1967), 302-310.

Kohn, M. L. "Social Class and Parent-child Relationships: An Interpretation," *The American Journal of Sociology* 48 (1963), 471-480.

Langton, Kenneth. "Peer Group and School and the Political Socialization Process," *American Political Science Review,* 61 (September, 1967), No. 3, 751-758.

Langton, Kenneth, and M. Kent Jennings. "Political Socialization and the High School Civics Curriculum in the United States," *American Political Science Review,* 62 (September, 1968), No. 3, 852-867.

Lefcourt, Herbert M. "Internal Vs. External Control of Reinforcement. A Review," *Psychology Bulletin,* 65 (1966), No. 4, 206-220.

Prewitt, Kenneth. "Political Efficacy," *International Encyclopedia of the Social Sciences,* Vol. 12. New York: The Macmillan Co. and the Free Press, 1968, pp. 225-228.

Rotter, Julien B. "Generalized Expectancies for Internal Versus External Control of Reinforcement," *Psychological Monographs,* Vol. 80, No. 1 (1966), pp. 1-28.

White, Elliot S. "Intelligence and Sense of Political Efficacy in Children," *Journal of Politics,* 30 (August, 1968) No. 3, 710-731.

Walters, J., R. Connor, and M. Zunich. "Interaction of Mothers and Children from Lower Class Families," *Child Development,* 35 (1964) 433-440.

Lucian W. Pye

Political Culture and National Character

Professor Pye is on the faculty of the Department of Political Science of the Massachusetts Institute of Technology.

ONE OF THE MOST DISTINCTIVE FEATURES OF MAN, AS A SOCIAL ANI-
mal, is his ability to distinguish between in-group and out-group. With
his social awareness comes the sense of the differences between one's
own community and that of foreigners. Within a domestic society people
learn to distinguish among ethnic, class, and geographical differences.
With greater sophistication comes an appreciation of differences among
foreign communities. It is, therefore, extremely natural for people to
discuss national differences.

It might even be argued that at the very beginning of the social
sciences there was a concern with differences in national character. In
both Herodotus and Tacitus one finds sharp and penetrating observations about the roots of national differences. The earliest Chinese annals
note the different traits of various foreign groups. Such writers as de
Tocqueville, Bryce and Emerson were centrally concerned with the
question of national temperament. The popular appeal of this tradition
of sweeping generalizations about national character is still powerful as
can be seen from the wide popularity of Luigi Barzini's discussions of
Italians, Lin Yutang on the Chinese, Fosio Maraini on the Japanese,
and V. S. Pritchett on the Spanish temper.

The current tendency of political science to move away from the
earlier fields of political philosophy and speculative theory has made
us forget the extent to which the best minds have contributed to our
tradition of national character. Herbert Spencer was convinced that "A
nation's institutions and beliefs are determined by its character."[1] Im-
manuel Kant and David Hume were serious students of the subject.
Indeed, Hume went so far as to suggest that a basic criterion for distinguishing political theorists is precisely the capacity to make intelligent
and not silly generalizations about national character. "The vulgar are
apt to carry all *national characters* to extremes; and having once established it as a principle, that any people are knavish, or cowardly, or
ignorant, they will admit of no exception, but comprehend every
individual under the same censure. Men of sense condemn these undis-
tinguishing judgments: though at the same time, they allow, that each
nation has a peculiar set of manners, and that some particular qualities
are more frequently to be met with among one people than among their
neighbours."[2]

And, of course, from Aristotle through Montesquieu there has been
a long tradition of seeking to relate political institutions and legal traditions to national temperament which in turn is related to geographical
and climatic considerations. The self-serving character of some of these
generalizations seems relatively obvious: Montesquieu with his feeling
that Europe provides the best environment for ideal political development and Aristotle arguing that Europe is too cold and Asia and Africa
too hot so only the Hellenic peoples can have the best government.

For the contemporary social scientist there is something slightly disturbing about these earlier exercises in describing national character. The suspicion often is that the authors are merely reflecting certain stereotypes or personal prejudices, which may easily change according to the political climate of the moment.[3] Subjective impressions should have no place in the social sciences, particularly, when they can so easily be merely the biases of the author who has not engaged in any form of systematic observation.

Yet objective considerations do suggest that people are more likely to be different than not. Fundamentally, assumptions about differences in national cultures are exactly the same as the assumption that attitudes and opinions differ according to age, sex, occupation and class, assumptions which are of the very essence of social science. Therefore, to pretend that national differences do not exist is as great, if not greater, violation of the spirit of empirical science as to make biased observations. In short, to suggest that all cultures are the same calls for an ideological commitment that is a form of prejudice. Hence, there is a basic dilemma for the social scientist: on the one hand, it seems inappropriate to make characterizations of national differences without sound objective information: but on the other hand, to pretend that national differences do not exist is to fly in the face of not only common sense but substantial evidence.

In the 1940s and early 1950s some anthropologists thought that we were moving toward a more scientific way of studying national character. The great advances that came from the work of Margaret Meade and Ruth Benedict in the application of psychoanalytic theory to the study of anthropology seemed to open the way to a much more sophisticated understanding of national character. The theories about the relationship of culture and personality suggested that there were solid intellectual bases for recognizing national differences. At the same time, advances in sample survey techniques made it possible to measure objectively differences in attitudes and opinions from culture to culture. Possibly because the subjects of many of these earlier studies were our former enemies—the Germans and the Japanese—there was little sensitivity to the danger that errors in our generalizations might be the cause of injustice. We seemed to be establishing a new rule of history: the losers of wars must pay the price of defeat by being the subjects of national character analysis.

Yet by the mid-1950s interest in national character studies declined sharply in the social sciences. In part, this was only a reflection of the decline in the influence of anthropologists in public affairs. Immediately after World War II it was possible for Clyde Kluckhohn to write in *Mirror For Man* that anthropology, by providing a broader and truer perspective in social life, was about to solve most of the problems of mankind. In a few years it was apparent that anthropology could not fulfill such exaggerated expectations, and the effort to apply the techniques for analyzing small primitive societies had proved inadequate for studying the large national cultures of the industrialized world. Indeed, it was the anthropologists themselves who became most aware of the lack of rigor and precision in these techniques.

A basic difficulty with the national character approach as it evolved in the immediate post-war period was precisely the problem of measurement. Wise and imaginative writers such as Geoffrey Gorer, Erich Fromm and Otto Kleinberg could make subtle and insightful observations about national differences, but when it came to systematic research there was no agreement as to standards for measuring such differences. If the study of national character was to become more scientific and more systematic there would have to be a change from the speculative interpretations to more systematic modes of observation and measurement. The difficulty with improving on measurements, however, is that it is extremely costly and demanding. In a sense, Nathan Leites confronted this problem in his classic article on psychocultural hypotheses when he suggested, that the difficulties of empirical testing could be met by recognizing, that most statements about cultural characteristics should be advanced in the spirit of tentative generalizations, for which there could be theoretical, if not practical, methods of testing.[4] This tolerant approach to the methodological problem, however, was ruthlessly dismissed by Alex Inkeles and David J. Levinson in their equally classic article when they adopted an agnostic view as to the existence of national character but called for such purist standards of measurement as to all but destroy the concept and to take much of the fun out of speculating about cultural themes.[5]

It is true that such concepts as "modal personality" may seem to violate some of the most elementary concerns of scientific analysis, for the concept does not build upon the measurement of immediate empirical phenomena—it is argued, for example, that no particular individual is likely to manifest all the characteristics identified in a modal personality type. We shall have to return to this problem of the aggregating of personality characteristics, but it is enough here to note that the concept of national character in political science at least, probably could have survived the issues of measurement if it had not been for a more serious difficulty.

The most critical weakness in the national character studies, as far as political analysis, was their failure to recognize that the political sphere constitutes a distinct sub-culture, and that all generalizations about a society are not necessarily equally applicable to the political realm. The rather casual way in which analysts of national character tended to move back and forth from the crib to the cabinet, from child training practices to grand strategy decisions, seems to suggest that they were uninformed or insensitive about many of the inherent realities of politics.

Political Culture and
the Socialization Process

In meeting this problem we have had to develop a more sophisticated view of the psychological dimensions of politics. Specifically, we have had to recognize that politics is a distinctive activity in all societies and that in each setting it develops a culture of its own; and, therefore, a distinction must be made between those people who participate in the political realm, and those who have little effect at all on politics. In all societies there is a significant difference between those who wield power and deal in public affairs and those who are mere citizens and unattentive observers. National character studies generally made no recognition of this inherent distinction.

Essentially what occurred with the development of political culture was to recognize that socialization and culture are inherently linked, and thus if there is a culture relating to the political sphere there must also be processes by which people are socialized to that culture.

In theory it is possible to conceptualize the individual being first socialized into his general culture, and then as he matures he passes through a second process of socialization as he takes on his political attitudes and becomes knowledgeable about public affairs. The process of political socialization can, in turn, lead the individual into an active role in the political realm itself, and thus there is a third process, that of political recruitment. Political socialization and recruitment are thus related to political culture in the same manner as the general socialization process is related to the culture of a society.

The concept of political culture as developed by Gabriel A. Almond stems from his observation that "every political system is imbedded in a particular pattern of orientations to political action."[6] Sidney Verba has noted that political culture "Consists of the system of empirical belief, expressive symbols, and values which define the situation in which action takes place."[7] In the International Encyclopedia of the Social Sciences I have written that, "Political culture is the set of attitudes, beliefs, and sentiments which give order and meaning to a political process and which provide the underlying assumptions and rules that govern behavior in the political system. It encompasses both the political ideals and the operating norms of a polity. Political culture is thus the manifestation in aggregate form of psychological and subjective dimensions of politics. A political culture is the product of both the collective history of a political system and a life history of the members of that system, and thus is rooted equally in public events and private experiences."

Thus, the innovation of the concept of political culture represented in part an attempt to achieve the more orderly and systematic way of noting differences in political styles and approaches. It represented a way of breaking away from the more sweeping generalizations associated with the approaches of national character. At the same time, the concept of political culture represents an effort to encompass more systematically in political analysis the findings of depth psychology.

As further empirical work has gone on with the use of the concept of political culture, it has become increasingly evident that while the concept may represent an advance over the national character approach there are still some very basic problems. These difficulties seem to be inherent in the larger problem of bringing together political analysis and modern psychology. While it is true that all forms of political analysis rest on some concepts, however crude, of psychology and the nature of man, it does seem that the advances of modern depth psychology has raised problems that have certainly not been resolved, and possibly they are ultimately unresolvable.

In the pages that follow we shall identify some of these problems. We must begin, however, by briefly noting the basic problem that has been plaguing political science ever since we made the effort to respond to the profound insights of clinical psychology.

Psychology and the
Political System

Although the insights of Freud and the new world of man which he inspired have given most people anxieties and trouble, they have been peculiarly troublesome to the social sciences with their strong commitment to the concept of nationality. From economics through government and politics the underlying assumption of human behavior has been that it should be valid to interpret all acts according to the calculus of the maximisation of interests. Freud suggested that man was infinitely more complex and that there was a logic of the subjective realm that did not necessarily match the logic of "objective considerations."

In seeking to apply the insights derived from the clinical situation to the understanding of history the basic question has been whether the new psychological knowledge required a reconstruction of our models of the "objective" political system or whether this knowledge only provided a deeper and more subtle understanding of individual behavior. Should the insights of psychoanalysis cause us to conceive of political and social institutions largely in characterological terms? Or are we given only a means of enriching our understanding of the individual while our models of the larger society-sized system remain largely intact?

Freud personally was convinced that his clinical discoveries were relevant for the understanding of history and society, especially because of the direct linkage between private fantasies and collective myths. In a sense, Freud treated the social world as merely an extension of the family situation. In the main, however, social scientists have tended to retain the concept of objective social and political systems and to treat psychoanalytical insights as relevant solely for understanding individual behavior. When Harold Lasswell took the initial step of incorporating psychoanalytic theory into political science he proceeded on the assumption that the political system had its own autonomy and had its own standards and rules. For Lasswell the political system had its own requirements and its specialized roles, and questions of personality were critical only in so far as they influenced the role performance of particular actors.

The concept of political culture represents a further step in the effort to combine psychological understanding with political analysis by seeking to establish a more subtle relationship between personality and political behavior. By conceiving of political socialization and recruitment as being equally related to personality development and general socialization on the one hand and preparation for role performance on the other, the approach of political culture seeks to avoid the question of the primacy of either personality or the role system of politics. Just as in sociology it is possible to conceive of personality and culture as the two sides of the same coin so in political analysis it should be possible by means of the political culture concept to see individual personality and aggregate political behavior as different manifestations of the same phenomena.

Although the ideal of political culture analysis is thus to achieve a balance between psychological and sociological considerations, in actual practice the stress from psychology is very strong. At present, there appears to be certain common distortions in our theory-building which need to be noted and which can be traced directly to the basic orientation of the psychological approaches that are being utilized in political science.

The Emphasis of
Continuity over Change

One of the most immediate effects on political culture theory of its dependence upon psychology has been a tendency to think of "explanation" as requiring only that current behavior be traced back to analogous behavior at an earlier stage of individual development. This in turn has tended to give emphasis to continuity and to leave change as being beyond explanation. Much of the artistry and "explanation" in psychoanlaysis has been in finding that the behavior of adults is firmly rooted in earliest childhood behavior. The fundamental assumption is that the discovery of similar behavior at an earlier stage of life provides a valid explanation of later motives. The stress is upon continuity of motives and feelings and since the spirit of analysis is highly deterministic there seems to be little point in seeking to explain change.

In part, the reason for this quality of "originitis" as Erickson once described it, is that a central concern in psychological theory has been to distinguish biologically determined behavior, learned behavior, and national innovations. Psychoanalytic theory has been committed to the view that behavior is not random, and that there is always some purpose behind what might otherwise be rationally quite inexplainable.

With the anthropologists the prime concern with personality development shifted from distinguishing between nationality and learned behavior to distinguishing between culturally learned behavior and social or biologically determined behavior. The anthropologists have been nearly unanimous in seeking to demonstrate the fallacies of using racial or biological considerations in explaining social behavior. Particularly in the late 1930's and early 1940's when Margaret Meade, Ruth Benedict and other anthropologists were seeking to counter any racist doctrines there was an understandable enthusiasm for psychoanalytical explanation of personality development because the theory provided an explanation for why learned behavior in the form of basic culture could be transmitted from generation to generation without any biological assistance. Psychoanalytic theory in suggesting how the personality was moulded and shaped and in explaining how cultures were transmitted, became a weapon for destroying racist "explanations." In a strange way the anthropologists' campaign against the "determinism" of racial views

resulted in an almost equally deterministic theory based on the perva-
siveness and prominence of culture.

Even before this development a central problem of anthropology
had been that of explaining continuity in behavior. If the basis of the
continuity of cultural differences does not lie in biological or gross environmental factors, then how is it possible to explain the long historical maintenance of such cultures as Chinese, Hindu, and Western,
to say nothing of the far more primitive ones? In seeking to account for
this continuity the anthropologists found great comfort in the powerful
theories of depth psychology which indeed suggest that personalities
were shaped at a very early stage and that cultures could be transmitted
effectively as they are built out of the same processes that produce the
individual personality.

It is worth noting here that this concern of the anthropologist to
give an explicit explanation for continuity is something which the non-
behavioral fields have simply ignored. For example, historians have
been on edge to trace the origins of behavior to earlier periods, but
they have not felt an equal need to explain how the pattern of behavior
could be transmitted over time. Historians of China, for example, often
observe that many features of Communist behavior are the same as
similar patterns common in traditional China. Indeed, historians often
believe that they have somehow "explained" Chinese Communist practices by simply noting that it is analogous to behavior found a hundred,
a thousand or two thousand years ago in China. In a strange fashion
historians often point to such examples of continuity as proof of the
importance or power of "history," but they do not usually feel compelled
to explain the mechanism which maintain such traditions. Clearly,
"traditions" cannot be preserved through the written words and the
reading of historical texts, for if this were possible Western scholars
who spent more time and energy working on Chinese historical material would have their behavior affected; yet it is Chinese who never read
the classical texts who are maintaining the traditions.

It is only through the empirical traditions of the behavioral sciences
that we have sought to be very explicit about the mechanism for
passing on social heritages. This in turn has meant, however, that the
emphasis in the social sciences on the relationship of generations has
been mainly in terms of continuities. This bias in cultural analysis has,
of course, been carried over into political science when we elaborated
the concept of political culture.

It is true that the theory of political culture has tended to emphasize, somewhat, more the later stages of political socialization, and,
hence, the more cognitive phases of learning. In the political culture

approach there is thus greater emphasis than in the earlier national character work on the learning experiences outside the family and what happens at school and through the mass media. Yet there is no escaping the fact that the power of any cultural theory lies in explaining continuity and not change, and, hence, the concept of political culture does, at present, have difficulties in throwing light on the dynamics of political change.

The Power of Personality Theory Versus the Necessity of Macro-Theory

This bias toward continuity is rooted in the impressive powers of psychological theories. Political science has had to respond in other ways to the sheer potency of modern developments in psychology, and the result has been a rising tendency to favor analysis that concentrates on the individual. Indeed, possibly the most significant basis for the success of behavioralism in political science is precisely the fact that this approach does exploit the inherent powers of psychological theories because it focuses upon the actions of individuals.

The strengths of psychological approaches lie not only in the insights from clinical analysis but also from the potential for measurement and quantification which comes from social psychology. For political science this advantage has led to wide ranging research in measuring the distribution and intensity of attitudes and opinions. The result has been an acute macro-micro problem in political science which the concept of political culture poses but does not resolve.

We can explain this problem best by comparing developments in political science with those in economics, a discipline that has amazingly ignored the behavioral revolution and still clings to the rational model of man by pretending that Freud never existed. The main thrust of economic theory has been at the macro-level and certainly they have never, as political scientists have, tried to construct their general system by aggregating the subjective feelings, sentiments and opinions of the individuals who make up the economic system. It is safe to say that had the economists begun their theory-building by trying to track down all influences that affect behavior within the economic system they would not have arrived at the extremely impressive general theory which they have today. Had the economists sought to measure the attitudes and opinions of all those who are involved in shaping the economic system they would not have been able to put them together into a coherent system that would be the objective economy. In short, what Keynes did was to ignore much of individual behavior and postulate quite abstractly a model of the national income flow. As far as Keynes was concerned the basic question of economics was how does the flow of money affect the economy and how do people in a sense adjust their behavior to the dictates of the system. Once macro-system is accepted on its own terms, the problem of analyzing the effects of psychological attitudes and opinions becomes a marginal problem with very set limits. Macro-economic theory thus provides the broad guidelines for predicting how the system as an economic system is likely to perform, while studies of the behavior of individual firms and customers serve mainly to modify the gross theory. In short, in economics the approach was to begin with a macro-model and fill in the behavioral dimensions.

In much of behavioral political science the approach has been the other way around as we begin with the behavioral dimensions and hope to aggregate individual acts and arrive at a picture of the larger system. If we were to follow the route that the economists have trod we would have to begin by characterizing the behavior of the larger political system, and then ask ourselves what are the critical attitudes that people would have to have for their larger system to perform the way that it does. The search would then be for, not the whole range of attitudes that a population may have, but for the existence of certain critical attitudes and values that makes it possible for the system to do as it does.

The Distribution of Attitudes Versus Critical Attitudes in Measuring Political Culture

We are, indeed, in a situation in which we are faced with a dilemma in our approach to political culture analysis. On the one hand, we do not want to give up the advantages that have come from the behavioral approach with its stress on the individual, but on the other hand the discipline, as we shall be shortly noting, is in even greater need to develop macro-theories. For political culture analysis this suggests the possibility of two different approaches. One approach would proceed on the basis of where our greatest strength lies—in measurement and quantitification—and would seek to depict as precisely and accurately the distribution of attitudes in a population and from this infer the nature of the political culture. The other approach would be to attempt to analyze the performance of the total political system, note its distinctive qualities and characteristics, and then turn to individual analysis of behavior to note the existence and the particular character of those psychological qualities that presumably make the system perform as it does. The advantage of the first approach is, of course, that it rests upon the tried and true methods of sample survey techniques, and with it there is a clear objective way of measuring differences from one culture to another. The great difficulty in this approach, however, is that it is hard to interpret the significance of differences in the distribution of attitudes and opinions or to suggest how such differences might actually affect the performance of the system as a whole.

The second approach has the advantage of focusing on the political system as the basic unit of analysis and, therefore, in the tradition of Harold Lasswell it treats psychological analysis as essentially enriching and strengthening other forms of observation and interpretation. Its weakness, of course, is that its success depends to a very great extent on the interpretative capacity of the analyst and thus there is always a danger that subjective considerations will color the study.

Basically, these two different approaches represent the classic micro-macro problem in political science. It might seem that it should make little difference whether we started with individual attitudes and aggregated them, or looked for the ideals of the system and found their support in individual sentiments. The difficulty, however, is that people have more attitudes, feelings and sentiments about politics than are reflected in their actual behavior. The richness of the human personality provides an extremely complex way for understanding and perceiving politics. The difficulty is to determine the criticality of any particular set of attitudes as far as performance of either the individual or of the system as a whole.

In short, the individual is in many respects far more complicated than the governmental system of which he is a part. As Karl Deutsch has noted in his *Nerves of Government* the individual brain has a greater potential for making "communication" linkages and connections than does the entire United States government. Therefore, a study of the political system that begins with a total inventory of individual feelings and attitudes runs into the danger of being unable to determine the limits of relevance.

A second problem of political culture studies that focus on individual attitudes is that of how to aggregate opinions in order to arrive at the collective body of attitudes and values that make up the system. The fact that it is possible to devise tests to measure individual opinions makes it very tempting to simply total up the distribution of opinions and arrive at cumulative figures which can then be assumed to represent the substance of the political culture of the system. The difficulty with this approach, however, is that we have no theories that explain the significance of any statistical differences in the distribution of attitudes in a population. How important is it that there is a ten or twenty percent difference in attitudes according to some instrument of opinion measurement? Is a five percent difference relevant or is a ten percent range of difference important or does it have to be a higher order of magnitude? Unfortunately, our theories about cultures do not provide guidance as to relevance of such percentage differences.

The limitations of such an aggregative approach are apparent when we try to deal with historical periods and the differences among generations. It is significant that in the behavioral approach to social science there is really no place for the concept of historic generations, only the discrete relationships between individual parents and children. This problem first struck me a few years ago when Sigmund Neuman was pressing upon me the value of the concept of "crisis generation." My problem was that from a behavioral point of view people are born every day and there is then a continuous and smooth age curve, so how is it possible to recognize from a societal point of view the "breaks" that would be equivalent to the gap between the individual father and son? Yet from an historical point of view there clearly is such a phenomenon as generation, just as there is the differences in the "decades" or in other historic periods. Historically there are certainly differences between one decade and another; the "gay 90's," the "roaring 20's," the "grim 30's," and the "soaring 60's" all have a reality that is hard to account for in social science theory, particularly if we have to use a simple aggregative approach. What proportion of men in the 1890's engaged in barbershop quartet singing, and wore striped sportcoats and straw hats to make that decade distinct from any other decade? How many people were in flappers and wore raccoon skin coats during the 1920's? Is this question of decades or generational changes and differences really a matter of quantitative changes, or is it a question of certain critical changes within certain limited elites?

For understanding the performance of the political system it may be more important to know whose opinions are changing them and what are the changes in total distributions of attitudes. Any aggregating approach is likely to miss the small critical changes, which when emphasized by the mass media, provide the bases for historical periodizations and system-wide changes.

This problem of the impact of small changes on the character of total systems was brought home to me vividly a few years ago when the late Norbert Weiner was commenting to a group of social scientists on a theme which preoccupied him in his later years: the decline of moral integrity and the increasing pretentiousness of intellectual life. He was recounting to the group how in the small town in which he grew up the two daughters of the janitor of the high school had devoted themselves to building and enriching the public library. The moral that he drew was that there has been a critical decline in the numbers of people who in modest and unassuming ways work to improve the world. At this point one of the empirical social scientists in the group spoke up and said, "Come, come, Norbert, how much of a change do you think there really has been in attitudes? How many people ever were like those two wonderful ladies you have described, and how many people do you think are like that today?" Weiner reared back and thought for only a second before saying, "Why I am sure that at one time about four percent of the population manifested such characteristics, and now I suspect there is only two percent; a shocking fifty percent decline. That changes the tone of our whole world."

Grand Abstractions and
Fuzzy Definitions

These are all serious problems that complicate the analysis of political cultures if we focus primarily on the individual. What are the problems if we begin from the other side and commence our study of the cultural dimensions by focussing on the performance of the total system?

Increasingly in recent years, political science has been moving back toward "holistic" or total system analysis. The principal reason for this trend is that since World War II and the expansion of new countries all over the world, we have become absorbed with the notion of political development. If political development has any significance at all as a concept, it deals with the performance of a total political system. Political development manifestly involves more than a few limited changes in attitudes and behavior; it must represent some kind of change in the total performance of the political system.

Thus we need to return to a grand abstraction such as the "political system" which is, unfortunately, not easily related to empirical phenomena. This creates within our discipline a basic methodological strain because the entire earlier trend of behavioralism was in the direction of rejecting such grand abstractions as the "state," "sovereignty" and the like and using only concepts that could be directly related to individual behavior and action. This was the trend that was sustained by the arguments of logical positiveness and the hope that the accummulation of tested "middle range hypotheses" would soon produce a growing body of truly scientific knowledge.

Our current dilemma in political science, which is sharply accentuated in the political culture approach, is that we feel compelled to deal with even larger systems of analysis, which means that we must work with very broad abstractions, and thus our "theories" tend to become less theories based upon testable propositions and more in the nature of heuristic formulations. On the other hand, our efforts on systematic proposition testing, which seemed to offer great potentials as a result of the disciplined work in psychology, has not gone ahead in a manner conducive to producing solid theories.

We are in a sense groping for a new paradigm which will make it possible for us to combine the capacities of heuristic formulations to illuminate large macro-systems of behavior and the scientific precision that rests with operationalizable propositions and quantitatively testable hypotheses.

In spite of all the difficulties which we have identified with the concept of political culture, it is possible that this approach may yet be able to provide the outlines of such a paradigm. For the concept of political culture does suggest that there may be a linkage between individual psychology and collective behavior that is based on more than a mere quantitative aggregation of individual sentiments and attitudes. Erik H. Erikson has, for example, subtly advanced a psychologically oriented theory about the relationship of a great leader's personal conflicts and his capacity to articulate a meaningful ideology for the people of his time who in lesser ways may be sharing his problems. In suggesting such a linkage between personal identity issues and public ideological successes, Erikson has advanced a new way of seeing the linkage between micro and macro-analysis.

The Critical Themes

It may be possible through political culture analysis to go beyond the Erikson theme of identity and suggest other themes that are basic to both personality development and the sentiments basic to the political systems. Indeed, there appear to be at least five such linking themes;

1. Identity

The demonstration of the value of this theme as a link between psychological considerations and historical processes lies not only in Erikson's study of Luther. We would note that basic to all politics is a strong sense of the parochial, of the distinctiveness of each community. In economic and social theories about development and stages of society it is possible to focus upon universal qualities, but in politics there are always the realities of particularistic histories which tie each polity to some time and place.

2. Loyalty and Trust

Beyond identity there is a larger issue of affection that is the basis of human relationship and the potential of trust in inter-personal associations. The base value of politics is indeed the question of loyalty: who belongs to whom? with what degree of commitment? and with respect to what issues? The capacity for loyalty and trust are matters that take both the basic personality of individuals and the fundamental climate of social life in any society. In politics there is always the need to identify with others, and indeed the only way a political actor can find his public role is to take on some larger identification, for the political self is always much more than the mere private ego.

3. Authority and Hierarchy

Power and authority are the fundamental staff of political life, and in personal development the dependency relationship between the child and the authority of parents is equally basic. It is not strange that in so much of the early work on national character there was an early tendency to link family experiences with public affairs, for in both contexts a common issue is that of how to manifest and in turn how to cope with authority. The mystique of authority which is basic to a functioning political system is, in a sense, a direct product of the early socialization experience.

4. Aggression and Conflict Management

A basic problem of the individual is to learn how to control and express human aggression and, in a sense, the most elementary purpose of the political system is to provide a social means for coping with this same phenomenon of aggression. All the different types of defense mechanism known to the individual personality seem to have their direct counterparts in collective patterns of behavior.

5. Cohesion and Integration

Finally, there is the very basis of ego psychology, the need for the individual to integrate all the strands of his personality, which is the same problem that a political system is confronted with, if it is to become effective. The dynamics of ego organization is remarkably similar to the dynamics of social cohesion and integration.

The Challenge

The challenge of political culture analysis is thus much more than just reducing some of the more obvious failings of national character analysis. Potentially political culture theory can provide a basis for resolving many of the most perplexing problems in contemporary political science. Through this approach we may be able to link together some of the oldest issues in political theory with some of the most recent findings of psychological research.

The basic strains in political culture analysis, in which we must try to cope with two equally vague abstractions—that of the political process and that of the entire subjective domain of man—will require that we appropriate canons of research and analysis which can become the guidelines for other fields of social science. The test of whether we can, in the spirit of the most rigorous and precise concept of science, move on to studying problems that lie beyond immediate empirical testing is, indeed, the crucial test that the social sciences generally face as we seek new paradigms for handling system-wide problems.

In striving to meet this test it is, however, to be hoped that political culture will not lose that spark of penetrating imagination that has given zest and spirit to national character studies. The pleasures and amusements of observing national differences will hopefully sustain us as we seek to become a new kind of scientist.

Notes

[1] *Social Statics*, Pt. II, Ch. 16, sec. 5. Quoted by Dhirendra Narain, *Hindu Character*, Bombay, University of Bombay, 1957, p. 2.

[2] "Of National Characters" in *Essays—Moral, Political, and Literary*, p. 244; Quoted in Narain, *ibid.*, p. 2.

[3] Harold Isaacs, for example, has graphically recorded the changing feelings that Americans have had toward China according to the state of American/Chinese relations. See His *Scratches On Our Minds*, New York, John Day, 1958.

[4] Nathan Leites, "Psycho-Cultural Hypotheses about Political Acts," *World Politics*, Vol. 1, No. 1, October 1948, pp. 102-19.

[5] Alex Inkeles and D. J. Levinson, "National Character: The Study of Model Personality and Socio-Cultural Systems," in Gardner Gardner Lindzey (ed.), *Handbook of Social Psychology*, Cambridge, Mass., Addison-Wesley, 1954, Vol. II, pp. 977-1020.

6 Gabriel A. Almond, "Comparative Political Systems," *Journal of Politics,* Volume 18, 1956.

7 Sidney Verba, "Comparative Political Culture," in Lucian W. Pye and Sidney Verba, editors, *Political Culture and Political Development,* Princeton, Princeton University Press, 1965, p. 513.

Political
Communication

Charles E. Osgood

Conservative Words and Radical Sentences in the Semantics of International Politics

Professor Osgood is on the faculty of the Department of Psychology of the University of Illinois.

ALBERT EINSTEIN, WITH THE FORESIGHT CHARACTERISTIC OF TRUE genius, had this to say at the dawn of the nuclear age: "The unleashed power of the atom has changed everything except our ways of thinking. Thus we are drifting toward a catastrophe beyond comparison. We shall require a substantially new manner of thinking if mankind is to survive." It will be my thesis that a new manner of thinking about our world will first require a revolution in how we talk about it.

In this paper I shall try to demonstrate that certain principles of psycholinguistics have relevance to the science, and art, of politics—particularly international politics. Psycholinguistics is that facet of the human sciences which deals with relations between the characteristics of messages and the states of the (human) organisms which exchange them. We shall be concerned primarily with the semantic aspects of these relations—with the meanings of word forms, with the rules by which words are combined into phrases and sentences, with the effects of one's utterings and scribblings upon others, with the semantic and valuative constraints upon what we ordinarily say with our words and sentences, and with how we can get out of this bind by some calculated rule-breaking.

The reader may well be wondering just what all this could possibly have to do with politics, particularly international politics. To satisfy this wonderment is, of course, the task I have set for myself. Throughout this paper I shall introduce each new notion with illustrations drawn from ordinary language and only then move into illustrations and analyses in the realm of international politics. I adopt this strategy for two reasons: first, because we are all most familiar with the ordinary language we use in communicating with family, friends and storekeepers, and the examples are therefore more compelling; second, because examples drawn from contemporary international relations, necessarily reflecting my personal political values, are liable to be controversial and hence lose their force. But since semantics is obviously an individual matter, we must assume that the principles involved can be transferred from Individual to Nation.

Personification of international relations is a common practice of social scientists and statesmen, just as it is among laymen. It is even to be found regularly in the writings of those scholars who would be the first to deny, as a matter of disciplinary principle, that laws of individual behavior apply to social groups. Such *implicit* personification—and consequent uncritical use of folk psychology in the interpretation of international relations—is both deceptive and dangerous. But there is a paradox here: Although one may deplore such naivety, if personification is in fact common practice in thinking and decision-making in international affairs, then it must be considered part of the subject matter of political science *and made as explicit as possible*. It is my hope that this paper will contribute something to this Individual-to-Nation process.

One can identify at least three typical modes of transfer from Individual to Nation as a means of interpretation. *Mode I. Social groups are merely individual humans operating within a social context.* This is the characteristic attitude of the social psychologist. Since there are no nervous connections between individual human islands, group decisions necessarily involve *communication* among individulas—and hence semantics. *Mode II. Key individuals are the determiners of national behavior.* This is the characteristic approach of many historians, novelists and, perhaps, statesmen. The crucial assumption is that the terminal behavior of any group is determined primarily by some focal individual —a Churchill, a de Gaulle, a Roosevelt. In this Mode, of course, the transfer from Individual to Nation is direct—being human, each key leader is entirely subject to the laws of human behavior, including laws of semantics. *Mode III. Multi-level system theory: systems at all levels of organization, from cell to individual to small group to nation, are subject to the same set of generalized organizational and information-processing principles.* This is also a direct mode of transfer, but it entails a number of assumptions that are difficult to meet in practice—for example, that such principles can be stated in sufficiently general terms, that the constructs to which the principles apply equivalently can be identified at the several levels, and that there are no "special principles" at a given level which drastically modify the operation of the general ones.[1]

For present purposes, I shall assume that principles of semantics discoverable at the individual level can be transferred to the national level by all of these modes—by the fact that individual humans do participate in the behaviors of nations, by the fact that certain individuals do play key roles in the "decisions" of nations, and by the fact that principles of information-processing (perceiving, interpreting, decision-making, executing) probably do have their analogues at all levels. It can be noted in passing that present technologies of communication and transportation undoubtedly serve to reduce the gap between ordinary individuals and decision-making individuals, thereby facilitating the transfer from Individual to Nation.

Conservative Words

Words are conservative. Although they do adapt to changes in the real world, they do so very slowly if left to themselves. Assuming a lawful and immutable relation between words and things, we humans keep trying to force *things* to conform to the meanings their *words* have acquired in the past. Thus were the semantics of World War I applied in preparing for World War II, and the French built a completely useless Maginot Line and a false sense of security behind it. So do we seem to be preparing for World War III, despite desperately not wanting it, by applying the semantics of World War II.

Wrapped up in the whole process as we are, it is difficult to perceive the lag between our language and the world it is supposed to describe and interpret. Occasionally a dramatic failure of events to conform with our expectations may jolt us into awareness that our world is changing—a rash of race riots in the slums or a score of people suffocating in the smog of American cities. The brighter among us may note that there is a constant conservative bias in our predictions about the future—sputniks appear in our skies and the Chinese test deliverable nuclear weapons long before these things were supposed to happen.

In periods of history when the rate of cultural change was slow, words could almost keep up with things and their mismatch was barely perceptible. But in the present age, with its exploding population and its exploding technology—which means increasing human interaction and accelerated culture change—our semantic maps of the real world become outmoded more and more quickly. Add to this the fact that most decisions in today's world are being made by men in their fifties, sixties, seventies, or even eighties—men whose maps were outlined at least 30 years ago—and the language gap threatens to become an abyss. Led by old men reading old maps, we are trying to find our way through the Wonderland of the Twentieth Century, having more contact with the phantasy of words than the reality of things.

The gap between word and thing also increases with the remoteness of things from immediate, individual experience. As one moves outward —away from the intimacy of family, possessions and the ordinary round of living, toward the community, the nation and the world—the map becomes a less and less reliable guide to the territory. For one thing, we become less able to correct our verbal maps against the facts of the terrain. For another, the meanings of our words become increasingly dependent upon the words of others. The words with which we talk about the most critical issues of our time—*megatons, mutual deterrence, aggression, Cuba, A Two Chinas Policy, the Vietcong,* and even *Ho Chi Minh*—are what in my business are termed "assigns." Their meanings are literally assigned by association with other words put together by other people (usually in the mass media) rather than from direct experience with things and events. We have immediate knowledge about what a *knife* can do; our knowledge about what a *nuclear missile* can do is rather remote and gutless. Thus, irrationally, knowing that one's city is targeted by a 10-megaton nuclear missile some ten thousand miles away is not as threatening psychologically as knowing that a madman with a carving knife is loose in the city streets.

The Power of the Word

Words may be conservative, but they can also be powerful. Wherein lies the power of the word? For that matter, just what *is* a word? The spoken word is an evanescent burst of noise, usually encountered in streams of other noises which we call sentences, all formed and arranged by a complicated set of rules of which most of us are blissfully unaware. The written word is a particular pattern of squiggles on the printed page, separated by spaces from the many others; it is not quite as evanescent as the spoken word, but nevertheless each of us throws thousands of them away in the trash can every day.

The power of words obviously does not lie in these noises and squiggles per se. It lies, rather, in a very remarkable relation between these physical manifestations, called "signs," and certain processes in language users, called "meanings." This is the *representing relation.* Words come to evoke in their users some distinctive representation of the things referred to, and these representations can be manipulated symbolically much more easily than the things themselves. Thus we can behave—appropriately or otherwise—with respect to the not-here and the not-now. I can devise strategies in which nation-names move about my mind like chessman on a board; words about things remote can give me hope (*Ho Chi Minh has announced a gradual withdrawal of troops to positions behind the DMZ*) or they can give me fear (*The Soviets are secretely developing an anti-missile missile*).

Exactly what noises and squiggles will be used to represent what things and events is largely arbitrary—which is one reason why human languages are mutually unintelligible. When one is born into a given language-culture community, he unwittingly assumes a social contract to use noises and squiggles the way others in his community do—to use the noise "man" to refer to adult male humans, for example. But once the myriad contracts of lexical and syntactic usage have been agreed upon, the relation of meanings to things is *not arbitrary*—which is one reason why human languages are mutually translatable.

The meaning of a word can be conceived as a simultaneous bundle of distinctive semantic features. These features represent those differences in reactions to things and events which, in human experience, have been found to make a difference in adjustment to the physical and social environments. Thus the representing or symbolizing process utilizes a kind of code for highlighting what properties of things and events have been found to be important in experience. Recent studies in comparative psycholinguistics are beginning to make it appear that human groups, regardless of differences in language or culture, tend to use very similar systems of semantic features—as if, in general, they have found the same kinds of distinctions important to make.

In some of our own research, for example, we have been finding that humans highlight certain properties of interpersonal behavior, but not others, as semantic features in their interpersonal verbs.[2] What is also interesting is that they use many of the same verbs with the same features to talk about international relations, as if nations were people. There is an Associative-Dissociative feature (*help* vs. *hinder, protect* vs. *attack*), an Ego-Alter feature (*exploit* vs. *aid, manipulate* vs. *educate*), a Superordinate-Subordinate feature (*dominate* vs. *submit to, lead* vs. *follow*), a Future-Past feature (*promise* vs. *apologize, threaten* vs. *retaliate*), and so on. Needless to say, there is considerable danger of *mis*representation when we apply, willy-nilly, the semantics of interpersonal relations to the things and events of international relations.

Since the semantic features on which words are coded can never exhaust the properties of things which might be represented, it is inevitable that words must be abstractions. In this sense, words are caricatures of things. Although this is most obvious for big, impressive symbols like *Colonialism* or *Black Power,* it holds also for little ordinary words like *dog* and *pencil. It is precisely in this selective abstraction from reality that the power of words lies.* Those properties of things that are semantically coded are sharpened in thinking; those properties of things that are not so coded are blurred in thinking. A man can freeze to death for lack of kindling wood and yet be found with a pocketful of wooden pencils—because pencils are coded "to write with," not "to make fires with."

What facets of reality are sharpened or leveled by words depends on what properties of things have made a difference *in the past use* of the language. This is the conservatism of words, and it can make us attent to features of events which are now irrelevant and be oblivious to features which are now critical. Bound by an antiquated semantics of Power Politics, diplomats keep wary eyes on the shifting patterns of alliances and scurry about trying to maintain *mutual security pacts*— NATO's, SEATO's CENTRO's and PREPOSTRO's. The semantic coding of *mutual security pact* simultaneously fixes thought on the solidarity of one group and on its antagonism toward another. But the differences *within* the groups so segregated and the similarities *between* their particular members are obscured. Within the so-called Free World there are members which, by most criteria, are more similar to members of the so-called Communist Bloc, and vice versa.

The semantic features of words may either define or imply. For English speakers, the term *father* includes Male, Adult and Parental among its defining features and Dominance and Goodness among its implicative features. Any human we call a *father* must be an adult male who has progeny, or else we are breaking our linguistic contract, but obviously he need be neither good nor dominant. Substitution of implicative for defining features—that is, the use of emotive language—is the trademark of propaganda. Buck teeth and a spider body obviously did not *define* a Japanese human, but it did make him more kill-able in World War II. Just as the same odor may be called an *aroma* or a *stench,* depending upon how one wants the listener to feel about it, so may the same guerrillas be called *freedom fighters, rebels* or *terrorists,* depending upon how one wishes the listener to feel about them.

Words of Power

Among the few remaining places where myth and phantasy still have power for modern man are advertising and international relations. Although we cannot eat words, smoke words or shave with words, the advertising industry makes a valiant effort to achieve that end; incantations, spells, contagious and analogic magic are part of the trade. International politics has its incantations (*the right to self-determination*), its spells (*we have a commitment*), its contagious magic (*a threat to freedom in Asia is a threat to freedom in Podunk, U.S.A.*), and its analogic magic (*another Munich*). Both have everything it takes for mythmaking—remoteness from the individual, conflict between ultimate Goods and Evils, and near-omnipotence of the storytellers. And in both the myths created do serve many social functions: They provide an illusion of understanding, simple prescriptions for ordering a complex world, and the promise that, if the illusions are believed and the prescriptions followed, everyone will live happily ever after. In the political arena, at least, the storytellers are often their own most gullible audience.

The words of international power politics are typically analogic. There are analogies from interpersonal relations; nation-states become *We*'s and *They*'s who assume military *postures,* who glare at each other *eye-ball to eye-ball,* who *harass* or *intimidate* each other, who *trust* or are *suspicious* of each other. There are analogies from 19th Century physics, with *balances* of power or power *vacuums,* with *slippery slopes* or *rows of dominos* along which vague forces operate with some natural inevitability, with *attractions* and *repulsions,* and centers toward which power *gravitates.* There are analogies from history—*another Munich, another Dunkirk, another Korea, another Dienbienphu* —although historians assure us that History never repeats itself. Analogies have the same sharpening and blurring effects upon thinking that ordinary words do, only more so; they raise the feature analogized to a dazzling prominence which obscures other, often more relevant, features.

The pseudonyms which pepper dialogue in the nuclear age carry this attentuation of word from thing even further, adding semantic features which do not exist in the thing and neatly countermanding features which do exist. The title CAMELOT conferred a romantic, even chivalrous, tang to an ill-fated U.S. Army Project designed to study the causes of revolutions.[3] To name an ABM system SAFEGUARD certainly must make its possessors feel more secure. A touch of nobility is added to raw power when intercontinental ballistic missiles are named THOR, JUPITER, ATLAS, ZEUS and POLARIS—although I miss the ultimate in semantic deception which would be a missile named VENUS.

Acronyms—short-cuts which compress the forms of phrases into their initial letters—carry the attenuation of word from thing even further. They also put a great burden on human memory. Debates on the status of NATO and on the merits of ABM can be carried on with only remote reference to the things involved. They become "things" of sorts on their own, things to be defended or attacked by partisans or critics with more reference to personal and political loyalties than to the complex events and arrangements in the real world they actually represent. When an acronym is devised *before* a thing is given an ordinary name, contact with reality is liable to disappear entirely. A playful example from the argot of military space scientists is EGADS, which names the system used to destroy a malfunctioning missile after it has been launched[4]—translation, *electronic ground automatic destruct sequencer!*

Much of military jargon is designed to dehumanize things and thus protect the speaker or listener from feeling moral qualms. In *The Doomsday Dictionary* of Kaplan and Schwerner,[5] for example, we find that the tertiary effects of nuclear blast are ". . . damage received by displacement of the biological target, or blast flight," and this is further analysed into "differential displacement" (which translates as violent separation of hand, arm, leg, head, etc.) and "total displacement" (which really translates as being tossed into the next block in one chunk). The military do have a way of juggling semantic features. We never bomb a simple village hut in South Vietnam, it is always a "VC

structure." Since attacking primitive junks and sampans with technologi-
cally sophisticated naval destroyers has a decidedly bullying feel about
it, we now attack "water-borne logistic craft"—which our sailor-boys,
of course, immediately and refreshingly referred to as WIBLICS!

There are fads in word usage just as there are fads in everything
else that is human. Items which acquire prominence and prestige in
one domain are borrowed for use in other contexts. We seem to be enjoying a military fad in American English. From the *missile gap,* made
prominent in the Fifties, we now have forms like *production gap, education gap, credibility gap,* and even—alas!—my own *word gap!* The
term *escalate,* recently prominent in discussions of policy in Vietnam, is
now heard in almost any context that includes the single semantic feature
of Increasing—*escalating prices, escalating traffic deaths,* and even an
escalating peace offensive. I came across an advertisement for a local
restaurant which goes like this: "Conquer the New Year . . . Reserve
your warlike end-of-year festivities to the lusty atmosphere of (our
Dining) Room and Lounge . . . Leave '69 in your wake . . . Charter
your reservations for dinner and the demolition of the old year . . ."
If such fads are any indication of the dominant mood of a society, this
becomes more than a bit frightening.

Here are a few words of power to conjure with: The word *Power*
itself is often confused, by those who think they have it, with the word
Force. The meaning of *Power,* unlike *Force,* includes the feature of
being able to produce a desired result.[6] According to Edelman,[7] "force
signals weakness in politics, as rape does in sex." If the use or threat of
force serves to create the very outcome it was designed to prevent—for
example, setting up military bases in Thailand resulting in a sharp increase in communist counter-activity—then it is self-defeating and certainly not a demonstration of power.

Peace and *Freedom* are nice words, but they are otherwise quite
empty semantically. And being empty, they lend themselves to rather
bizarre uses. Is *Peace* a world spinning toward eternity triggered for
mutual annihilation and kept from it only by mutual fear? This is what
the phrase "peace through military strength" really means today. The
name of *Freedom,* along with the resounding phrase "law and order," is
often used to justify its exact opposite—to rationalize subservience to
authority and condone suppression of the freedom of others.

The term *Coexistence* does reflect an awareness of the irrationality
of mutual nuclear annihilation—but what more than this does it mean
to people? At an International Convocation on the Requirements of
Peace, held in 1965 by the Center for the Study of Democratic Institutions,[8] distinguished scholars from a number of countries focussed on
the implications of this term. Adam Schaff, semanticist from Poland,

observed that coexistence only has meaning in the context of competing political, economic and social systems—it is somehow anomalous to speak of coexistence between the United States and Canada. He went on to say that "coexistence is a fight, a competition, a noble competition for the hearts and minds of people." According to Paul-Henri Spaak of Belgium, "coexistence means only that you and we renounce war. For the rest we fight, trying to make the best demonstration we can that one system or the other is best."

It is interesting that most participants in the conference used the phrase *peaceful coexistence* to describe this state of affairs. Surely, *competitive coexistence* would more aptly represent what they had in mind. There are many ways one can enliven the word *coexistence*, and by so doing point forcefully to quite different real-world possibilities: one could talk about *fearful coexistence*, pointing to the inherent nature of mutual nuclear deterrence; one could talk about *aggressive coexistence,* pointing to everything short of all-out nuclear war; and one could talk about *tolerant coexistence*, pointing to acceptance of differences without trying to change them, and even *cooperative coexistence*, pointing to cooperation rather than competition despite differences in systems. Note that by insertion of varying adjectives we are ringing changes in meaning of the whole phrase, within the semantic framework established by *coexistence*—a process of word mixture to which we will return at a later point.

Socialism and *Capitalism* are certainly words to conjure with. Some people reason that *Socialism* equals communism and is therefore evil, that Russia and China are the leading socialist countries and are therefore unalterably evil. Other people reason that *Capitalism* is evil, that the United States is the leading capitalist country and therefore unalterably evil. In a survey conducted in Western Europe and the United States, Ralph K. White[9] found that 88% of the Europeans sampled believed the U.S. to be extremely capitalistic—by which they apparently meant private control of industry; 65% of them favored a moderate degree of socialism for themselves—by which they apparently meant government regulation of industry and social welfare legislation. Most Americans, reviewing the increases in government regulation and social welfare legislation in the U.S. over the past few decades, judged their own country to be moderately socialistic—precisely what most Europeans favor! Thus do words divide us.

In Defense of Ambiguity

Ambiguity can hurt. It does when the same word is used *in the same context*, but with different meanings for different people. Such is the case with *Socialism* and *Capitalism* above, to say nothing about *Democ-*

racy. Another example from the contemporary scene would be the phrase *Black Power*: it is obvious that for many Blacks it means the exercise of legitimate power of numbers, at the polls, in the market-place and in the community, whereas for many Whites it means an open threat to use physical force to gain objectives. But for most ordinary words, potential ambiguity is effectively eliminated *by context.* When someone says *duck* in the barnyard, I will not crouch as I will when the same word is uttered in a ball park. The sentence, *Support of the Israeli in the U.N. debate was unexpected,* is ambiguous when presented by itself—were the Israeli supporting or being supported?—but, in the context of a news report of Israeli air attacks on Lebanon, and U.N. censure thereof, there is no ambiguity.

Proponents of one World Language as the salvation of Mankind often include eliminating ambiguity as one of the planks in their plat-form—one word one meaning! Not only would this increase the size of our working vocabulary inordinately—the little word *play*, for example, has some 40 different meanings, at least 15 of which are quite common —but a language free of ambiguity would be like sand in the fluid coupling of man-to-man and man-to-government. Some degree of am-biguity is necessary for a smoothly functioning society.

Political scientist Murray Edelman[10] makes the insightful observa-tion that administration of laws governing ordinary social behavior tends toward a compromise between the letter of the law and the vagaries of human nature—too loose administration sets man against man and too strict sets man against government. When law is enforced as if it were a command rather than a virtuous generalization, around which a game can be played, it becomes a trial of force rather than a trial of wits.

In international politics there appears to be little tolerance of ambiguity. Negotiators strive for months to over-specify the inherently unspecifiable, to wring all possible ambiguities out of every statement in every language. At the Peace of Westphalia in 1648 it took six months for delegates to decide in what order they should enter and be seated in the negotiating chamber. How long did it take to decide on the shapes and markings of tables for the Vietnam negotiations in Paris? Inter-national politics *is* more a trial of force than a trial of wits, and ambigu-ity is therefore more threatening than challenging.

A prime example of intolerance of ambiguity is reification of *The Nation* as the unit in international affairs. Since the flowing forests and oceans do not recognize these creations of the human mind, we put up boundary markers, erect walls and fortifications, establish border-cross-ing restrictions, try to impose language homogeneity within boundaries, define invisible territorial extensions into the seas, and brightly color our maps in different hues so that children can learn just what is really

where—all to reaffirm that *The Nation* is indeed a unitary thing like
other things that have names. It then becomes easier to personify nations as Actors in a great global game and harder to appreciate either
the similarities across boundaries or the differences within.

Part of any semantic revolution must be an *increase* in the ambiguity of nation-names, by using language which deliberately levels distinctions between nations and sharpens differences within them. This implies
gradual dissolution of the nation-state as the prime political unit, which
surely is heresy. But in a nuclear age there may be more security in
disunity; out of creative chaos there could come both a greater tolerance
of ambiguity and more accurate semantic mapping of the complexities
of the real world—paradoxical as that may seem. Fortunately, human
languages contain the seeds for their own revolutions, so let us turn now
from words to sentences.

Radical Sentences

We refer to our species as *Homo sapiens*, but *Homo loquens* would be
more accurate. Other animals have been shown to symbolize the not-
here and not-now to some degree—witness the way honey bees can represent the distance and direction of new food sources by their dance;
other animals certainly manipulate the environment toward their own
ends—witness the dams built by beavers. But no other animal really
talks, in the sense of using a shared set of abstract rules for making
propositions about the world. This is at once our great advantage as a
species and, potentially, our downfall. Ability to propositionalize about
things leads to control over them, but control over things without understanding and control over ourselves invites disaster.

Humans share many needs with lower organisms—needs to pro-
create, to feed, to avoid pain, for example. But the fact of propositional
language creates uniquely human needs, particularly the need to know
and the need to do something about what is known. When one can
conjure with the not-here and not-now, one usually assumes some
responsibility toward it. Myths, religions and ordinary daily news are
testimony to the need to know, or at least have some illusion of knowing, and knowing impels doing things in anticipation of events—making
an offering at the shrine of one's God, planting crops at a time deemed
propitious by omen or science, or even building a fall-out shelter in
anticipation of a nuclear attack.

Valid propositions about the environment, either informal ("com-
mon-sense") or formal ("science"), have given humans considerable
freedom *from* its harsh constraints. But as Michael Mason put it to

me,[11] scientific control of the environment has already reached the point where we now have a new kind of freedom—a freedom *to* which is positively embarrassing in its riches: freedom to make deserts into gardens, freedom to manipulate our own numbers and even our own genetic make-up, freedom to bring any part of the world to any doorstep by satellite communications. The possibilities are staggering to the imagination, but choice among them demands fresh and apposite propositions about the world.

Rules for Creating and Understanding Sentences

We make propositions by combining words into sentences of a particular type. Propositional sentences make assertions about their topics, and they can be signaled by *I state that, I assume that, I claim that* and the like—but we are rarely given this warning. Unlike words, such propositional sentences can be tested for their truth value. Take, for example, the sentence *Tom is a thief.* One can ask significantly, *is it true that Tom is a thief?* One cannot ask significantly, *is it true that Tom?* or ask *is it true that thief?*

When propositional sentences come from prestigious persons and make assertions whose truth values cannot be readily tested—either because of the remoteness of the things referred to or because of the inherent ambiguity of the concepts involved—their power of conviction is compelling. Faced with the assertion of a Pentagon expert that *a missile gap exists and threatens our security,* what is hapless Mr. Congressman to do but vote for a bigger defense budget—even though this assertion eventually proves to be false? Interestingly enough, resistance to such assertions, when it comes, is usually not so much based upon the truth-value of the assertions *per se* as upon the veracity of the speaker as a source. *The peculiar power of sentences comes from the fact that they do assert something about the topic to be true*—even this sentence, *what I say* (topic) *is not true* (commentary).

The meanings of words are constrained by the sentences in which they appear. Let us represent, for convenience, the meaning of a word as a string of plusses, zeros and minuses—a strip-code for its bundle of semantic features—and then ask ourselves what may transpire when two or more words are forced to interact within phrases or sentences. (1) If the coding of one word is the same on a certain feature as another word with which it is pressed into syntactic combination, it will intensify that feature of meaning—as the adjective *sudden* does for the noun *surprise* in the phrase *sudden surprise.* (2) If one word adds distinctive codings where the other has zeros, then it serves to modify the meaning of the whole—as in the phrase *sudden anger* (one can also experience *slow, burning anger*). (3) If one word has codings opposed to those in another word on the same semantic features, then what are called "semantic anomalies" are produced—as in *sudden complacency* or *meek contempt*. This "feeling of incongruence" is a most significant human capability, of which I shall have more to say momentarily.

The assertion *Tom is a thief* momentarily punches some of the semantic codings of *thief* onto the topic of the sentence, *Tom,* thereby modifying the meaning of *Tom*—quite congruously for the arresting officer but completely incongruously for Tom's mother! Yet they both understand what the speaker intends, whether believing or not believing him. This momentary fusion of semantic features is essential for understanding phrases and sentences, but it would be disastrous if the change in word meanings were permanent. Fortunately, words tend to snap back into their normal semantic shape after being bent to the purposes of sentences. Otherwise our semantics would become a murky, meaningless shambles.

But when the same words are used together again and again, a kind of *transprinting* of their code-strips takes place— contamination of one word by another, if you will. In the hey-day of McCarthyism (the ex-Senator McCarthy from Wisconsin), the phrase *Fifth-Amendment Communist* appeared repeatedly in the press; it was possible to actually measure a gradually increasing negative evaluation of the concept *Fifth Amendment*—even among college students who should think better. Phrases like *imperialist war-mongers,* on the one side, and *Communist aggressors*, on the other, serve to keep the semantics of both sides purely contaminated.

The influence of word upon word within sentences can be quite subtle. In English the word *neighbor* is not coded for sex. Yet if I say *My new neighbor is pretty*, you automatically assume that I am referring to a female, and if I say *My new neighbor is handsome*, you assume that it is a male. The sex codings of *pretty* and *handsome* are being momentarily conferred upon neutral *neighbor*. Sentences graced by the phrase *most people* carry a sense of ubiquity that far exceeds its casual method of calculation. Use of the phrase *Administration Spokesman* confers an aura of intimate access and sophistication upon the source which is hard to escape (be it news secretary, just secretary or even chambermaid). Conversely, one of the many ways of "belittling" sources is to make the propositional nature of their assertion explicit. To report that *The Russians claim that the Communist Summit Conference was a demonstration of unity within the world of socialist societies* is to cast the shadow of doubt upon what they are claiming. Propositional sentences are most compelling when their propositional status remains implicit.

Students of the Oxford School of Philosophy, notably Wittgenstein and Ryle,[12] have suggested that words can only have meaning when used in sentences. But surely this is a two-way street. Just as sentences constrain the meanings of words, so do the meanings of words constrain the sentences that can be produced in ordinary language.

At the grossest level there are *syntactic rules*: correctly speaking English, I cannot create sentences of words coded grammatically as Object-Subject-Verb in that order—for example, *Garlic I taste*—although ordinary speakers often do produce just such non-sentences when highly motivated toward the logical object (garlic). At a somewhat finer level there are what Noam Chomsky[13] has called *selectional rules*, clearly in the hinterland between syntactics and semantics: compare the sentence *Revolutionary new ideas appear infrequently* with the pseudo-sentence *Colorless green ideas sleep furiously*; the latter is a perfect series of anomalies—negative *colorless* clashes with positive *green* on a color feature, the concreteness of *green* clashes with the abstractness of *ideas,* and so on through the string of words.

At the finest level there are strictly *semantic rules*: It is semantically anomalous to say *She plead with him tolerantly*, because *plead with* is coded for a Subordinate relation of *she* to *him* whereas *tolerantly* implies a Superordinate relation of *she* to *him*. This is the level at which language can most subtly constrain how we think about things, and some semantic juggling is often necessary to make true propositions. I think it would be accurate to say that *Prime Minister Wilson plead tolerantly with Prime Minister Smith of Rhodesia—tolerantly* because of relative power status of the nations involved—but many Britishers found this state of affairs just as anomalous as the sentence.

There are, finally, *pragmatic rules* of usage—rules which reflect what we know, or think we know, about the real world. Thus the sentence *He shot the man with a Wallace sticker* is unambiguous only because we know that you can't use bumper stickers to shoot people with. Similarly, the assertion made by some right-wing Birchites that *President Eisenhower was a Communist* is ludicrous—not because there is anything wrong with its semantics, but because of what we think we know about the late President Eisenhower and Communism.

Why do I claim that sentences are potentially radical? For one thing, whereas the words available to us at any time are finite, the number of potential sentences we can create with them is infinite. For another thing, most sentences we encounter are novel as wholes; I know that most of the sentences in this paper were novel to me as I wrote them, and I assume they are novel to the reader, yet I have reason to hope that both understand them. Furthermore, sentences can be both whimsically nonsensical and deliberately non-factual—we can lie with sentences. But most importantly, sentences "do things" to the words they use, forcing new and sometimes revealing interpretations of reality. When, of a certain woman, I say, *She will make someone a nice husband,* I am breaking semantic rules, to be sure, but I am also offering a thumbnail personality sketch of the lady in question.

Sources and Effects of Sentences

Now let us return to the world of international politics. Precisely *what* sentences about this world are we likely to create and how are people likely to interpret them? The actual sentences about nations and their relations that we hear are a very small sub-set of the possible sentences which could be produced, even within the rules of sentencing just outlined. The reason is simply that we usually say "what is on our minds" —but this will require a bit of elaboration. In my analysis of why we create the sentences we do and interpret them the way we do, I shall emphasize only one semantic feature—the evaluative or attitudinal feature. But this aspect of meaning certainly carries the most weight in politics.

Try to imagine a space of some unknown number of dimensions within which the concepts we talk about appear as points. The dimensions of this space are the semantic features already discussed. The most prominent dimension of this space—let's say the up and down of it—is the evaluative, or *good-bad*, dimension. This dimension of meaning is based upon the human bedrock of pleasures and pains, of rewards and punishments, of threats and promises.

One's own Ego, or self-concept, is *good* by virtue of biological imperative—at least until one is taught about sin or becomes old and cynical—and this Ego early becomes the arbiter for evaluating other concepts. Signs of *immediate things* like MOTHER, FOOD, and SAFETY, which please and support Ego, tend to move upward toward maximal Goodness, and signs of immediate things like PAIN, DIRT, and DANGER, which hurt, shame and threaten Ego, tend to move downward toward maximal Badness. These concepts in turn become pivotal evaluators, pushing and shoving other, *more remote things,* like MY FRIEND vs. A STRANGER and MY GOD vs. THE DEVIL, into appropriate positions along this evaluative dimension—simply by virtue of being associated, positively or negatively, with them in propositional sentences. Exposed to assertions like *My Daddy says Niggers are lazy* and *My teacher says policemen protect us from thieves,* race concepts, occupational concepts, nation concepts, and all the rest gradually acquire values. The underlying principle in this primitive mapping of semantic values onto things is *pressure toward cognitive consonance* (or, if one prefers the negative, *avoidance of cognitive dissonance*).

It is by such a basic process that the Unfamiliar is assimilated to the Familiar, and thereby given meaning. Rebellions of Have-not peoples in Limboland against foreign domination and revolutions of Have-not peoples in Mysterica against domestic tyranny are only too easily rotated into congruence with the familiar Good-AMERICAN/Bad-COMMUNIST polarity—with the Have-nots characteristically being pushed into the Bad regions of the semantic space. The Cold War is steadily fired by application of its own tired rhetoric, which regularly appeals to the pivotal concepts of GOD and DEVIL for its sustenance —thus being a kind of Holy War. And this process is not by any means restricted to the remote world of foreign relations; it operates with equal force on one's way of conceiving civil rights movements and student protests—in the eyes of some a part of the all-pervasive Holy War against Communism.

Assertions connect topics with commentaries. The connectors (verbs) may be either associative (A *is* B, A *likes* B, A *helps* B) or dissociative (A *is not* B, A *dislikes* B, A *hinders* B). If both topic and commentary have the same evaluative sign (both *good* or both *bad*), associative assertions will be consonant and dissociative assertions dissonant. If both Russia and China are held to be communist and therefore evil, it is cognitively consonant that *Russia should support China*; it took many Americans a long time to accept the Sino-Soviet split, and some still believe it to be a diabolical hoax. If France is an American ally (both *good*), then it is cognitively dissonant that *France should support Russia and China*; needless to say, from the State Department on down, many Americans found de Gaulle's associative moves toward both Russia and China most unsettling.

If topic and commentary have opposed signs (one is *good* and the other *bad*), then dissociative assertions become consonant and associative ones dissonant. In human conflict situations it is easy to believe aggressive dissociative assertions made by one's opponent (*We will bury you*) and hard to believe his concilliatory associative assertions (*We can coexist peacefully*). It just simply is congruent in Black-and-White thinking for BAD GUYS to threaten GOOD GUYS, and vice versa. This creates a constant bias in credibility which encourages escalation of conflicts.

Stability of this Black-and-White inner world is maintained by a process called *implication of opposition*. Once a polar evaluative opposition has been set up between two topics, commentary which attributes properties to the one implies attribution of the opposites of these properties to the other. Before the United States became actively involved in World War II, American commentators from London often employed this mechanism, probably quite unconsciously: *England and Germany are at war* (polarization of topics). *The English are a decent, home-loving people, and they look upon America as their friend* (commentary on one topic). Nothing negative is said about the German people, nor need it be.

Most people, most of the time, create sentences that are consonant with their own systems of attitudes and beliefs. This is one reason why they produce only a small sub-set of possible sentences about the world. If someone believes that Capitalism is evil, he is not likely to produce sentences like *I favor the capitalist system* or like *Capitalists can be trusted* and so forth for myriads of other potential sentences. But what happens when a person is constrained to produce assertions that are inconsistent with his own attitudes and beliefs? What happens when he is exposed to assertions made by others that are inconsistent with his own system?

This is where what I call *psycho-logic* enters the picture. This is an entirely illogical, but very potent, psychological process. It is designed to restore the comforting state of mental equilibrium—with all the Goods and Bads in their right places—whenever this state has been disrupted by incongruity. Incongruity creates cognitive stress, and the victim is driven to do something about it; when he does something to the world or to himself which restores cognitive balance, it gratifies him and makes him feel secure. Psycho-logic may not follow logical principles, but it is nevertheless peculiarly significant for an understanding of the dynamics of international politics.

When a person is constrained by his own self-interest to talk and act *as if* he agrees with certain people and believes certain things, his behavior is inconsistent with his own values and he is under constant cognitive stress. One resolution is simply to tolerate the dissonance, rationalizing it as leading to a larger goal—but people differ in their tolerance of ambiguity. One wonders if the late Mr. Adlai Stevenson suffered just such prolonged cognitive stress while functioning as U.S. Ambassador to the United Nations. Another resolution is to change one's behavior, get out of the situation, say what one really thinks; people in public life do commit suicide sometimes, politically as well as physically. The most likely resolution, however, is a form of psycho-logic: the person gradually and unconsciously changes his values and beliefs toward consistency with what he feels he must say and do. Men on the accession routes to power are peculiarly susceptible to such self-induced "brain-washing."

It can be hypothesized that the same dynamics influence relations among nations. If the people of nations A and B really dislike and distrust each other, but they are constrained by their mutual self-interest to repeatedly behave *as if* they liked and trusted each other, their mutual perceptions should become more consistent with their mutual behaviors. Is there any evidence in recent history for such processes at the inter-national level?

In a significant paper titled "The Kennedy Experiment," Amitai Etzioni[14] documents a real-world test of this hypothesis. Beginning with the late President Kennedy's speech at the American University on June 10, 1963, in which he announced the first unilateral initiative (that the U.S. was stopping all nuclear tests in the atmosphere), a series of reciprocal unilateral steps were taken (the Soviets stopping production of strategic bombers, the Americans approving the sale of $250 million worth of wheat to the Russians, and so forth), culminating with conclu-sion of the Test Ban Treaty—clearly to the self-interest of both sides. Did the predicted psycho-logical side-effects occur? A correspondent to the *New York Times* has this to say on June 16, near the beginning of the experiment—". . . there was a new threat of international peace in the air this week, the kind of threat that leaves sophisticates smirking and the rest of us just dumbfounded"; but on September 22 the same correspondent had changed his tune—"We have cleared the air and cleared the atmospheres and warmed the climate and calmed the winds." The Kennedy Experiment came to an abrupt end—in Dallas, Texas.

There are more complex inter-nation interactions that display the same forces at work. The rapid favorable change in American attitudes toward Germany after World War II was undoubtedly, in part, a shift toward cognitive consistency with the developing Cold War polariza-tion against Russia at that time. More recently, the warming of attitudes toward Russia has undoubtedly been facilitated by the incongruous split between Russia and China and the new polarization against the latter, accompanying our deeper and deeper involvement in Asia.

Is it possible to deliberately manipulate the cognitive stress applied to nations and its form of resolution? Suppose, for example, that the U.S. were to initiate a calculated series of steps designed to harden relations with Nationalist China—criticism of the dictatorial government on Taiwan, enforced demilitarization of the off-shore islands of Quemoy and Matsu, explicit statement that the Nationalist regime is no longer considered the legitimate government of all China. For the Mainland Chinese, such assertions by word and deed would be dissonant with their image of the U.S. as an implacably hostile power and incongruent with their psycho-logic of relations between two Bad Guys (the U.S. and Nationalist China). Such steps would therefore be expected to create cognitive stress in the Mainland Chinese—stress toward making at least one of the Bad Guys better. Simultaneous softening of the U.S. posture toward Communist China—eliminating trade embargos, encouraging exchanges of journalist, scientist and tourists, invitation to participate in negotiations on the control of nuclear weapons—should influence the resolution of this stress, in the direction of less hostility toward the U.S. rather than toward Nationalist China.

When a person is exposed to assertions from others which cause him cognitive stress, psycho-logic offers a number of defensive mechanisms. He may simply deny the assertions and stop thinking about them. More subtly, he may accept the assertions intellectually but deny their emotional implications; many Americans have become quite callous about the use of napalm, crop-destroying sprays and other indiscriminate weapons against living things in South Vietnam. For insurance against cognitive stress, one may selectively expose himself to information that is consistent with his own belief system and selectively avoid information that is inconsistent.

But the real world has a way of re-presenting itself to the mind. If the disturbing incoming assertions cannot be avoided, then the familiar conceptual framework can be bolstered by associating prestige symbols with what is congruent and derrogation symbols with what is incongruent. In the flare-up of criticism about the Warren Commission's report on the assassination of President Kennedy, political leaders, religious leaders, and even the chief of the Federal Bureau of Investigation, J. Edgar Hoover, came forward to reinforce the credibility of the Commission's report. But if *Castro* were to criticize the Warren report, it would be even more firmly believed. When Castro asserts the nobility of the cause of some political group in Latin America, this group becomes automatically suspect in the U.S.A.—a process known as the "Kiss of Death."

By attributing different *motives* to ourselves and our opponents—benevolent motives to WE and malevolent motives to THEY—*exactly the same behavior by both* can be rationalized into the value system. Psycho-logic thus creates a double standard of national morality. During the Cuban missile crisis, the American government defined the weapons being implanted in Cuban soil as "offensive" in nature, whereas essentially similar American weapons in West Germany, Italy and Turkey were defined as "defensive"—and the Soviets, of course, applied exactly the same definitions, but in reverse. In the Vietnam conflict, both the U.S. and North Vietnam have trained, armed and supported their own factions in the South—yet, when the WE's do it, it is fulfilling a moral commitment, and when the THEY's do it, it is naked aggression. Both sides have taken advantage of truces to strengthen their positions—yet, when the WE's do it, it is practical military realism, and when the THEY's do it, it is crass deceitfulness.

Once unleashed, words and sentences fly about willy-nilly in all directions. This is particularly true with modern electronic communications and it poses particular problems for political messages. From the viewpoint of the political speaker, he is always dealing with multiple audiences which have multiple interests and multiple relations to him. When a head of state makes a speech, he can be sure that his own party, the opposition party, labor union members and industrialists, one's own military and the opponent's military, to say nothing of general publics both at home and abroad, are all listening in, and what falls harmoniously on the ears of one is bound to fall gratingly on the ears of another. Occasionally one may be able to use a private code for the benefit of some segment of his audience, as when Secretary Rusk has referred to the Chinese capital not as Peking but as *Peiping*—the name favored by the Nationalists and an insult to the Communists, of which the American public is quit unaware.[15]

From the viewpoint of the political listener, there is a continuous bombardment of conflicting assertions. He expects this from within, and indeed this is one index of democracy. But since the ordinary citizen, no matter where he may be, identifies other nations as monolithic personalities, conflicting voices from abroad become most confusing. When the hard-line assertions of a militarist are interlaced with the soft-line assertions of a U.N. diplomat, and both are attributed to the same national entity, that nation obviously is guilty of deliberate double-talk.

Now, it may be argued that human individuals of even ordinary intelligence, although susceptible to psycho-logic, certainly are more sophisticated in their thinking than this analysis implies. This is quite correct. But when all of the complex interplays among the *individuals* who make up nations have worked themselves into the amalgam of national policy, what appears in the dialogue between *nations* seems to represent something close to the lowest common denominator of its individual ingredients. I once suggested to a friend, who uses individuals to simulate nations in experiments on strategy, that his simulations would be more realistic if he substituted 8-year-old boys for adults as players. But even for a sophisticated individual, the remoteness of the events talked about and his nearly complete dependence upon the mass media render him peculiarly susceptible to psycho-logic when he thinks and talks about international affairs.

Toward a Semantic Revolution

Rules are made to be broken. It is only through breaking them when necessary that we can force our language into a more faithful portrayal of things as they are. When a young lad, accused of a felony, exclaims, "Ah ain't nevah done nothin' to nobody nohow!", he is guilty of a quintuple negative at the very least—but his claim to honorable character is being vividly made. Winston Churchill's coinage of the phrase *Iron Curtain* broke pragmatic, if not semantic, rules of English, but it certainly provided an apt characterization of the Cold War situation of the time. We need a more lively language to revitalize the stale rhetoric of international politics.

But if rules are made to be broken, then there must also be rules for breaking rules—otherwise we have not revolution but chaos. "When I use a word," Humpty Dumpty said, in rather a scornful tone, "it means just what I choose it to mean, neither more nor less." "The question is," said Alice, "whether you *can* make words mean so many different things." "The question is," said Humpty Dumpty, "which is to be master, that's all." There are grains of both truth and untruth here. Being master of one's words is not synonymous with being arbitrary in one's use of them. Adaptation of a language to the rapidly changing world is essential, but so is continuity of a language with its past.

As to novelty or innovation in language, a continuum can be traced from monotony, through coinage and metaphor, to verbal magic, and ultimately into chaos. The stale rhetoric of international politics approaches the nadir of novelty; words and phrases predict each other, redundantly semantic features are all in rapport, and little new information is communicated by the parading sentences. If there is too much unpredictability—if too many semantic features are in conflict—a pinnacle of novelty may be approached, but again little is communicated because of sheer chaos. Just as there is an optimum degree of unpredictability in the arts—variations on the theme—which maximizes aesthetic pleasure, so is there an optimum degree of rule-breaking in language which maximizes communication of fresh ideas, whether it be in poetry or politics.

Effective metaphors break semantic rules optimally. In the literal use of English, one cannot say *the panther shouted* (only humans can *shout*). Speaking poetically, however, one might say *the thunder shouted down the mountainside,* thereby humanizing the thunder; but I, at least, could not say *the brook shouted down the mountainside*—without making it a torrent. *Thunder* and *shouting* share enough features to allow over-riding of the Humanness distinction, but *brook* and *shouting* do not. I use the term "verbal magic" to refer to the case where a false context is used to support a semantically anomalous assertion. My favorite example is a TV beer advertisement: After dropping bottles of the brew from sky-scrapers, running them over with steam-rollers, and flinging them against brick walls—with nary a scratch to the glass bottles—the assertion is brightly made that *this beer has indestructible flavor!*

One ingredient of a semantic revolution is *a healthy suspicion of familiar words and phrases.* By way of example, let us analyse the now-familiar phrase, NUCLEAR DETERRENCE. The assertion *A deters B* carries the implications that B must be aggressive, since he requires deterring, and that A is both non-aggressive, since he merely deters, and actually benevolent, since he is opposed to a potential aggressor. The phrase MUTUAL NUCLEAR DETERRENCE, demanded by the real-world fact of Soviet nuclear capability, is a bit more sophisticated—for one thing, it neutralizes A and B with respect to just who is benevolent and who is potentially aggressive—but this phrase also has subtle connotations. It has a stable, reassuring feel to it—almost like being in a medieval suit of armor—but given its foundations on the shifting psychological sands of mutual fear and distrust, nothing could be much less stable or reassuring. In other words, the semantic implications of this phrase simply do not fit its referent.

Another ingredient of a semantic revolution is *imaginative flexibility with and tolerance for unfamiliar words and phrases.* Returning to the concept of MUTUAL NUCLEAR DETERENCE, with its illusory assurance of stability, it is refreshing to note that one well-known strategist[16] has dubbed it *the delicate balance of terror.* In coining this phrase our strategist was deliberately violating semantic proprieties; *terror* is certainly not something our language implies can be *delicately balanced,* and yet this is precisely the state of affairs, as the Cuban missile crisis so amply demonstrated. Creating radical phrases is not restricted to academic types, of course. When asked by CBS News on February 20, 1967, to explain the latest military escalation in Vietnam, an Administration spokesman said it represented a "calculated outburst of impatience" on the part of President Johnson!

If the referent of CIVIL DEFENSE in our time has become fallout and blast shelters designed to protect part of the population temporarily, while anti-missile missiles try to discriminate and intercept ever more sophisticated attack missiles, then a more appropriate term than civil defense would be *civilian elimination*. This term would have double significance: it refers at once to that part of the population which perishes, either immediately or in the aftermath, and to the reduced resistance of civilians (who believe themselves protected) to military adventurism in the new nuclear dimension. However, I doubt if any politician would care to be associated with an *Office of Civilian Elimination*.

New words and phrases rush into the spaces left by the mis-match of language to reality. The greater the rate of culture change the greater the pressure on speakers to innovate. In a paper titled *Speaking of Space*,[17] David McNeill demonstrated this convincingly by comparing the frequencies of novel nominal compounds in samples of articles in space engineering, in psychology, and in the humanities—the percentages being 19%, 8% and 3% respectively. The nuclear age is creating many empty spaces in our semantic maps of the world, but linguistic innovation is more apparent in its technological than its political aspects. In the *Doomsday Dictionary*,[18] we find that a *beach* is a unit of fission energy equaling 3,000 billion tons of dynamite, or enough to kill half the earth's population by fallout (a term derived from the motion picture, *On the Beach*), and that a *kahn* is the more modest quantity of fission energy required to liquidate the entire population of one major country without any shelters—300 *kahn* equals one *beach*.

The term *kahn*, of course, is taken from the name of one of the most provocative, innovative—and macabre—writers about strategy in the nuclear age, Herman Kahn. His several books[19] are replete with lively concepts like *catalytic war* (conflict between two major nuclear powers deliberately started by a third power), *escalation ladder* (steps ranging from subcrisis disagreements to all-out nuclear war and its aftermath), and *stark deterrence* (capacity of *overkill* by a factor of 10 or more, so that miscalculation or wishful thinking by an opponent becomes most unlikely). Of course, there are apposite coinages, which highlight the truly significant properties of things, and inapposite ones, which obscure them. The term *overkill* is not particularly apposite, suggesting degrees of killing humans when humans can only die once; it is actually used to refer to the extra intensities of attack required to liquidate a defended target as compared with an undefended one.

Another ingredient of a semantic revolution is *respect for the distinction between words and things.* This, of course, is the central theme of General Semantics. A State Department expert on Asian affairs and I have been carrying on a debate by correspondence. In one letter he writes, "I submit that you simply cannot read the public statements made by the Chinese Communist . . . leaders . . . without having an unmistakable impression of implacable hostility." True enough: the controlled Chinese press rattles like the bones of a skeleton with tired, dusty old phrases—*imperialist warmongers, criminals in the Pentagon,* and so on *ad nauseam.* But this State Department official's opposite number in Peking can easily find statements in our press displaying equally implacable hostility. The danger lies in using such ideological jargon as proof of intentions in the real world.

Actions should speak louder than words, but in international politics actions are often ambiguous as to interpretation. They may be expressive as well as instrumental. Dean Acheson's interpretation of the Berlin crisis of 1961 was in global rather than local terms—that Krushchev had forced a test of wills upon an untried American President, and any willingness to negotiate would be interpreted as a sign of weakness. The assassination of John F. Kennedy was interpreted variously as a communist, a military-industrial, or a right-wing conspiracy, depending on where the observer stood politically himself. The conflict in South Vietnam, at the time of U.S. escalation in February, 1965, was officially interpreted as "aggression from the North" and unofficially interpreted by many unattached experts as a "civil war." Nevertheless, we would be wiser to pay more attention to what nations do and less attention to what they say. As long as the feet of Chinese soldiers and their weapons stay on Chinese soil, for example, we can afford to shrug off their blustering words.

Yet another ingredient is *substituting empathy for projection in predicting the effects of our words upon others.* Since most of us do most of our talking to people in a community which shares a common set of meanings and values, we have usually been successful in predicting their reactions to our words simply by projecting on to them how we would react ourselves. When we extend this normal process to people of other cultures using other languages, however, we inevitably get into trouble. Projection makes it easy for Americans to assume that the South Vietnamese people see the conflict there as we do—as part of a massive confrontation between the Free World and Communism. In

terms of Vietnamese experience it is probably, first and most immediately, a struggle for sheer survival in a war they hardly comprehend
and, second but more remotely, a struggle for national independence
from colonialism. Developing empathy for others requires exposing
oneself to their conditions and experiences—directly if possible but
mediately through well selected descriptions if not—and then role-
playing the effects of our messages while standing in their mental shoes.

A former official of the Agency for International Development,
Byron Johnson, has called the acronym AID a hypocritical misnomer,
charging that American "aid" consists mostly of self-promoting, arro-
gantly-administered loans that offend the pride of people in other nations.[20] Despite the benevolent intent, it is depressing how often AID
is given or taken away for military and political reasons, how often it
foists useless goods on bewildered people in order to relieve gorged
American markets, how often it ends up in the pockets of the relatively
well-to-do in foreign countries, thereby actually widening the gulf
between Have and Have-not people within the countries being "aided."
The very term UNDERDEVELOPED is an insult to people whose
written histories may go back much further than our own, for it equates
material, technological progress with cultural development in general.
We would be wiser to speak about *unevenly developed countries*—a
phrase which at least admits of the possibility that we Westerners are
also underdeveloped in some respects and overdeveloped in others, to
the extent that our society could die from it.

Another revolutionary phrase I would recommend is *benevolent
subversion*: There is no question but what the West—and particularly
the United States in the past few decades—has been the most effective
force in history for subverting the governments, the economies, and the
whole ways of life of other peoples throughout the world. And there is
no question but what we have been benevolent in intent, at least as we
see ourselves. But when forced into anomalous confrontation, the words
benevolent and *subversion* bring into mind obscure but significant
features of each—the potential selfishness of benevolence and the potential altruism of subversion.

Perhaps the most important ingredient in a semantic revolution is
using radical sentences to compensate for conservative words. Although
new words can be coined and old words can change their meanings,
they remain essentially conservative and inept for the fresh purposes of
the moment. Sentences can crunch words together into phrases which
highlight new features and irradicate old; they can formulate assertions
about the world which question tired assumptions and suggest new
truths. Of course, the phrases may be bizarre and the assertions incredi-

ble upon close inspection, but the potential for fresh ways of talking, and hence thinking, is there.

For about ten years I have been espousing a general strategy for international behavior modeled upon what I think I know about interpersonal behavior—a strategy which seems appropriate for a nuclear age. Its formal and descriptively accurate name is *graduated and reciprocated intiatives in tension-reduction*. But early-on in the game I discovered that very few people, including myself, could easily remember this complex nominal compound correctly. While doodling at a conference one day I came up with the acronym, GRIT—which not only provided cues for the salient features of the strategy but also seemed quite appropriate, since grit is exactly what it requires.

This strategy is a form of calculated de-escalation of conflicts: A nation caught in a conflict spiral deliberately initiates sequences of small, tension-reducing moves, these moves being well within its margin of security and being designed to elicit reciprocating steps from the opponent. To the extent that reciprocation is obtained, somewhat larger, more significant steps can be taken, and both parties move cautiously toward a political rather than a military resolution.

My original paper on this appeared in a book, sponsored by a group of Democratic congressmen, titled *The Liberal Papers;*[21] the Republican National Committee described my contribution as "surrender on the installment plan"—to which, in the present context, I can only say "touche." Debating the feasibility of such an untraditional approach to conflict resolution—at least as far as sovereign nations are concerned—forced me to question certain unquestioned assumptions about national security in this nuclear age,[22] and in doing so create a few radical sentences of my own. They will provide a final illustration of my thesis.

I had to assert that *the primary motive behind the threatening behavior of nations toward others is usually fear*. The traditional assumption, consistent with the dynamics of psycho-logic, is that one's opponent is always motivated by aggressive impulses. Accepting even the possibility of fear motivation enables one nation to respond more rationally (and less fearfully) to the blustering behavior of another.

I had to assert that *there is no real security in military superiority in a nuclear age*. The traditional assumption is that a nation is secure only when it is so strong militarily that no other nation, or combination of nations, would dare to attack it. But, of course, the possessor of such superiority becomes the focus of fear for others and thus the stimulus for continuing the nuclear arms race—which in our time is an invitation to common suicide. I would even go so far as to recommend a strategy of "calculated nuclear inferiority": when two (or more) nations can destroy each other ten times over, as far as continuing as a viable society is concerned, a calculated degree of inferiority probably offers *more* security (by virtue of being less fear-producing) and certainly gives one an advantage in initiating arms controlling and limiting agreements. Whether because of political intent or economic necessity, I think that this has been the strategy of the Soviet Union vis-a-vis the United States over the past decade or so.

I had to assert that *having an invulnerable nuclear deterrent makes it possible for a nation to take calculated risks, risks designed ultimately to eliminate the need for the deterrent itself.* The usual assumption is that such capability is merely a deterrent against others, and the possessors stand frozen in their mutual threat. But the simple fact of deterring others also provides a nation with a margin of security within which to take calculated risks. Rather than being seen as simply a continuation of the military tradition of discovering bigger and better ways of destroying opponents, the grisly fact of nuclear weaponry can be viewed as the impetus toward erradicating the very tradition that gave rise to it.

I had to assert that *in the reduction of international tensions, POST commitment by reciprocation can be substituted for PRIOR commitment by negotiation.* Although in our ordinary relations with wives, children, neighbors and colleagues we almost never *negotiate* a prior commitment before starting tension-reducing actions ourselves, it has been traditionally assumed that under conflict conditions one *nation* cannot be decent to another without first obtaining from the other an iron-clad prior commitment that it will be decent in return. Not only can patterns of intiatives and reciprocations (post-commitments) reduce mutual hostilities, but they can create an atmosphere within which serious negotiations on critical issues can be successfully undertaken. Both of these propositions were demonstrated in The Kennedy Experiment, and there have been some other demonstrations in human history.

And, finally, I had to assert that *goodwill among nations is a result of, rather than a prerequisite for, de-escalation of tensions.* The traditional assumption has been that a nation cannot risk making even conciliatory *gestures* toward another unless some degree of mutual goodwill and trust exists between them—since otherwise such gestures are likely to be interpreted as "signs of weakness." Quite to the contrary, as I argued earlier in this paper, given even a modicum of mutual self-interest, the reciprocal actions taken in its service can literally create mutual goodwill where little or none of it existed before.

Interlocking assertions like these can provide a framework for re-thinking our relationships to each other on this shrinking little planet at the dawn of its nuclear age. The assertions may be proven false, of course, but so may the tenets of any theory. The important thing is to use the potential radicalness of our sentences to at least reach for a clearer perspective on our own time and place. Revolutions do not guarantee a better world—they only make it possible.

Notes

[1] These notions are taken from a draft of a still unpublished paper by Robert C. North and myself, titled *From Individual to Nation.* It is an attempt at an explicit transfer from individual to nation via Mode III, a general systems model.

[2] Technical Report #39. Communication, Cooperation, Negotiation in Culturally Heterogeneous Groups. ARPA Order No. 454, under the Office of Naval Research, Contract NR 177-472, Nonr 1834 (36), September, 1966.

[3] As reported in *Science.*

[4] McNeill, D. "Speaking of Space," *Science,* 152 (1966), 875-880.

[5] Kaplan and Schwerner. *The Doomsday Dictionary.* New York: Simon and Schuster, 1963.

[6] Larson, A. "Power and Law in World Affairs." *The Progressive,* 30 (1966), 12-15.

[7] Edelman, M. *The Symbolic Uses of Politics.* Urbana, Illinois: Univ. Illinois Press, 1964, p. 114.

[8] *On Coexistence.* Occasional paper, Center for the Study of Democratic Institutions, February, 1965.

[9] White, R. K. " 'Socialism' and 'Capitalism'; an international misunderstanding." *Foreign Affairs* (January, 1966), pp. 216-228.

[10] Edelman, *op. cit.,* Ch. 3.

[11] Mason, M. (Producer), Talks Department, BBC. Correspondence.

[12] Cf., Ryle, G. "The Theory of Meaning." in C. E. Caton, ed., *Philosophy and Ordinary Language.* Urbana: University of Illinois Press, 1963.

[13] Chomsky, N. *Aspects of the Theory of Syntax.* Cambridge, Mass.: M.I.T. Press, 1965.

[14] Etzioni, A. "The Kennedy Experiment." *Western Polit. Quart.,* 20 (1967), 361-380.

[15] Nelson, B. *Science,* 154 (1954), 246.

[16] Wohlstetter, A. "The Delicate Balance of Terror." *Foreign Affairs* (January, 1959).

[17] McNeill, *op. cit.*

[18] Kaplan and Schwerner, *op. cit.*

19 Kahn, H. *On Thermonuclear War* (Princeton, N. J.: Princeton Univ. Press, 1960); *Thinking about the Unthinkable* (New York: Horizon Press, 1962); *On Escalation* (New York; Praeger, 1965).

20 Johnson, B. L. "Let's Stop Calling it *AID.*" *War/Peace Report,* 6 (1966), 10, 8-9.

21 Osgood, C. E. "Reciprocal Initiative," in James Roosevelt, ed., *The Liberal Papers.* Chicago: Quadrangle Books, 1962.

22 Osgood, C. E. "Questioning Some Unquestioned Assumptions about National Security." *J. Arm. Cont.,* 1963, *1,* 1-13. Cf., also in *An Alternative to War or Surrender* (U. Illinois Press, 1962) and *Perspective in Foreign Policy* (Pacific Books, Palto Alto, California, 1966).

Melvin Manis

Experimental Studies in Communication

Professor Manis is on the faculty of the Department of Psychology at the University of Michigan. The research reported in this paper was supported by the Veterans Administration and by National Science Foundation Grant-1116. Some of the material in this paper appeared originally in Professor Manis' book *Cognitive Processes* (Belmont, California: Brooks/Cole, 1966).

FOR THE PAST TEN YEARS OR SO, MY COLLEAGUES AND I HAVE BEEN engaged in a program of research concerned with social judgment and communication. This effort has yielded some promising information regarding the impact of attitudinal and cognitive variables on social perception. My aim in this paper is to describe some of the systematic phenomena in this field, and to raise some implications that are perhaps relevant within the realm of political perception and communication. The discussion will be focussed on two main areas of investigation: (1) the effect of the recipient's attitudes on his decoding behavior; and (2) the impact of contextual variables on the communication process.

In a provocative paper published in 1950, Leon Festinger noted that people are normally motivated to validate their opinions. That is, since they wish their beliefs to be veridical (to conform to some standard of *correctness*), they engage in informal methods of verification, somewhat along the lines of the social scientist who wishes to test a proposition of interest through empirical research.

For some beliefs, the checking procedure can be carried out rather directly. If I think that a given political candidate is evasive, but wish further confirmation of this view, I can make it my business to observe him in public meetings, or in discussions on television. For certain beliefs, then, it is possible to carry out verification checks through reasonably direct procedures. This can often be accomplished with reasonable efficiency in the realm of physical objects, where, for example, I can test the durability of a plastic cup by simply dropping it on the floor, to see if it is in fact "unbreakable," as the commercials claim. While it is true that my encounter with a political candidate (in the earlier example) may be similarly direct, social judgments of this type are often rather complex; the observations that signify "evasiveness," for example, are less clearcut than those that signal "unbreakability."

Moreover, many of our beliefs cannot be verified directly. My views concerning the political consequences of the Civil War are simply not testable through direct observation. Similarly, there is no possibility of empirically validating my beliefs regarding the probable course of political events had John Kennedy lived to serve out a full two terms in the Presidency. As these examples may suggest, there are a vast number of beliefs that engage our interest and attention, but are nevertheless difficult or impossible to verify in any direct sense. Beliefs of this sort are normally checked through a process of *consensual validation,* in which we compare our own views with those held by others. In this form of verification we are particularly sensitive to the views of various reference groups, whose opinions we value either because of their specialized knowledge, or because of such general attributes as trustworthiness, likability, and prestige.

Consensual validation is heavily reliant on the communication process. I may, for example, compare my own beliefs with the written opinions of Walter Lippmann, or with the views of the colleague on campus, and may indeed engage in directed reading or face-to-face questioning in order to elicit relevant information. This process can be carried out by both of the interacting parties, and I can ultimately attain social verification (if there is initial disagreement) through a variety of procedures. I can, for example, change my own views, to bring them in line with what others believe, or I can (if I am persuasive) convince others of the validity of my beliefs. A third mechanism, which I will amplify later, is the possibility that I can achieve what *appears* to be consensual validation (or at least partial validation) by systematically distorting the significance of someone else's remarks.

There are, of course, boundary conditions that delimit the applicability of this theory. For example, once-validated beliefs are not immutable, and may be subject to further checking and correction as we become familiar with the views of new reference groups, or acquire additional relevant information. There are also important personality differences in the individual's ability to maintain his own views in the *absence* of social support. Despite these qualifications, it seems safe to conclude that for most people, the consensual validation of their beliefs by relevant reference groups remains a matter of some concern.

A Simple Model
of Communication

The communication process can often be represented in terms of a simple paradigm. Assume, for example, that a communicator has certain opinions or information that he wishes to convey to his neighbor. A common view suggests that this type of information transmission is achieved through a shared linguistic "code," whereby the speaker symbolizes that which he wishes to convey within the framework of patterned sounds that we call language. Upon receiving this coded output the listener simply decodes what he has heard, transforming it into a set of inferences regarding the information or attitudes that the speaker sought to convey (along with other information that may have been communicated *unintentionally*).

Communication is not, however, uniformly successful, for there is good evidence to suggest that the listener's inferences may be affected by many variables apart from the verbal message he receives. As a consequence, a message designed to convey a particular content (the speaker's attitude, for example) may be variously interpreted, depending upon a variety of other factors. It is important to note that these effects are not simply the result of *random* processes, but instead, represent *systematic*, replicable phenomena.

The Recipient's Own Views as a Determinant
of His Decoding Behavior

One line of research that has, I believe, clear relevance for a proper understanding of the processes involved in political communication concerns the impact of the individual's *own views* on the interpretations that he places upon others' statements of opinion. This is a problem that is frequently recognized, but one that has not always been formulated with adequate precision. I would like to review some of the representative data in this domain, along with a theoretical analysis that I have found provocative and researchable.

One of the most famous studies relating attitude to social judgment was conducted in Oklahoma during a campaign to repeal the prohibition laws in that state (Hovland, Harvey, and Sherif, 1957). The investigators first selected several groups of people who held quite divergent views concerning the dangers of alcohol. Some of these people were members of the WCTU; others were active in the campaign to loosen the prohibition regulations, and still others were essentially neutral. People from these various groups were all presented with a persuasive message that took a mildly anti-prohibition stand, and were asked to indicate the writer's preferred location on the attitude continuum. The results indicated that there were systematic differences between the various groups with respect to their understanding of the writer's views. People whose own beliefs were rather similar to the views expressed in the message generally minimized what little difference there was; that is, they interpreted the communicator's views as being even closer to their own beliefs than was actually the case. This type of distortion, in which the meaning of a message is "displaced" toward the receiver's preferred poistion, has been termed the *assimilation effect*. Not all subjects showed assimilation, however. Those whose views clearly conflicted with the contents of the message typically exaggerated the existing discrepancy; they interpreted the communicator's stance as being even more opposed to their own views than in fact it was. This type of distortion, in which the speaker's intended meaning is displaced *away* from the recipient's preferred stand, has been termed the *contrast* effect.

I have always been struck by the possibility that attitude-related distortions of this type may result from the individual's attempt to reduce the persuasive impact of the incoming information. This approach is closely related to the postulates underlying the consensual validation idea, for it assumes that a certain amount of discomfort will be produced when the receiver of a message is presented with a statement that conflicts with his own views. Moreover, if we consider messages that are increasingly divergent with the listener's preferred stand, he should feel *increasing* pressure to change. When the discrepancy between the receiver's views and those embodied in the message becomes sufficiently large, however, the available evidence from the attitude change literature suggests that the recipient may feel somewhat *less* pressure to change. This reduction in the communicator's influence potential is most likely to occur when the communicator is not identified in any way. Under these conditions of anonymity, if a statement of opinion is clearly at variance with the recipient's views, the unidentified speaker will often be dismissed as a "crackpot," or some otherwise misguided individual whose divergent beliefs can be comfortably ignored. As I have suggested, these assumptions regarding the recipient's felt pressure to change are all reasonably congruent with the available information on attitude change.

What does all this have to do with attitude-related distortion effects? Figure 1 shows how these assumptions may enable us to explain

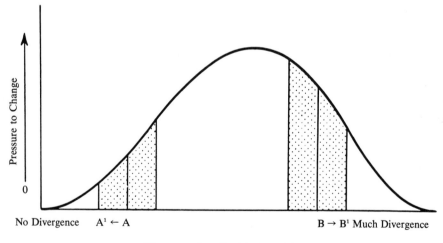

FIGURE 1

A SCHEMATIC DIAGRAM SHOWING THE RELATIONSHIP BETWEEN
(A) COMMUNICATOR-RECIPIENT DISCREPANCY AND (B) PRESSURE
TO CHANGE, ASSUMING AN ANONYMOUS COMMUNICATOR

the occurrence of assimilation and contrast effects. In this graph, the horizontal axis represents various degrees of discrepancy between the views of the receiver and those of the speaker. The vertical axis shows the amount of pressure to change that the recipient would normally feel upon receiving persuasive messages that differ from his own views by these varying amounts. Assume, for example, that the recipient favors an extreme position at the far left of the horizontal axis. The graph suggests that pressure to change first rises and then falls, as our recipient is faced with messages that diverge more and more from his preferred stand. Since an incoming message is almost always ambiguous (to a greater or lesser degree), the receiver must choose from a range of "possible" interpretations. Moreover, since he is presumably motivated to maintain his existing views with little or no change, it is reasonable to predict that each message will be interpreted in such a manner as to minimize the resulting pressure to change. Consider a message that, given a *proper interpretation*, might be moderately discrepant with the listener's views; the "true meaning" of this message might be at position A in Figure 1. While there is a range of *plausible* interpretations that might be associated with this message, as shown by the vertical gray band at the left of the graph, the model suggests that our hypothetical recipient will probably interpret the message as espousing position A', rather than any of the other reasonable alternatives, since messages at A' are associated with less pressure to change than any of the other possibilities. Note also that the displacement from A to A' constitutes an *assimilation effect,* since it reduces the apparent discrepancy between the receiver's views and those that he attributes to the message source.

Figure 1 also shows how contrast might occur. Consider a message that deviates *markedly* from the receiver's views; assume that its actual location is at B. As before, we assume that there is some ambiguity concerning the communicator's true position, as indicated by the vertical gray bar at B. Since, according to our model, the recipient should choose an interpretation that minimizes pressure to change, we are led to predict that the message will be interpreted as advocating position B', rather than one of the other possibilities, thus resulting in a *contrast effect.* Note further that as in our example of assimilation, this distorted interpretation helps the recipient to maintain his own views, for it effectively reduces the pressure to change that is associated with the message. The idea that we can reduce the force of another's views by exaggerating the discrepancy between our own beliefs and the position that he appears to espouse derives informal support from the frequent use of the *reductio ad absurdum* strategy in political and other discussions.

While assimilation and contrast have frequently been reported in studies of this sort, they do not always appear, nor should they, according to the theory proposed above. First, let us recall that in our previous examples we have always assumed that the message source is *unknown* to the receiver. Under this condition, messages that the receiver sees as being highly discrepant with his views can easily be discounted, since they may be interpreted as evidence that the source is unreliable. Obviously, however, the message source is often well-known. How might this affect our results? Consider, for example, a speaker who is well-liked and respected by his audience. Under these conditions, regardless of the discrepancy between the message content and the views of the listener, it is unlikely that the speaker's opinion can be easily discounted. Indeed, there is evidence to suggest that with a "high-prestige" communicator, the recipient of a persuasive message feels more and more pressure to change his views, as the incoming message shows increasing divergence from his initially preferred stand (Aronson, Turner, and Carlsmith, 1963).

Figure 2 graphically depicts this state of affairs. As in our previous examples, let us again assume that the recipient is presented with messages at positions A and B, remembering that in this case he knows the

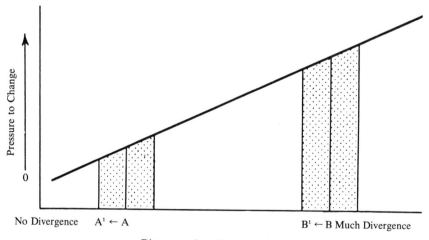

FIGURE 2

A SCHEMATIC DIAGRAM SHOWING THE RELATIONSHIP BETWEEN
(A) COMMUNICATOR-RECIPIENT DISCREPANCY AND (B) PRESSURE
TO CHANGE, ASSUMING A HIGHLY PRESTIGEFUL COMMUNICATOR

communicator to be a person worthy of his respect. As before, the messages are assumed to be somewhat ambiguous, thus permitting a variety of interpretations. Note that under these conditions, for both messages A and B, pressure to change can be most effectively reduced by minimizing the apparent discrepancy between the recipient's *own* views and those of the communicator, who is seen as favoring positions A' or B', through an assimilative process. It should also be noted that according to this interpretation, contrast effects should *never* be obtained, providing the speaker is highly regarded by his audience. Regardless of how discrepant his message may be (when compared with the recipients' views), assimilation effects should be generated, since this type of displacement will consistently reduce the listener's tendency to change his views. This prediction is reasonably well-supported by the available experimental evidence.

In one experiment (Manis, 1961), several groups of college students who varied in their attitudes toward college fraternities were presented with a series of short essays, each of which described the author's views on the fraternity issue. Although the authors were not personally known to the subjects, they were often described in rather glowing terms. Some were said to be excellent students, others were described as very popular, and still others were described as being exceptionally stable and personally mature. When the subjects attempted to infer the authors' attitudes toward fraternities after having read their messages, clear-cut assimilation effects were obtained *regardless* of the discrepancy between the reader's views and those of the authors. That is, there was a consistent tendency for the pro-fraternity students to interpret the messages as being more pro-fraternity than did those who opposed fraternities. It is interesting to note that when these same messages were presented as coming from *less* reliable sources, no consistent relationship was found between the subjects' own views and their interpretations of the messages. One might have expected that this second condition would lead to consistent contrast, for we often believe that our own views are rather different from the opinions of those we hold in low esteem. However, in a subsequent study of this sort (Berkowitz and Goranson, 1964), contrast effects *were* obtained when persuasive messages were attributed to a disliked source. Taken as a whole, these results seem encouragingly consistent with the postulates sketched earlier.

In considering the relevance of this research for the political scientist, it seems appropriate to reflect on the fact that the data in these studies are often collected from college students, who are quite consciously serving as experimental subjects, and are often paid for their efforts. My own view, based on sheer conjecture, is that the results obtained from these highly-selected self-conscious people quite possibily underestimate the magnitude of the effects that might otherwise occur. There are several reasons for believing this. First, our student-subjects are well above average intellectually, and generally free from gross personality disturbances. They are also motivated to be dispassionately accurate, and to avoid wishful thinking, since they are frequently led to believe that for each message they read, there is one "correct interpretation," and that their job is to find it, so as to demonstrate their social perceptiveness. I cannot help but believe that this intellectualized approach probably serves to diminish the impact of various distortion-producing factors. For example, it is unlikely that many experimental subjects are willing to permit themselves the luxury of reaching a conclusion about the communicator's intended meaning before completing his message; in our everyday reading, on the other hand, it is quite common to put an article down, through boredom or disgust, after developing some notion (however hazy) of the author's point of view.

Context Effects

Let us now consider some of the ways in which the environmental context may affect the communication process. Generally speaking, there is a great deal of evidence to support the conclusion that the individual's perception and interpretation of a given stimulus or event may be significantly affected by the context that is provided by *other* stimuli and events to which he has recently been exposed. More particularly, these context effects normally take the form of an apparent contrast between the prevailing level of stimulation and the stimulus that is subsequently experienced. Much of the early research on this problem centered on simple sensory phenomena. We are all, for example, quite familiar with the fact that on a hot day, the cool water of a swimming pool may initially seem quite cold (although we may eventually find it more tolerable). In cooler weather, on the other hand, even if the water temperature has been artificially maintained at a constant level, it may feel soothingly warm. Similar effects can be readily demonstrated in a variety of sensory modalities (Helson, 1964).

In my own work (Manis, 1967), I have attempted to study the implications of this type of context phenomenon within the realm of verbal communication. In this research, I have made extensive use of a series of photographs, showing the face of a male actor who portrays a variety of emotional states—some pleasant, some neutral, and some unpleasant (see Figure 3). Our subjects are simply instructed to describe selected pictures from this set. To assess communicative accuracy, the resulting descriptions are typically given to *other* subjects, along with an array of the original photographs. This second group, the decoders, is instructed to pick out the particular photograph (referent) described

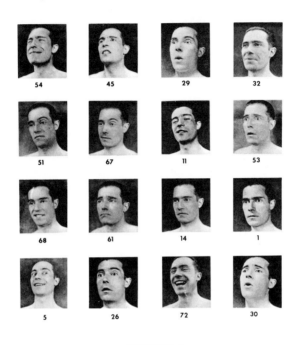

FIGURE 3

PHOTOGRAPHS USED IN THE REFERENTIAL COMMUNICATION STUDIES.
(MANIS, 1967; MANIS, ARMSTRONG, AND RIGER, 1969)

in each passage; when a subject succeeds in this task we may conclude that communication has been achieved, since the speaker's intended referent has been accurately conveyed. Moreover, by studying the decoder's errors, we can often trace the operation of various cognitive biases.

In one experiment, we studied the impact of contextual variations on the decoding process. There were three groups of decoders. One group was given a series of descriptions based on predominantly *pleasant* emotional expressions; in the second group, most of the descriptions were concerned with *unpleasant* emotions, while the third group received a *full range of* descriptions, based on both pleasant and unpleasant expressions. In addition, all subjects intermittently received several "test" descriptions, based on expressions that were neither pleasant nor unpleasant. The decoders were simply instructed to indicate the particular photograph (out of nine possibilities) that was described in each passage. We were mainly interested in seeing if the neutral test passages would elicit different choices (or interpretations), depending upon the *other* messages that the subjects had read. Figure 4 shows that the results parallelled those normally obtained in similar psychophysical studies. Subjects who were given descriptions that were mostly unpleasant tended to assume that the neutral passages were

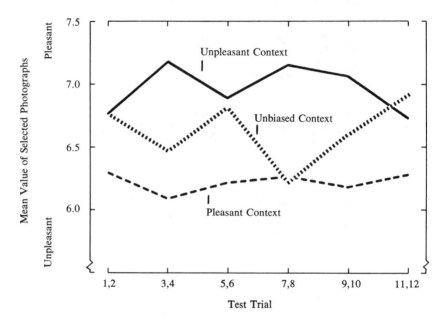

FIGURE 4

THE EFFECT OF EXTREME CONTEXTS ON DECODING BEHAVIOR

based on relatively *pleasant* poses; those assigned to the pleasant context, on the other hand, responded to the neutral test passages by choosing faces that were relatively *unpleasant*, while the unbiased group generally fell between these two extremes.

It is interesting to note that these effects were generated rather quickly and did not require a long period of conditioning, for the group differences were manifest from virtually the very beginning of the experimental session. Translated into the realm of political attitudes, these results imply that our inferences concerning the views espoused by various communicators may be significantly affected by other relevant materials that we have recently read or heard about. A speaker who focuses on the themes of justice and domestic security might thus seem to be favoring rather different positions if his talk has followed a statement by George Wallace, say, rather than Dick Gregory. In both cases, if the present approach is applicable, the listener should displace the speaker's apparent position *away* from the views previously expressed.

Our study of context effects in the realm of communication revealed a second important finding. The decoders who were given an *unbiased* array of messages (including both pleasant and unpleasant descriptions) did a significantly better job in selecting the proper referents for the test passages than either of the other two groups; decoders who were presented with a biased array of messages (whether pleasant or unpleasant) were thus handicapped in their attempts to interpret the neutral test passages. The implications of this result are most intriguing. If these data can be safely generalized, the present evidence suggests, for example, that an individual who is continuously exposed to a narrow and extreme range of political opinion, may subsequently find it difficult to interpret properly the comments of a more moderate communicator. Unfortunately, I am unaware of any serious attempts to test this proposition.

Most studies on context phenomena are rather brief, lasting no longer than an hour or so. There has thus been relatively little work concerning the long-term consequences of contextual biases. It seems most reasonable to expect that these effects would simply dissipate with the passage of time. However, while I have little doubt that this pattern would be demonstrable in the *long run*, there is some evidence that this simple "attentuation" model may be only partly correct.

Several years ago I was interested in the phenomenon of persuasive immunization. Earlier researchers in this field had compared various methods of strengthening the individual's resistance to subsequent influence attempts. In a study concerned with attitudes toward various noncontroversial medical topics (e.g., the use of penicillin), McGuire (1962) found that one effective immunization technique was to provide people with counter-arguments against the various points that were subsequently to be raised in messages designed to change their opinions. My own research (Manis, 1965), was concerned with the impact of these immunizing messages on the receiver's *interpretation* of the change passage.

For example, we wanted to see if the opinions imputed to an author who criticized the routine use of penicillin might be affected by prior immunization. In performing these experiments, we varied the time that intervened between (a) the receipt of the immunization attempt and (b) the subsequent presentation of the change message. In one experimental condition there was virtually *no delay*, with the immunization and change passages appearing on successive pages in a mimeographed handout; thus, one page might warn the reader against some of the "misguided" criticisms that had been levelled against the widespread use of penicillin, while the next page contained a rather complete *attack* on penicillin, based on these very charges. In a *delay condition,* a period of 3-5 days separated the presentation of the two opposing passages. In all cases, both the immunization and the change messages were attributed to trustworthy sources—physicians affiliated with major medical centers.

The results were striking. When the change messages immediately followed the immunizing information, clearcut contrast effects were obtained. For example, immediately after immunization, the author of the anti-penicillin message was thought to be particularly critical (as compared with his perceived view when there had been *no* prior immunization). This result closely follows from the context phenomenon discussed earlier. The immunizing information apparently provided a pro-penicillin context, which produced a displacement of the subsequent change (i.e. anti-penicillin) message toward the opposite (anti) pole of the attitude continuum.

When the immunization procedure was followed by a 3-5 day delay the results were drastically different. Under these conditions the anti-penicillin passage was interpreted as being *less* critical than it was in the control (no immunization) condition. The significance of the change message was thus displaced *toward* the view expressed in the previously received immunization passage.

Unfortunately, we do not yet have a satisfactory understanding of this delayed effect. One possibility (among several) revolves about the hypothesis that the results obtained in the delayed condition may reflect the subject's attempt to minimize the apparent conflict between the immunization and change passages. For example, it may be disconcerting to learn that two well-trained physicians are in radical disagreement concerning a matter of medical practice; the situation may seem more sensible, however, if the second of the two passages is interpreted as being only *moderately* discrepant (rather than *totally* discrepant) with the information previously provided. This account must be further elaborated, however, to explain the strikingly different results which were obtained depending upon the time interval that separated the immunization and change passages.

Context Effects and
Verbal Output

Our discussion up to now has focussed on contextual factors that may affect the recipients' interpretation of incoming messages. Contextual factors can also exert a systematic influence on the *communicator*. This often seems to come about because the context affects the speaker's perception of that which he wishes to convey, which in turn is reflected in his verbal output.

In one of our recent experiments (Manis, Armstrong, and Riger, 1969), we provided several groups of communicators with a 10 x 12 page on which were shown 16-24 posed photographs of various emotional expressions. By asking different communicators to describe a common subset of neutral expressions, while varying the context provided by *other* photographs, it was possible to explore the effects of different visual contexts on the communicators' descriptions. For example, some subjects were instructed to describe various neutral photographs when they were embedded in a sample of predominantly pleasant expressions, while others described them when presented in a predominantly unpleasant array. To determine the impact of these distinctive contexts, the resulting descriptions were rated by a group of judges who were simply instructed to indicate the degree of pleasantness of the emotional state described in each passage. The results showed clearcut evidence of contrast. The neutral faces were described in relatively unpleasant terms when they appeared within the context provided by the array of predominantly pleasant faces, while these same expressions were described as being relatively pleasant when embedded in an unpleasant array. In a subsequent experiment, similar effects were obtained when the communicators simply *read about* pleasant (or unpleasant) emotions, before writing their own descriptions.

Extrapolating into the political realm, these results suggest the intriguing possibility that the way in which we perceive and describe our own political views may be significantly affected by our awareness of other "possible" positions that we recognize, but do not necessarily endorse. Consider, for example, two people who hold to similar liberal values in the domain of welfare legislation; let us further assume that these people *differ* in the range of possibilities that they recognize as alternatives to the position they have chosen. Mr. Smith may thus be a liberal for whom the range of possible options is relatively constrained; the conservative alternatives that some find attractive may never enter his mind. If we assume that these "other" positions provide a context that contributes to Smith's perception and description of his *own views,* we are led to anticipate that in stating his opinions, his comments may convey a noticeably different impression than the statements of a colleague who shares his (Smith's) beliefs, but recognizes a broader range of plausible alternatives. According to our context model, Smith should express himself in more conservative terms than his like-minded friend. That is, because Smith views his beliefs against an undiluted background of liberal alternatives, he should underestimate his own liberalism.

Conclusion

Laboratory experiments suggest that the communication process can often be systematically distorted through the operation of various motivational and social psychological influences. It seems plausible to anticipate that these influences may play a significant role in the political realm, and may affect both (a) our assumptions regarding the views held by others, and (b) the manner in which we express our own views.

References

Aronson, E., Turner, Judith A. and Carlsmith, J. M. "Communicator Credibility and Communication Discrepancy as Determinants of Attitude Change," *Journal of Abnormal and Social Psychology,* 67 (1963), 31-36.

Berkowitz, L. and Goranson, R. E. "Motivated and Judgmental Determinants of Social Perception," *Journal of Abnormal and Social Psychology,* 69 (1964), 296-302.

Festinger, L. "Informal Social Communication," *Psychological Review,* 57 (1950), 271-282.

Helson, H. *Adaptation-Level Theory: An Experimental and Systematic Approach to Behavior.* New York: Harper & Row, 1964.

Hovland, C. I., O. J. Harvey, and M. Sherif. "Assimilation and Contrast Effects in Reaction to Communication and Attitude Change." *Journal of Abnormal and Social Psychology,* 55 (1957), 244-252.

Manis, M. "The Interpretation of Opinion Statements as a Function of Recipient Attitude and Source Prestige." *Journal of Abnormal and Social Psychology,* 63 (1961), 82-86.

Manis, M. "Immunization, Delay, and the Interpretation of Persuasive Messages." *Journal of Personality and Social Psychology,* 1 (1965), 541-550.

Manis, M. "Context Effects in Communication." *Journal of Personality and Social Psychology,* 5 (1967), 326-334.

Manis, M., G. W. Armstrong, and Stephanie Riger. "More Context Effects in Communication: Determinants of Verbal Output and Referential Decoding." Unpublished manuscript, 1969.

McGuire, W. J. "Persistence of the Resistance to Persuasion Induced by Various Types of Prior Belief Defenses." *Journal of Abnormal and Social Psychology,* 64 (1962), 241-248.

Political
Therapeutics

Christian Bay

Human Development and Political Orientations: Notes Toward a Science of Political Education

Professor Bay is on the faculty of the Department of Political Science of the University of Alberta.

IN THIS PAPER I SHALL EXPLORE SOME PROBABLE RELATIONSHIPS between human development and the shaping of political orientations and commitments.

Admittedly this is a dangerous terrain to enter, with all kinds of methodological pitfalls, quite apart from the absence of maps as well as compass. Yet I believe it is necessary to venture into this morass, even with only a makeshift compass, and to encourage others to be equally defiant of certain time-honored conventions of political inquiry. Without serious study of the psychological basis of political beliefs that manifest varying degrees of realistic concern for the public interest, I contend, we shall never develop a meaningful concept of political education, let alone a body of scientific knowledge about political education and how to promote it.

I am starting out with the proposition that some political orientations are better, *in some sense,* than others. We all accept this as an assumption in our role as citizens, but the usual stance of social scientists is to reject it in the realm of our professional work.

Now, there are some excellent reasons for this stance: the variety of political orientations in our society is large, and it would indeed appear rash, if not downright totalitarian, to seem to suggest that political orientations are misguided to the extent that they differ with our own. Moreover, many of us value diversity of opinions as an indispensible aspect of a civilized polity, and to suggest that some opinions are right, others wrong, might seem to challenge the value of diversity. Moreover, as John Stuart Mill argued eloquently in *On Liberty*, only by the free expression of *all* opinions, in a competitive market of ideas, would it be likely that well-founded opinions would gain in acceptance over erroneous opinions, or indeed that any opinions, even true opinions, would come to be entertained thoughtfully rather than superficially.

But there are also some excellent, and, I think, persuasive reasons for rejecting the premise that we as social scientists cannot evaluate or rank political opinions in terms of better or worse, or healthier or sicker, or better or more poorly justified, according to reasonably explicit *and* reasonable criteria. If the attempt that follows should deserve attention, that in itself would justify at least an open mind on the issue. And we note that John Stuart Mill's argument, just referred to, supports tolerance of diversity of opinions while it at the same time assumes that out of the clash of opinions will emerge better, more well-considered, more valid opinions.

To be sure, the social scientist might insist that only in matters of fact, in empirical matters, does it make sense to believe that "truth will combat error." The argument here is that empirical issues are not all that readily distinguished from normative issues; that even clearly normative propositions are not as immune to validity checks, or to scientific evaluation, as is frequently assumed.

It will be for the reader to judge whether the present effort is just another piece of ideological advocacy, or whether it is a constructive attempt to clear some of the ground for a scientific study of the development of concern for the public interest, and of political education. All I can urge at this point is an open mind; only by making serious attempts should we determine, and always only tentatively, what are the limits of the realm of scientific inquiry. Let me add that by "scientific inquiry" I mean the application of the best available, most replicable and measurable observation techniques, logically (or mathematically) interrelated and accumulated toward increasingly general, well integrated, well supported and testable propositions and theories. In this sense the present paper is pre-scientific rather than scientific; it is a foray, not a systematic investigation; but the foray aims at contributing to general theory, not to ideological affirmation.

In what follows I shall first of all (I) define "political orientation," and briefly describe some general attributes of these phenomena. This will lead up to (II) my attempt to rank the most common varieties of political orientations in the western world by categories of different degrees of compatibility with what I shall refer to as "humanistic commitment"—while attempting to demonstrate that this is a *rational* standard of judgment rather than just another philosophical position.

I don't expect to be immediately persuasive in arguing for the "naturalness" of that standard of judgment; at any rate not in that part of my argument. But the following parts might help. I shall next (III) develop a theoretical framework for a theory of *optimal human development* that will associate "more developed" with "more humanist." Then follows a section (IV) in which I attempt to show how general propositions can be developed within that theoretical framework, and, with three illustrations, how such propositions can yield hypotheses and how data can be brought to bear, directly on the hypotheses and indirectly on the propositions.

In conclusion (V), I shall discuss a conception of political education, as distinct from political socialization, and try to show that political education is urgently needed, especially in our time. The usefulness of the present paper hinges on whether I shall have succeeded in contributing toward a better understanding of the requirements of effective political education.

Aspects of Political Orientation

"Orientation" is here defined rather broadly and loosely as the sum of the individual's attitudes, beliefs, opinions, values, predispositions toward action, or nonaction. For some purposes Charles L. Stevenson's distinction between verifiable beliefs and non-verifiable attitudes is important, but not on this occasion (Stevenson, 1944). Again, Milton Rokeach's distinction between general values and specific attitudes, and between value systems and attitude systems, while of great significance in the advancement of our understanding of political orientations (and some of his work will be discussed below) is not sufficiently fundamental to affect my use of the term "orientation," which will encompass the whole range of values and attitudes (Rokeach, 1960).

Orientations are "political," for present purposes, to the extent that they bear on public problems (Mills, 1959, Chapter 1). I have elsewhere developed a distinction between "political" and "pseudopolitical," the former term to refer to behavior perceived to be in the interest of justice, or in the public interest, while the latter is to refer to behavior in the same arenas which seeks to foster the private interest of individuals or groups (Bay, 1965 B). This distinction, too, will be referred to again later on in this paper, but "political orientation" will cut across it.

Again, Gabriel A. Almond and his collaborators have developed a typology of political roles, from embryonic and inactive to more developed and active —namely "parochial," "subject," and "participant" (Almond and Powell, 1966). And Robert J. Pranger has distinguished between "participants" in politics dominated by concentrated power and "participators" in political decision-making in more democratic polities (Pranger, 1968). For my purposes these roles all encourage, and are in turn influenced by, various types of political orientations.

Political orientations of all denominations and descriptions can be more or less articulate; and for a given individual they are usually more articulate in some areas of interest and less articulate in others. By "more articulate" is here meant relatively well explicated, explained, or justified or rationalized. Degrees of articulation surely depend in part on educational attainments as well as "intelligence" (in a sense that is operationally defined in terms of high scores on certain verbal and logical achievement tests). But articulation levels also depend on general experience and motivation. The greater the individual's exposure in the past to words and events requiring a certain type of discourse, the more his ease and facility with that type of discourse will expand. The

Eskimos, to cite the old standby example, have a great many words for "snow".

In addition, present motivations surely must influence degrees of articulation. We tend to be satisfied with mouthing clichés if that is all that is expected of us by significant others, on issues that we have little or no interest in.

Other things being equal, then—including educational attainments, types of experience, intelligence etc.—we may expect the political orientations of individuals to differ not only in types of commitment or "political color," depending on their personal values (in Rokeach's sense, to be discussed below); they also will differ in degrees of articulation, accordingly. And within an individual's political orientation, if we know on what kinds of issues the highest levels of articulation are exhibited then we also know in what areas have been the bulk of his past experience or are his principal present motivations, or both. Reflectiveness and vocabularies do not develop at random; like muscles, their development reflects exercise and needs.

We all know people who seem highly articulate on some issues but appear naive and cliché-prone in other fields. If we know ourselves reasonably well, we are bound to realize that the same contrasts, to some extent at least, characterize our own minds. Nobody can realistically aspire to be highly articulate, as distinct from being glib, in all areas of discourse; the best that the educated person can hope to achieve is an acute awareness of the limitations of his own knowledge and perspectives, and a corresponding proneness to speak more hesitantly beyond those limits. For psychological reasons many people, but hopefully not ourselves included, often exhibit the opposite tendency, namely of speaking with what appears to be the most cocksure sense of certainty in areas in which they are reduced to repeating the clichés of others. This can happen when private anxieties are aroused, for one thing, for example by scare campaigns in anti-communist mass media; the result can be that individual defense mechanisms of innumerable citizens come to project private anxieties on to the political arena. Or socially insecure persons can develop a great facility with the clichés of the conventional wisdom, or whichever of them seem appropriate at each place and at each time; without necessarily taking a personal interest in the substantive issues, many individuals can develop a style of easing their daily social relationships by way of continually demonstrating their knowledge of and "sound judgment" on contemporary problems.

Already in the last couple of paragraphs I have exhibited, I trust, one kind of normative bias: I think that, on important social and political issues, articulate and reflected on political orientations are superior to cliché-ridden conformist or neurotically fixated orientations. I believe anyone seriously involved in the educational enterprise—as teacher, parent, or citizen—ought to share this bias in favor of rational reflectiveness, particularly pertaining to issues of major significance to the public welfare.

On the same ground I espouse the related norm of *autonomy*, in David Riesman's *et al.*'s sense: the capacity to choose whether to conform or not to conform to particular beliefs or institutions (including, I would add, laws), on the basis of individual standards of right and wrong (Riesman *et al.*, 1953). This autonomy should according to my position also apply, incidentally, to standards of professional judgment in political science, for example to the common belief that we as professionals must not speak to the relative validity of political commitments.

The norm of autonomy, thus conceived, is closely related to a norm of *rationality*, which may be formulated as follows: it is desirable that political orientations should be internally consistent and utilize all available and relevant evidence, and they should in principle be falsifiable by given categories of unexpected new evidence. While the citizen should be free to choose to conform or not to conform to a given belief or institution, he should base his choice on knowledge rather than ignorance, and on valid rather than erroneous inferences.

Humanism and Political Orientations

Most of my colleagues will agree, implicity or explicity, that political orientations can to some extent be evaluated in terms of their levels of articulation and degrees of autonomy and rationality. Professionally and not just privately, we may find political statements faulty with respect to errors of fact or of logic, or with respect to evidence of narrow indoctrination. But my argument goes much further: articulateness, autonomy and rationality are necessary but far from sufficient as criteria in the proposed scheme for evaluating types of political orientations.

My additional and crucial normative standard is "degree of compatibility with a humanistic commitment." I define "humanistic commitment" very simply as *a commitment to the sanctity of human life prior to all other commitments*. That ancient mathematician of Syracuse, Archimedes (287-212 B.C.) is supposed to have said, "give me a fixed point, and I shall tilt the earth." I like to tell my own students that I shall give them a fixed normative point with which we can tilt the liberal pluralist ideology, which most political scientists of my generation, and certainly most of our literature, seem to share. If the preservation and protection of human life, with the optimally free growth of all human beings, is taken to be the overriding aim of legitimate government and of politics, then every social institution can be judged as means to this general end. A makeshift compass, perhaps, but I use it and I recommend it.

In practice such judgments are not all that simple, of course, and in the following, perhaps rash and certainly sketchy attempt to formulate judgments on types of political orientations, on this basis, I am bound to over-simplify. But I trust I will at least succeed in making the point that such judgments are not impossible to make, on a professional basis; and also, by implication, that in the absence of a substantive point of departure the norms of autonomy and rationality alone are not of much utility in formulating commonly acceptable standards for responsible politics. On other occasions I have argued along similar lines by way of urging that "formal rationality" must be supplemented by "substantive rationality"; I have stated that we as political scientists must strive to become as rational, systematic and research-oriented in choosing ends as we traditionally have been trained to be regarding the choice of means (Bay, 1965 B, p. 41, and 1968 A, p. 224).

Let me now divide the majority of political orientations in the western world into five general categories, and rank them in terms of degrees of compatibility with the humanistic commitment just outlined.

(1) Least compatible with a humanistic commitment are *fascist* political ideologies, in that they tend to prejudge categories of human beings as superior and inferior, or the latter even as expendable. If the sanctity of human life as such is to be aim of politics, then all lives are equally sacred, and political redress must be given first to those who are the most oppressed and stymied, economically, socially or politically, and whether by historical accident or by economic or ideological design.

There may have been individuals who have thought of themselves as fascists who basically have been nationalists and have been compassionate toward underdogs within the nation as well as toward foreigners in general; but the prevailing tendency has been toward brutal elitism. Taking "fascism" in this general sense, there have been and are many rightwingers in this category who may think of themselves as democrats, or republicans, or belong to parties with such names, but who share the same contempt for human beings perceived as outsiders or outgroups. All race haters are in this sense and to this extent fascists, and quite a few religious bigots are too.

(2) The second lowest level of political orientations, in terms of my humanist standard, is what I would call *conservative parochialism,* —the stance of uncritical defense of past traditions or present institutions, or even glorification of the past or present. Far from all who call themselves conservatives are in this category; some conservatives, as a matter of fact, are interested in conservation of natural resources, or even of human resources as well. But the parochial conservatives I have in mind here are primarily interested in preserving privileges, and are afraid of every idea or movement that might undermine the present system of privileges. On this basis they tend to close their eyes and hearts to social problems, except perhaps by way of supporting private charity; and they tend to oppose vehemently all movements that seek to promote social or economic or racial equality. They lose as little sleep, probably, as the fascists do over the miseries of, say, the slum-dwellers in most major cities in the western world, or over victims of colonialist oppression. They do claim to be upset by the brutalities of communist oppression, but one suspects that their greatest aversion is to communism as an egalitarian ideology; communism might have been quite acceptable to many of these people if not mainly the middle class but the working class were seen as constituting the oppressed class.

(3) A middle category is represented by what I would call *conservative liberalism* (I could as well have called it "liberal conservatism"); most people in North America who think of themselves as conservatives or as liberals, or as being in between, or "middle of the road," have in common a basic sense of satisfaction with the existing political system. Professed liberals tend to emphasize blemishes more than do professed conservatives, but as democratic pluralists and moderates both have much in common: a commitment to "democratic processes" prior to substantive principles of legislation; a commitment to the "rule of law" prior to social justice; a commitment to "patriotic loyalty" prior to world peace, non-aggression or anti-militarism. What I would call the master myth of democracy is uncritically accepted by most liberals and conservatives: the belief that "the people," or the majority, are the ultimate rulers, and that the political system makes the government dependent on the will of the majority. That this belief is palpably in error need not be argued here (Bay, 1965 B, 1967 A, and 1969).

This democratic ideology is at odds with humanism in that not the sanctity of life but the preservation of a political system, or "way of life," becomes the end. Not justice for the oppressed but respect for the courts is the prior concern. The suffering of others is rationalized by attributing entirely hypothetical or illusory powers to the underprivileged as democratic citizens. Even the inarticulate and often immature young men, too young even to vote, let alone run for office, who are conscripted to kill or be killed in suppression of revolutions abroad, say in Vietnam, come to be seen, through this looking-glass, as citizens exercising their democratic obligations: And starvation and other social calamities abroad are of concern to most liberal-conservatives, except on Sundays perhaps, less in terms of human suffering than as a problem of susceptibility to anti-Americanism or communism.[1]

There are proportionately very few fascists in North America, and even the proportion of parochial conservatives is not very large, especially not among those under fifty. In my view the most fundamental obstacle to political and economic change in the United States is the massive preponderance of liberal-conservatives, who are as a rule personally righteous and well-meaning, but who by their unconditional commitment to the rules of the so-called democratic game have made it virtually impossible to achieve real changes, within a system that in fact is anything but democratic. Our political system serves the interests primarily of the most economically overprivileged minority in history, at the cost of vast deprivation among the poor in America, and of far worse suffering in the poorer countries, whose economies often are at the mercy of American corporate giants. This, however, is an analytical perspective which does not dispute the moderately humanistic nature of the personal political orientations of most North American liberals and conservatives. The problem is not a lack of good will toward all their fellow men on their part, but their having become socialized into an ideology that tends to make them committed to an allegedly democratic system, at the expense of a commitment to justice and human rights for those who are in fact oppressed under that same system.

(4) A more humanistic orientation is *revolutionary activism:* the stance that rejects the established institutions entirely; or the people who are working for radical upheavals, with the aspirations of the ancient Christian prophecy: the last shall be the first, and the first shall be the last!

There is no doubt but that a passionately humanistic commitment has been the basis of many a conversion from a comfortable acceptance to a complete rejection of our political institutions. Yet there is always the hazard that what began as a love for the oppressed ends up as mainly a hatred for those perceived as oppressors, who may well personally, as Marx taught, be well-meaning products and in a sense victims of the system that superficially seems to benefit them: it may have deprived them of their humane consciousness. And there is the further hazard that in preparing for the revolution other men come to be perceived as means rather than ends, or even as expendable means.

This is not to deny the possibility that in certain times and places, and perhaps in many countries today, revolutionary efforts must be supported, as a lesser evil compared to a cruel status quo. What I assert is that the effective revolutionary and his uncritical followers are likely to be less than fully committed to humanism in the sense developed here.

(5) The highest level of political consciousness, according to my standards, I would call *militant humanism*. It is essentially the consciousness that Albert Camus developed in *The Rebel* (Camus, 1954). It is the constant readiness to combat oppressors and to side with the oppressed, and to be open to evidence of oppression on our own side as well. It is the willingness to be a renegade, a traitor, to the winning side at the time for victory and for revenge, in the spirit of Christopher Fry's *The Dark is Light Enough* (Fry, 1954). It is a commitment in principle to the notion that laws are to be obeyed only to the extent that they do not oppress, or discriminate unjustly against the oppressed. It is a commitment to the view that politics should serve the same priorities as medicine, in the sense that governmental redress must be given first to those who are least privileged, just as the doctor is supposed to tend to the sickest patients first. It is the position that all human lives are ends, and that all social institutions are means, which must be constantly studied and evaluated, and abandoned, adjusted or reformed to the extent indicated by study and evolution.

Let me now confess that I do think of my own basic political commitment as being the most consistently humanistic one available to me. But why else should I hold my views? I have chosen, not invented these views. Like everyone else I have many political opinions and attitudes, which may be well or poorly founded, and consistent or inconsistent with each other or with my basic commitment. Opinions and attitudes must be, if we are rational, tentative only. But, and this is where I differ profoundly with most pluralist liberals, there has to be one basic, *a priori* commitment, subject of course to analysis and interpretations but not to challenge; and that commitment, in my view, can only be to the value of each human life itself, freely evolving. And one cannot consistently choose this commitment and also be fully a patriot, or fully a democrat, or even fully a revolutionary perhaps.

A Theory of
Optimal Human Development

I have pointed elsewhere (Bay, 1968 B) that current concepts of political development lack reference to notions of human development.

In my view this omission should be seen in a more general context of neglect of the study of psychological aspects of politics, or particularly of motivational and personality aspects. Part of the explanation is surely the greater ease with which the social aspects of political behavior, including socio-psychological, can be studied with quantitative methods. Another part of the explanation, possibly, is that systems theorizing is less subversive when criteria of good policies can be sought only within the system itself, in terms of "functional" *vs.* "dysfunctional," rather than judging policies and indeed the whole operating systems on the basis of outside criteria. Once we develop a conception of man and his needs, the natural consequence is to insist that a political system should have our allegiance only if and to the extent that it serves man and his needs, and does so better than alternate systems; the familiar conventional assumption today, that our "democratic system of government" must be rationalized and defended, will subsequently be more widely recognized as an irrational proposition.

If we feel free to take our chances on the issue of whether "western democracy" has given us the best of all possible worlds, in terms of human freedom and welfare, then we may proceed to formulate our conception of human development. This conception is not "our" or "mine" in the sense that I would claim originality; it has not been invented but chosen by this writer—and chosen as a general working hypothesis, not as a commitment. As I have written on this topic before, and the primary sources will be referred to, this section of my argument can be very brief.

Social psychologists, notably Daniel Katz and M. Brewster Smith *et al.* (see especially Katz, 1960 and Smith *et al.* 1956) have been the most important contributors toward this theory of human development, together with two great personality theorists, Abraham H. Maslow and Erik H. Erikson (see especially Maslow 1946, 1954, 1962 and 1965, and Erikson 1950, 1958, 1962, 1964 and 1969). And in a sense all these writers stand on the shoulders of Sigmund Freud.

Perhaps the best point of departure is their question, which is a common sense question in its simplicity but has been pursued by these writers with the intellectual radicalism of uncommon sense: *what good does a particular opinion, or orientation, do to the individual?* Only when and to the extent that we discover the motivational nature of political orientations can we learn how to make forecasts about the prospects for influencing them. And once we have adopted the view that political orientations *ought to be* more humanistic; a view that runs counter to conventional pluralist assumptions, and in a sense could be called a anti-democratic view; then it becomes desirable to discover ways of influencing orientations and their development toward more humanism.

There are essentially three categories of motivations that determine our opinions, according to Katz, and to Smith *et al.*: rationality motives; conformity motives; and ego defense motives. To take these in reverse order, and elaborate briefly with an example, one may be an anti-communist for ego defensive reasons. That is, one may project on to "the communists" all the violence and evil that one cannot tolerate seeing in oneself, or in one's own, or God's, country; one dogmatically divides the world into the good guys or nations, and the bad guys or nations, and would feel not only confused but threatened if someone argues that perhaps the world is not this simple. Alas, political decisions about the ABM and other issues of national life or death often appear to be influenced by otherewise eminent scientists who all their adult life have been fighting paranoid caricatures of communism.

Again, one can be an anti-communist for conformity reasons. We may discover, often quite early in life, that to express conventional anti-communist sentiments yields returns, whether by way of good grades, pats on the head, connections, good business, or career advancement. If one participates in conventional electoral politics one is bound to make this discovery. Not that one becomes a professed anti-communist while privately maintaining a more critical perspective. Academics may occasionally take this way out, but most people try to avoid hypocrisy: since opinions in this field are not really that important to most of us, we tend to adjust our views to whatever views seem palatable to significant others.

Again, one can be an anti-communist on a perfectly rational basis, psychologically speaking. If, as in North America, most people are exposed to apparently diversified but in fact almost uniformly anti-communist mass media, then most people will become anti-communists for very sensible reasons. This perspective will make sense to them; it will help to make order in their universe and to explain events. And, I must add, also persons with unencumbered access to pro-communist views as well may become anti-communists on entirely rational grounds. I am not about to make any pronouncement, either categorical or tentative, on what is the right attitude to take to that extremely complex phenomenon, communism in our time—or, if you prefer, modern USSR, or modern China.[2]

Instead of anti-communist attitudes I might have chosen pro-communist attitudes as my example, although in North America the former choice has the didactic advantage for present purposes, because there are far wider conformist pressures in that direction. Also, there are indications that anti-communism is an ideology more available to satisfy ego defensive needs, compared to pro-communism (Rokeach, 1956, p. 39). And it may well be, furthermore, that in anti-communist circles no cognitive activity is required at all, while in pro-communist circles, at least in the western world, a fair amount of reading and of familiarity with marxist concepts is expected.

But the point to stress is that virtually all our attitudes and opinions reflect, according to this theory, our motivational pattern, which in turn reflects our needs, or the tensions resulting from their frustration. A second, equally important point is that no human being is entirely rational, in the motivational sense applied here, as has been suggested above (p. 6). Perhaps some scientists approximate the ideal of complete rationality as researchers in their own fields, although even here approval-seeking and perhaps even neurotic motivations are unlikely to be entirely absent. Most of us in our daily lives surely exhibit mixes of rationality, conformity-orientations, and neurotic hangups, with our personal mixes varying from field to field and from one time to another. The less our substantive interest in a particular issue, the less likely that we will make up our own minds on it and take the trouble to select the most rationally satisfying perspective, according to the evidence available to us. And the stronger the conformist pressures on an issue, or the more closely it is linked with anxiety-provoking themes, the less likely that rationality-motives will prevail, when we develop our beliefs and attitudes.

Compared to our beliefs and attitudes, our values, in Rokeach's sense, are more permanent elements in our orientations, and are more likely to be rooted in childhood experience. Attitudes are directed to specific objects and are therefore (and for other reasons) likely to be more subject to being directly influenced by events. The problem with Rokeach's measurement of values, for present purposes and at this time, is that neurotically fixated assumptions may influence value preferences but are not directly measurable with Rokeach's instruments; yet one can infer their presence, possibly, to the extent that values like "freedom" or "mature love," for example, are given low ratings by individual respondents to Rokeach's questionnaires (Rokeach, 1969 and 1970).

Maslow's most valuable contribution for present purposes is his theory that posits the existence of a basic value hierarchy common to all human beings, which is unidirectionally dynamic, in the sense that "higher needs" become activated and pressing only after the experience of having had "lower needs" satisfied. In addition, his suggested basic need hierarchy does seem plausible and useful as a working assumption subject to being tested, in years to come: (1) biological sustenance, (2) physical security, (3) affection, love, belongingness, (4) self-esteem, self-regard, and (5) growth, development (Maslow, 1946, 1954 and 1962).

At the most elementary levels of human deprivation it is unrealistic to expect, as James C. Davies has pointed out, that *political* orientations in our sense are feasible (Davies, 1963). In our society, on the other hand, the handicapping deprivations are less likely to be starvation or fear of physical violence (although in some of our cities the trend may go in the opposite direction), compared to a sense of alienation, of being treated with contempt, or of being trapped and stymied; in other words, the more salient problems are deprivations of belongingness needs or of self-esteem, or stunting of growth.

The ultimate test of any theory is in its power to explain phenomena. I shall touch on problems of deriving hypotheses and designing relevant research in the next section, but must here make the general point that the sketch to be outlined, toward a theory of human development, will be of value only to the extent that the approach will yield hypotheses that can be tested, while at the same time it will provide plausible explanations for data that cannot as readily be explained by other theoretical perspectives available.

Very tentatively, then, may I contribute an extremely simple description of five developmental stages on the way toward a mature humanistic political commitment:

(1) Emotionally very deprived children may become authoritarian personalities, or occasionally anti-authoritarians. That is, they come to repress their aggression against parents *and other authority figures*, to the extent of becoming uncritical adulators of leaders and groups perceived as their own. Or, in the case of anti-authoritarians, they repress their dependency needs instead, and become hostile to all perceived authority figures; this would seem a far more difficult style to get involved with, for most children, and probably happens with less frequency (Bay, 1965 A, pp. 206-7).

To focus on the authoritarian personalities for a moment, not all respect for authorities is neurotically motivated, obviously. But, as Theodor W. Adorno *et al.* were the first to demonstrate empirically, authoritarianism that is ego-defensively motivated is associated with anti-semitism, race-hatred, and, in general, ethnocentrism and hostility to outgroups and deviants of many kinds (Adorno *et al.,* 1950). If the authoritarian personality has any political orientation at all, he is likely to be a right-winger, perhaps even a fascist at heart.

(2) Most people in our culture perhaps outgrow or learn to cope with anxieties about their own worth as human beings. The rise of secularism has led to a declining concern with questions of "sin," and there certainly has been a fast advancing process of liberation from guilt associated with sexual desire and its fulfillment. Moreover, the teachings of Freud and psychoanalysis, and of Benjamin Spock in child-rearing and of John Dewey in education, to name but the most obvious names, have all contributed to reducing the more crushing obstacles to psychological security and freedom in the process of growing up, for most youngsters. The levels of healthy self-esteem among young men and women in North America today could be considerably higher, but are probably as high as those achieved in any other country up to now, and higher than in most parts of the world.

But social anxieties remain, at the conscious or subconscious level. The "lonely crowd," as Riesman *et al.* have pointed out, tends to consist of individuals who are terribly concerned with whether or not they are liked by or even respected by others (Riesman *et al.*, 1953). To the extent that we share this preoccupation, we all tend to become, in a generic sense, pseudo-politicians; *i.e.*, we keep utilizing our opinions, attitudes, cognitive processes not as tools of comprehension of the external world, but as instruments for gaining acceptance by others. In short, we embrace the conventional wisdom, not because it does something for us intellectually but because it does something for us socially.

People differ, of course, with respect to what groups they want to be accepted by. The more diffusely anxious are concerned with gaining approval from virtually everybody, perhaps excepting small children, the insane, and those with obviously low social status. The more manipulatively anxious, say the narrowly ambitious career-seekers, will be more selectively concerned with the gaining of approval, and may even take apparently bold stands in defiance of conventions if that is thought to be pleasing to their reference groups or reference persons.

Our agencies of socialization, including most notably our schools, are geared to stimulating and utilizing these common social anxieties. "We adults destroy most of the intellectual and creative capacity of children by the things we do to them or make them do. We destroy this capacity above all by making them afraid, afraid of not doing what other people want, of not pleasing, of making mistakes, of failing, of being *wrong*. Even when we do not create children's fears, when they come to us with fears ready-made and built-in, we use these fears as handles to manipulate them and get them to do what we want." (Holt, 1964, p. 167).

As adults we try to get children to think the way we want them to. And even in the universities, perhaps especially in education and in the social sciences, this process of socialization toward conformist, uncritical patriotism continues full blast, for all the festive orations concerning the cultivation of critical faculties. Exams and grades, right up to the Ph.D. level, make sure that anxieties continue to have their impact on opinion formation.

If the proportion of North Americans who are deeply enough disturbed to become rightwingers appears fairly small, especially in the younger age brackets, I believe good majorities are sufficiently socially anxious to be psychologically predestined to become conformists, essentially apolitical in the sense that their political attitudes are determined mainly by what seems the best protective coloring for the individual, considering his private environment and his personal worries and problems, and not, or much less, by observations and reflections on public issues.

Essentially apolitical conformists might well be communists in societies governed by communists, but in North America they are likely to be either conservatives or liberals; *i.e.* either strongly identified with the perceived status quo, or identified in a more openended way with established institutions and ideals.

Conservatives are probably first of all those within this broad category whose occupations and careers would seem particularly exposed to rational challenge; for example, people whose standards of living seem particularly contingent on an arms race, or on the continuing subjugation of minority ethnic populations; or on the absence of effective governmental regulation of privileges, such as control of air waves, or of mass media, generally, or of large advertising funds. The weaker the rational case for particular privileges, and the more massive such privileges, in terms of income and economic power, the more those who hold them will tend to develop a defensive solidarity against the intrusion of progressive ideas and people; and essentially apolitical people with their income and careers to worry about will tend to assimilate the same staunchly conservative attitudes.

Others who tend to become strong conservatives are men and women with some neurotic predispositions to fascism or rightwing positions, who are nevertheless sufficiently flexible to dissociate themselves from the more rigidly anti-democratic and self-defeating kinds of opinions.

(3) The large majority of essentially apolitical conformists in the United States and Canada, especially among those now under fifty, are most likely to think of themselves as moderates, independents, or liberals, rather than conservatives. They find it the best policy not to offend anybody needlessly, and they have been around sufficiently to

know that not all people with power and influence are conservatives. In academic circles, as a matter of fact, and in quite a few other milieus as well, there may well be more power and influence on liberal than on conservative hands. And a moderate liberalism can seldom be attacked as un-American or subversive, outside the Deep South. This stance also has the advantage over conservatism of being compatible with fidelity to some youthful ideals of social justice, truthfulness, or the like, at least in constricted areas.

I do not mean to sound patronizing, or even contemptous, when attempting to describe conformist liberals as a species of the genus I have called, in effect, *homo apoliticus.* I believe most North Americans belong in this category, inside as well as outside academia (and most Europeans, too). And I consider most North Americans generous, civilized, basically nonviolent individuals with a sense of fair play. Their problem, from my point of view, is that they have been made to believe that the rules of the political and economic game are fair, and of their own making. They have been rendered politically impotent by the democratic myth asserting that popular rule exists, as well as by their private economic and social anxieties. The latter type of cause of political emasculation is to be sure declining among the very young today, but among their liberal and affluent parents social anxiety and political moderation have tended to become a way of life beyond questioning. It is given for rather few parents to learn in any radical sense from their children, although it can and does happen, particularly when social anxieties are moderate. Some able academic people I know have been very good learners.

But the tragedy of conformist liberals is at least twofold, in my opinion. Politically their tragedy is in their failure to question *radically* the *system* to which they habitually give their allegiance; their failure to discover that *because* the majority consists of moderate individuals who let themselves too easily be governed, in democracy's name, the conservatives and rightwingers in the Pentagon, the war industries etc. have been unable to make of the United States a bulwark of reaction and privilege, and a dispenser of death and destruction wherever the poor try to liberate themselves even from local oppressors, in Vietnam or in almost any other country in the so-called (of all names!) Free World.

The personal tragedy of *conformists* of any political coloring is in their declining intellectual ability to be independent and curious. This decline probably begins as soon as any youngster is made to suppress his own doubts, as a matter of social convenience (Freud, 1928). This easily leads to a *habit* of choosing the easy answers, as an alternative to cultivating the arts of hard thinking and the joys of intellectual independence. By definition, conformists tend to be careful not to offend anybody who might be influential, and to restrict the range of their political thought and the expression of their humane feelings accordingly. As they become older, their powers of political analysis, and perhaps most of their critical faculties, will tend to atrophy by disuse; just as their ability to feel strongly about injustice, or even to react against human suffering outside their own immediate experience, will tend to be reduced.

(4) Anti-authoritarian personalities have been referred to above; they may be psychologically compelled to become leftwing activists (or sometimes rightwing activists, depending on who the salient authority figures are). But most people on the left would appear to be on that side of the political spectrum by choice. Some, to be sure, are recruited less by the power of ideas than by the charisma of leftists, of the same or the opposite sex. "Activists have more fun."

But people on the left tend to be more interested than others in books and ideas, too. This is natural, as it takes more cerebral effort to criticize than to applaud. Moreover, political deviants so often experience being challenged that they tend to get their cognitive muscles exercised more often than do their more moderate or conservative peers.

Yet on the left, too, there appear to be factors at work that limit rationality. For one thing, the romanticism of warring for righteousness may tempt to develop a concern for role-consistency that reduces openness to new data, new experience, and alternative strategies of action. Daniel Katz has in a more general context described what he calls "the value-expressive function" of attitudes "in which the individual derives satisfaction from expressing attitudes appropriate to his personal values and to his concept of himself" (Katz, 1960, p. 170). The desire for this kind of satisfaction is not necessarily a source of irrationality, but it can be, to the extent that the individual has come to develop a rigid, stereotyped conception of himself, or of his political role.

This is where political ideologies come in. Like sectarian religion, ideological politics present essentially closed systems of thought for total acceptance. I am not disputing the fact that revolutionary dogmatism in some times and places can provide the best hope for building the movements that will overthrow an awful regime and install a better one in its place. But I am arguing that an effective soldier in the struggle for a just cause is not necessarily a maximally developed human being.

Even within the New Left, a movement that for some time had been relatively free from the doctrinal hair-splitting that had reduced the Old Left to ineffective, squabbling or warring factions, there are today very bitter disputes over strategies and priorities—disputes that are too often made irrational and unsolvable by way of competing ego-investments in different conceptions of political style. More than once I have heard otherwise rational radicals discuss issues of activist strategy not in terms of what course is wise but in terms of what course, and what people, are strong. This is just one of many examples that could be cited, of tendencies toward romanticizing the role of revolutionary action, or toward making it an end in itself.

(5) The fully developed political individual, according to my idea conception, is essentially similar to Albert Camus' Rebel, as I have stated (above p. 157). To be sure, Camus was a moral philosopher rather than a political theorist; and his political opinions are not always compatible with mine.[3] But the moral imperatives of his rebel also define what I take to be the basic commitment of the mature political man—as distinct from his counterfeit, the pseudopolitical man, the seeker after power, wealth, status or other personal satisfaction: the rebel's constant is commitment to the defence of the oppressed.

I have argued for the sanctity of human life as the only commitment that should be unconditional and predominant, for the person and for the polity. I believe this is a "natural" commitment, as does Camus, though in a different sense of "natural" and on different grounds. Camus seeks to prove, rather tortuously in my judgment, that a sense of human solidarity follows logically from the individual's commitment to his own life. My approach is to argue on more empirical grounds that *to the extent that* individuals in their developing years are secure and free, they tend to develop, or recognize in themselves, strong feelings of empathy with the oppressed. To the extent that they become educated, and not just socialized and trained, they will develop a desire for knowledge, and the ability to digest and accumulate data for purposes of comprehension as well as political action.

I have in this section sketched out certain very general types of psychological obstacles to the development of political maturity in this sense. It is time now to speculate about what kinds of propositions, hypotheses, and data would appear most promising, as ways to develop, test and improve on the theoretical perspectives outlined.

General Propositions About
Optimal Human Development

Let me now try to chart the way from a general theoretical framework toward propositions, hypotheses, and examples of relevant empirical research.

What has been sketched out above could be called a theory of human growth toward maturity, in some sense; or, in Maslow's sense, toward self-actualization (Maslow, 1962). I prefer to speak of an incipient theory of *optimal human development*, without indicating any end state to be anticipated, at least at the outset, by definition. "Maturity" I consider a useful colloquial shorthand term, but no attempt will be made to define it, let alone define it precisely enough to serve theoretical purposes.—"Optimal human development" implies that development in certain directions is desirable, at least up to a point; also implied is an empirical proposition to the effect that human beings do tend to develop, in some ways, unless they are incapacitated by self or environment. That children grow into adults in a physical and biological sense is obvious; that their ability to master many kinds of tasks tends to increase in the years from childhood to adulthood is almost equally obvious.

Beyond that, the present conception of optimal human development implies the mainly empirical assumption that children as well as adults, of all ages, under favorable conditions can improve their mastery, their wisdom, their ability to do good to themselves and others.

The implied normative premises are of a psychological-political nature: for the individual, maximal insight into himself is desirable, for what is denied and repressed is thwarted and killed, and I have always assumed that human life itself is the end, in its optimal fullness. Optimal insight into the environment is desirable because lack of realistic knowledge in effect hampers and thwarts; yet I use the term "optimal" rather than "maximal" because man is a social being, and is probably better off by accepting less than a total freedom to even think, let alone act, destructively (unlike, for example, Dostoyevski's *Raskolnikov*, who claimed for himself as a superior person the right to kill). The sanctity of human life, and our solidarity with all oppressed and disadvantaged members of the human race, are premises better not questioned, except possibly for very specialized philosophical purposes. Beyond this, realism about people and institutions is only desirable, I would think, up to the amounts with which each individual can live comfortably enough to avoid bitter despair; religious and other illusions cannot be categorically condemned as medicine for the soul, as Henrik Ibsen, for one, has taught us in *The Wild Duck* (Ibsen, 1950). Within the limits of the amount of anomie that the individual can stand, then, or the amounts and kinds of ambiguity that he can tolerate, an optimal insight into the real nature of the individual's environment is desirable. Self-insight on the other hand, is desirable to the maximum possible degree, because the individual is equipped with mechanisms of defense that bar him from seeing more than he can stand to see of himself; the more capable an individual is to face his own full range of motives and desires, and past experience, the more capable he will be to face up to and to cope realistically with the external world.[4]

Viewed from a classical philosophical perspective, the purpose of all political activity is to cope with problems, so that the City of Man can be safeguarded and improved in the quality of the social life it offers. It follows that it is in the public interest that those who take part in politics should have the maximal psychological prerequisites for optimal realism about the nature of the society and of its problems. Since political activity is almost synonymous with moral activity, and each citizen according to the classical tradition is a political and moral being, it further follows that all citizens, for the good of themselves as well as their community or society, should be maximally capable of realistic self-insight, optimally rational about public issues, and optimally capable of coping realistically with each of them. I believe this classical perspective is widely accepted or acceptable today, by those colleagues who are willing to speak as professionals to normative issues. The one classical notion that we all, I believe, tend to reject in our time, is the assumption that some categories of men by ascription are fit to rule, while others are fit only to be ruled: in our time we like to think of *all* men and women as fit to rule themselves, *i.e.* as capable of being citizens, not mere subjects.

If optimal citizenship requires maximal psychological freedom and optimal rationality about society, it also requires an optimal commitment to some conception of justice based on a maximal respect for human life. My argument is that the sanctity of human life should be the absolute, indeed the only master norm from which all others are derived, and that all other norms are therefore in principle arguable; this is why I believe in an "optimal" rather than a "maximal" commitment to any particular conception of justice, or any particular ideology, or any particular patriotism. One may dedicate one's life to a cause based on one particular conception of justice, and yet there ought always to be an openness to challenges which are based on the master principle of timeless humanism: that the securing and freeing of all human lives must be the ultimate end of any civilized order and the only legitimating basic task of any government.

So much for the value assumptions and empirical propositions presupposed in the very conception of Optimal Human Development— from now on to be referred to as OHD.[5] Now to the question of what kinds of data or research can improve our knowledge of the nature of and the conditions for OHD to the maximal extent, *i.e.* for the largest possible proportion of a given population. But here I can only give a couple of illustrations, sufficient only to establish that the theoretical approach developed here can in the long run be sustained only if data can be brought to bear on hypotheses related to this theoretical framework. I have in a previous paper on political and apolitical students referred to some categories of past data that gain in significance (*i.e.* explanatory power) if pluralist assumptions are discarded in favor of the present approach (Bay, 1967 B). The present paper tries to expand on the theoretical perspective developed in that one, which was subtitled "Facts in Search of Theory." At a later time I hope to add to the range of facts that will be accommodated and utilized in theoretical construction (Bay, Harvey, and Harvey, 1972).

In passing it should be said that I see nothing to be gained by drawing a distinction between research bearing on the nature of OHD as against research bearing on the conditions for OHD. It makes didactic sense to draw the distinction, but an effort toward making it clear and precise is not warranted, at least for present purposes, since most research bearing on OHD will bear on its nature as well as its conditions.

Let me now very briefly discuss three successive empirical propositions bearing on my conception of OHD, and in each case illustrate the feasibility and value of research by way of one hypothesis and one set of research data bearing on it.

Proposition I

Human development involves gradual liberation from the pressure of the most basic needs, and consequently reduces the individual's dependency on rigidly defensive beliefs.—Among many other formulations that could be derived, let us pick the following *hypothesis I:* The less preoccupied an individual is with problems relative to deficiencies in the satisfaction of his own basic needs, more specifically within the range of the four basic need categories in Maslow's scheme, the lower he will score on Milton Rokeach's Dogmatism scale.

Jeanne N. Knutson has confirmed this hypothesis, albeit with a somewhat special and non-representative sample consisting of employees of a wood and paper processing plant, school teachers, and hospital personnel, 495 in all, from Eugene, Oregon and a neighboring town. On the basis of an ingenious series of measures of indicated need deprivations on various levels in Maslow's need hierarchy, she came up with the following table, collapsed by Knutson into the three categories of "psychically deprived," "low self-actualizers" and "high self-actualizers" for the rows, and with respect to the columns comparing six levels of dogmatism from low to high. For simplicity let me here collapse the dogmatism categories, too, into four columns:

TABLE 1
CONTINUUM OF MENTAL HEALTH vs. DOGMATISM

| | Dogmatism | | | | |
	Low 2-3	Medium 4	5	High 6-7	
Psych. depr.	4.0	36.3	45.8	13.9	100 %
Low s-a	3.3	55.8	35.0	5.8	99.9%
High s-a	10.8	62.7	24.5	2.0	100 %

As the author points out this shows up a strong negative relationship between Rokeach's Dogmatism Scale and Knutson's combined measures of mental health, in this particular sample, at a level of significance of better than .001. There are no doubt wide open opportunities for improving both measures, and for testing this relationship out in more representative samples (Knutson, 1968).

Proposition II

Education, as distinct from training in skills and molding by rewards for conformity, involves the freeing of the mind from externally imposed thought patterns and their supporting anxieties. This freeing of the mind is more likely to take place, the more secure the person, and the greater his exposure to liberal or humanistic ideas. *Hypothesis 2:* The natural leaders among student radicals (*i.e.* those who insist with the deepest conviction on their own generation's right to live according to their own rules, democratically agreed on, and to learn according to their own sense of priorities, freely chosen by each) tend to be those who themselves are relatively secure and free, so that they can be maximally realistic and concerned about the outside world.

On the American scene in particular there is much evidence to support this hypothesis: radical student activists have been shown to come from relatively socially secure and well-educated homes; they have been shown to do rather better than most of their peers academically, in spite of time invested in extracurricular politics; they have been shown to be relatively low on neurotic traits. Moreover, it has been shown that tendencies to student activism increase with time spent in a college or university, and that they also increase with amounts of exposure to the humanities and social sciences, as contrasted with fields like engineering and business administration (see Flacks, 1967, and research summarized by Bay, 1967 B).

Here, too, much more work is needed. For one thing, we need to become more empirically sure of what kinds of exposure to the world of intellect are most likely to "grab" students at particular stages of development and with particular types of worries and anxiety patterns. Dr. Alexander W. Astin's and his team's massive researches ought to shed some light here, and also on what kinds of institutional character- istics and what patterns of conflict on the campuses might be most beneficial for educational ends. (Astin and Panos, 1969).

Proposition III

People tend to develop mature (*i.e.* disinterested) conceptions of justice to the extent that they learn to cope with anxieties and become edu- cated. Physically and psychologically deprived people may be aware primarily of their own troubles, perhaps including their own victimiza- tion by "society," or whatever; but with an increasing sense of security individuals can, unless they have bought their good fortune with their personal integrity (*i.e.*, have embarked on careers that penalize and effectively bar intellectual independence), develop a sensitivity to and indeed a revulsion against seeing others, even strangers, victimized, whether in Vietnam or in one's own society.— *Hypothesis 3:* In most American student populations it should be possible, by way of gently pointing out evidence of apparent indifference to the plight of under- privileged people, to stimulate among them the development of a mani- fest concern. This kind of concern is latent in all of us, the theory asserts, to the extent that we enjoy at least a minimum of personal security, freedom, and education. This is not to say merely that people who are themselves well off, economically and psychologically, will develop a willingness to make financial contributions to good causes. The present hypothesis asserts also that a real cognitive dissonance is latent and can be made manifest, *i.e.* demonstrated in social action, when individuals are made aware of not being just or consistent in granting to others the good things in life that they want and expect for themselves.

Milton Rokeach has in his most recent work by ingenious yet clearly professionally sound techniques managed to demonstrate that this latent cognitive dissonance exists and can be made manifest among college students by way of very limited stimuli. Let me by way of example mention only one among a variety of series of experiments which has confirmed the feasibility of exerting actual influence that utilizes and incidentally confirms this hypothesis.

What Rokeach did in two consecutive experiments was the follow- ing: Having found that large proportions of student respondents tend to rank "freedom" high and "equality" low, in relation to the universe of 18 values in his personal value-ranking questionnaires, he made an apparently innocent remark, in class, to both experimental groups among these students, a remark to the effect that these students appeared to value freedom for themselves but not for others, judging by that response. To the control groups he said nothing of any judgmental import.— Three months later all these students received *bona fide* invitations to join the local branch of the National Association for the Advancement of Colored People, a mail solicitation of the kind that anyone could receive from any organization that seeks public support and new members through the mail. There are no grounds for believing that any student in either group believed that Dr. Rokeach was in collusion with the NAACP, as of course he was. An impressive confirmation of his hypothesis was achieved when it turned out that in both experiments there were significantly larger proportions of experimental than of control subjects who decided to join the NAACP and paid their dues; it seems clear that this difference in behavior must be attributed to his own low-key remark in class to the experimental subjects (Rokeach, 1969, Chapter 7, and 1970).

Rokeach's newest work opens fresh possibilities not only for gaining new knowledge of value hierarchies in many populations; it also makes it possible to explore how value structures tend to change with human growth and development, and how various kinds of natural or experimental stimuli do or can promote optimal human development.

The value of any theoretical paradigm depends on the explanatory and predictive powers of theory and hypotheses engendered within it. No sure case for the validity of the OHD approach toward the understanding of the development of political orientations has been made in this paper. Limitations of space as well as of knowledge have made it possible to present only the contours of the paradigm and a couple of illustrative examples of relevant research that would acquire added significance (by confirming hypotheses derived from theory of high explanatory power) in this theoretical perspective.

While there remain grave doubts about the validity of the OHD approach to the study of political orientations and behaviour, it surely can be said that the conventional pluralist paradigm has been found severely limited in explanatory power. In other contexts I have pointed out that the increasingly fashionable concept of "political development" has been left hanging in the air within authoritative political science literature, because the pluralist value-vacuum has barred any connected concept of human development, and also left obscure what is "political," anyway, as distinct from, say, economic or organizational development

(Bay, 1968 A and 1968 B). As a result, the tendency has been to hide behind academic jargon the reality of a simpleminded hierarchical scheme in which "high development" would be specified according to present achievements or operations of Anglo-Saxon democracies. In my view the obvious desirability, which few would care to deny explicitly, of getting away from this posture by way of linking political development with some theory of human development, should in itself recommend the present approach as worthy of further exploration. Unless empirical political theorizing is to continue to accept present institutions as the ultimate givens, or in effect as the normative fence that keeps blocking alternative institutions from our horizon, surely we must seek in some conception of human development the rationale for evaluating political development, or political behavior and institutions generally.

A Conception of
Political Education

Suppose now that we were to accept the probable validity or value of the present approach to the study of political orientations; we are then assuming not only that psychological factors influence political opinions, which is hardly a controversial assumption. We assume, too, that there is an optimal human development, in an empirical and a normative sense, and that different levels toward OHD will tend to stimulate (and reflect, perhaps) different political orientations between the extremes of fascism and humanism. If this perspective were widely accepted, what would be some of the consequences for political education, and for university curricula more generally? Let us indulge in a few speculations within the brief space that is left.

One of the drawbacks to the pluralist paradigm is the muddle in which conceptions of political education have remained, probably by necessity. On the one hand, the value of "democracy," and by implication of the present allegedly democratic institutions, is assumed to be beyond question as a basic norm, and as a frame of reference for how to evaluate specific institutions and decision categories. Also, it is assumed that certain categories of opinions are bad, or perhaps sick: say, white (or black) supremacy, anti-semitism, fascism, communism. On the other hand, within "the democratic spectrum," from social democracy to rightwing conservatism, one opinion is held to be as good as another; to be politically educated, it is assumed, is to know the essential "democratic" institutions, to know how to perform "democratic duties" like voting, and to be willing to "choose" political opinions. How one chooses, by imitation of parents, by whim, by perceived class or group or personal interest, by response to a candidate's charisma, or by reason and reflections on who or what is just, is really beyond the pale of "political education"—or "citizenship" or "civics" as it is more often called in the schools.

In the last decade a literature on "political socialization" has emerged, which seeks to describe and analyse how in fact individuals, and especially children and youngsters, acquire their political perspectives, in the schools as well as in the homes and elsewhere. This literature has filled a real need, for we now know much more than before about the ways in which established political norms are implanted on nonsuspecting youngsters, who by and large become molded toward accepting what exists, rather than educated toward questioning and judging the present and seeking better ways for the future (see especially Hyman, 1959; Greenstein, 1965; Easton and Dennis, 1965 and 1967; Brim and Wheeler, 1966; Hess and Torney, 1967; Lane, 1962; Lane 1969).

Robert Pranger has been the first to argue, as I read him, for applying the term "political socialization" only to the molding process just described, while reserving "political education" for a type of political communication that "emphasizes above all the artificiality of political order and the citizen as a creative actor within this order" (Pranger, 1968, p. 44). "Artificiality" refers not to the general phenomenon of political order, I take it, but to any particular order, suggesting that it should not be considered necessary and irreplaceable; for the object of political education is to equip us to seek and promote the best political order. The "best of all possible worlds" assuredly must be in the future, if indeed it ever will be transferred from our imagination to the real world.

There will always be political socialization in this sense, by sociological necessity. The powerful will always seek to shape the behaviour and the minds of the less powerful, and most parents will always seek to impress their own values and concerns on their children. What responsible education must seek to make sure is that there will also be political education, in Pranger's sense, which as he points out is close to the classical conception of the teaching of civic virtue. The aim of political education is not to produce the knowledgeable, law-abiding citizen who merely knows his rights and obligations under the established system, but to produce "the free man armed with enough political sophistication to participate in politics as a person with the capacity for independent judgment, despite the pressures from political socialization" (Pranger, 1968, p. 44).

It is evident that effective political education requires something more than exposure to philosophical principles and political history. "Capacity for independent judgment" requires mental health, or human development, to use the term applied in the above discussion. Persons low on OHD may perhaps become sophisticated about facts, given the right kinds of amounts of theoretical and practical exposure, but will have a low capacity for independent political thought and action; they may in some cases be anti-authoritarian rebels rather than authoritarians or timid conformists, but they cannot be non-authoritarians, non-dependent on external direction.

If the argument above is valid, something more than *independence* of judgment will be achieved by persons high on OHD, namely *humanity* of judgment, or *justice* of judgment. Not only capacity for being rational but sensitivity to issues of justice improve with human development. And the citizens to be produced by political education are conceived of, ideally speaking, as persons capable of being not only independent but just also—indeed, as persons who feel compelled to be just because they are, in Camus' sense, revolted by injustice.

I believe the large majority of today's American youth are free enough and secure enough to have the psychological prerequisites for becoming citizens in the sense of becoming knowledgeable, rational, just, and humane individuals, to degrees substantial enough to create a far better society for themselves. Their prospects for accomplishing this are dim mainly for sociological reasons: their organizational environment inevitably seeks to perpetrate itself, and many of the organizations the individual is up against are extremely powerful, above all the state, or the economic powers for which the state is a facade; in short, the established powers, with their schools, armies, churches, corporate and public bureaucracies, etc., which between them apply always the same carrots and sticks to youngsters with anxieties and ambitions for status or security: shape up, conform, go along, play ball, be a nice guy; don't rock the boat, don't protest, never mind the other fellow, it's not your business what happens in Vietnam, or Brazil, don't make a nuisance of yourself.

All such do's and don'ts promote political socialization and discourage political education. And they are many and powerful. No wonder most Americans of my generation have swallowed whole all the civics pap about democracy achieved and America the glorious leader of the Free World; no wonder that they have behaved like obedient subjects, not free citizens, and cheerfully sent their well-socialized sons to Vietnam to participate in the crimes that have been revolting large proportions of the young generation, and increasing proportions of their own as well, in recent days, at last.

The hope in our time is that increasingly the young are becoming politically educated, even in the United States, where the forces of socialization have in the past succeeded so extremely well in producing de-politicized subjects. Young Americans have perhaps more psychological potential for effective political education than their contemporaries in most other countries, for a number of reasons. One is that the political worries of their elders (*e.g.,* "communism," "socialism," "atheism") have become obsolete to the point of looking ridiculous to the alert among the young much faster than in former days, with faster rates of technological change. Another is that public problems, at least to young people, have assumed a much more pervasive importance, now that every reflective person knows that the terror balance, the population explosion, the cumulative poisoning of the soil, air and water, including our own bodies, all add up to grave doubts whether our civilization, or indeed mankind, shall exist much longer. Naturally, most young people tend to worry less about their private futures than used to be the case, also on account of their private affluence, keeping in mind the liberal tradition that Louis Hartz has described. The corporate establishment that young Americans are up against is of course gigantic; while not as visibly ruthless at home as the Chinese or even the Russian, its powers of control and destruction internationally have no match. And yet it may be peculiarly unstable, precisely because it has come to rest at home on the democratic myth as a basis for its legitimacy, and is not well equipped for resorting to terror against its own citizens —except possibly in some of the ghetto areas.

But to the extent that the sons and daughters of the rulers themselves and their class become the revolutionaries, machine guns and weapons cannot alleviate the threat to the social order that effective political education will bring about. It is trite to say that the young are bound to take over, sooner or later. The important point is that among the young increasing proportions seem to have become politically educated, under circumstances that indicate their education will stick, in the sense that they will not easily become corrupted by the traditional carrots and sticks. If this is true, then even the power of the Pentagon may be curtailed sharply in the next ten or twenty years, with drastic consequences for foreign clients whose terror regimes have prevented political education for the vast majority of their subjects.

In any event, across the civilized world the obsolescense not only of old issues but of old justifications for political rule is becoming embarrassingly clear with ever greater rapidity, due in part to the rapid technological development, with the mass media and the growing international awareness of monstrous crimes in the name of high principle, with fast-budding development of protest movements and even countercultures among the sensitive and the young. The democratic myth as justification for Pentagon power around the world is crumbling fast.

Will international chaos, or some kind of a world communist order, be the result? Very likely not. Assuming the Pentagon will have its nuclear claws cut before they blow up the world (a risky assumption, to be sure), we are more likely to see national liberation movements take very different courses in different parts of the world. No doubt there will be much bloodshed in long-oppressed nations, but probably not in the West, where the new, younger leaders will feel strong enough to do without blood purges (although some bloody racial fights, even racial wars, may be almost unavoidable).

We have concluded that our civilization has produced accelerating processes of technological and social change which have made established ideologies and beliefs clearly obsolete at a faster rate with every few years, and thereby have undermined the actual authority of those who rule, who are almost all relatively old men. In addition, as Kenneth Keniston has been the first to observe and formulate, our affluent society has produced a new stage of development for increasing proportions of young people; he calls it "the stage of youth." As industrial society had freed the children from the need to work and made possible a separate teenage stage of development and a "teenage culture," so our emerging technological society has made it possible for many youngsters after their teens, through a good part of their twenties, to take the time to "find themselves" by way of a moratorium on future role commitments.

Keniston argues that "affluence is producing more and more families who bring up their children to be idealistic, responsible, and *serious* (my italics CB) about the creedal values of our society—children who are therefore dismayed and outraged when they discover the societal lapses between principle and practice. Social change erodes the institutionalized hypocrisies that in other eras helped conceal this gap between social creeds and deeds." (Keniston, 1968, p. 265). Not all young people achieve the stage of youth—only those whose anxieties about themselves and their own future are sufficiently limited, or effectively coped with, to permit them to define their own identities and their own attitudes toward their society. The stage of youth is a developmental stage beyond conformism in my terms, it is a stage of protest against injustice and of affirmation of humanist ideals. In so far as youth is explicitly political, its place is invariably on the left. If the social order seems to bar effective political action on the left, young people may seek escapes from society in various ways, or else become revolutionaries who tend to reject humane values on the road to the anticipated cataclysms; but to the extent that effective political strategies seem to them to have a fighting chance to pay off, now or later, they will tend to be political activists, in their schools, places of work, or neighborhoods.

"A man who is not a radical at twenty is likely to be a police spy at forty," Clemenceau is reputed to have said. Keniston's theory affirms this hypothesis in more general terms: "With the successful resolution of youth, a man or woman is more able to compromise without feeling compromised and, conversely, to stand alone on principle without feeling isolated" (Keniston, 1968, p. 271) because he will have determined his own identity and will know exactly the rightness or wrongness, *in his own terms,* of what he is doing. He has achieved a self-knowledge that is not gained by those who move from adolescent lack of serious responsibilities into given adult roles that have been defined *for* them, not *by* them.

Youthful radicalism of the past, certainly in America, has tended to be sporadic and to become socialized, *i.e.* transformed into adult-accepted channels (occasionally into leftwing channels, to be sure). What is new and immensely hopeful is that youthful radicalism nowadays so often appears to have the psycho-social quality of a real developmental stage, which opens the prospect of continuing resistance to the conventional political socialization pressures, and thus may permit the individual throughout his adult life to keep taking his own ideals seriously, and to preserve also for political issues his rational mind, his sense of justice and his integrity.

If I am not mistaken in these observations, and if there is time enough before nuclear or biological catastrophe catches up with us, then we can indeed expect a new breed of citizen to take effective control, in the years to come, not only of our universities and colleges, but of our political and eventually our economic institutions as well. I can think of no other viable way of insuring ourselves against an early end to civilized life on this planet. Our private corporation-dominated society has spawned the technology that is likely to do us all in, unless we can arrest the drift toward the ultimate catastrophe by way of effective politics, as distinct from pseudopolitics. But this requires an end to the dominance of the pluralist ideology, which has relegated politics, in effect if not in official pretense, to the menial task of regulating conflicts between the private interests which between themselves dominate our economic life. America's giant resources have been exploited, consequently, mainly for private ends, with law and order, the police and ultimately the armed forces too at the service of the corporate interests. This is the system into which youngsters still become socialized by way of the democratic myth; deception is necessary, for healthy young people would reject this reality if they were left in control of their own eyes and could see it.

I have observed that increasing proportions of young people are refusing nowadays to become politically socialized into a system that would doom their own future or that of their children. Political education has been taking hold in our universities and colleges, and is beginning to be felt even in our high schools. Like de-Stalinization in the USSR, the process of liberation from ideological oppression is probably irreversible, barring a global catastrophe; unlike the situation in Russia, America has an officially liberal tradition that handicaps the forces of military and paramilitary suppression, which means that the liberating processes probably will make progress much faster in this country. But there is no time to lose, for time is fast running out, it would seem, on the human experiment.

Notes

[1] Biafra was an exception; Christian churches have done much to publicize this tragedy, and to support the Ibos, among whom the Christian missions have established a great deal of influence. By contrast, the Christian churches have taken little interest in the continuing mass slaughter of non-Moslem Sudanese, or of "backward" Indians in South American countries.

[2] I trust it has been made clear that I intend to be categorical only in my affirmation of the supreme value of all human lives; and a tentative judgment here on the merits of communism would require a spelling out of premises first, and amount to a major digression.

[3] In his great debate with Jean-Paul Sartre, the latter had in my view the better of the argument (Sartre, 1965).

[4] There is bound to be a high correlation between degrees of self insight and of realistic coping, because coping can be realistic only by accident if or to the extent that self-insight is deficent. On the other hand, as M. Brewster Smith reminds me in a letter, self-insight is not a sufficient, only a necessary condition for effective coping. For one thing, neurotic syndromes such as obsession-compulsion can combine good self-insight with inability to act freely.

[5] One further empirical proposition, which cannot be discussed in the space available, is that opportunities for increasing OHD are not limited in any zero-

sum game kind of direction; it is not necessary, in other words, to raise the issue
of how to choose between achieving, say, 80% of OHD for 40% of the population as against 40% of OHD for 80% of the population. This for two reasons:
(1) the more of OHD is achieved for some, the stronger the forces that will
promote OHD for others; (2) clear priority issues arise only concerning the more
basic preconditions for OHD, such as in the realm of violence or economic
deprivation. Here the answer is to take the human rights approach: increased
freedom first for the least free (Bay 1965 A, pp. 4-7 and *passim.*)

References

Adorno, Theodor W., Else Frenkel-Brunswik, Daniel J. Levinson, and
  Nevitt Sanford. *The Authoritarian Personality.* New York: Harper,
  1950.

Astin, Alexander W., and Robert J. Panos. *The Educational and Vocational
  Development of College Students.* Washington: The American Council
  of Education, 1969.

Almond, Gabriel A., and G. Bingham Powell. *Comparative Politics: A Developmental Approach.* Boston: Little, Brown and Co., 1966.

Bay, Christian. *The Structure of Freedom.* New York: Atheneum, 1965. (A)

Bay, Christian. "Politics and Pseudopolitics," *American Political Science
  Review.* 59 (1965), 39-51. (B)

Bay, Christian. "Civil Disobedience: Prerequisite for Democracy in Mass
  Society," in David Spitz, ed., *Political Theory and Social Change.* New
  York: Atherton, 1967. (A)

Bay, Christian. "Political and Apolitical Students: Facts in Search of
  Theory," *Journal of Social Issues.* 23 (1967), pp. 76-91. (B)

Bay, Christian. "The Cheerful Science of Dismal Politics," in Theodore
  Roszak, ed., *The Dissenting Academy.* New York: Pantheon, 1968. (A)

Bay, Christian. "Needs, Wants, and Political Legitmacy," *Canadian Journal
  of Political Science.* 1 (1968), pp. 241-60. (B)

Bay, Christian. "Behavioral Research and Democratic Theory," *Berkeley
  Journal of Sociology.* 14 (1969), pp. 18-34.

Bay, Christian, Susan K. Harvey, and Ted G. Harvey (1972). Citizenship
  and Human Development (tentative title). Forthcoming.

Brim, Orville G., Jr., and Stanton Wheeler. *Socialization After Childhood:
  Two Essays.* New York: Wiley, 1966.

Camus, Albert. *The Rebel.* New York: Knopf, 1954.

Davies, James C. *Human Nature in Politics.* New York: Wiley, 1963.

Easton, David, and Jack Dennis. "The Child's Image of Government," *The Annals of the American Academy of Political and Social Science.* 361 (1965), 40-57.

Easton, David, and Jack Dennis. "The Child's Acquisition of Regime Norms: Political Efficacy," *American Political Science Review.* 61 (1967), 25-38.

Erikson, Erik H. *Childhood and Society.* New York: Norton, 1950.

Erikson, Erik H. *Young Man Luther.* New York: Norton, 1958.

Erikson, Erik H. "Youth: Fidelity and Diversity," *Daedalus,* 91 (1962), 5-27.

Erikson, Erik H. *Insight and Responsibility.* New York: Norton, 1964.

Erikson, Erik H. *Gandhi's Truth.* New York: Norton, 1969.

Flacks, Richard. "The Liberated Generation: An Exploration of the Roots of Student Protest," *Journal of Social Issues,* 23 (1967), 52-75.

Freud, Sigmund. *The Future of an Illusion.* New York: Liveright, 1928.

Fry, Christopher. *The Dark is Light Enough.* London: Oxford University Press, 1954.

Greenstein, Fred I. *Children and Politics.* New Haven: Yale University Press, 1965.

Greenstein, Fred I. *Personality and Politics: Problems of Evidence, Inference, and Conceptualization.* Chicago: Markham, 1969.

Hess, Robert D., and Judith V. Torney. *The Development of Political Attitudes in Children.* Chicago: Aldine, 1967.

Holt, John. *How Children Fail.* New York: Dell, 1964.

Hyman, Herbert H. *Political Socialization: A Study in the Psychology of Political Behavior.* New York: The Free Press, 1959.

Ibsen, Henrik. "The Wild Duck," in *Three Plays.* London: Penguin, 1950.

Katz, Daniel. "The Functional Approach to the Study of Attitudes," *Public Opinion Quarterly.* 24 (1960), 163-204.

Keniston, Kenneth. *Young Radicals: Notes on Committed Youth.* New York: Harcourt, Brace & World, 1968.

Knutson, Jeanne N. "Motivation and Political Behavior: An Attempt at Synthesis." Unpublished Ph.D. Dissertation, University of Oregon, Eugene, 1968.

Lane, Robert E. *Political Thinking and Consciousness: The Private Life of the Political Mind.* Chicago: Markham, 1969.

Maslow, A. H. *Motivation and Personality*. New York: Harper & Row, 1954.

Maslow, A. H. *Toward a Psychology of Being*. Princeton: D. Van Nostrand, 1962.

Maslow, A. H. *Eupsychian Management*. Homewood: Richard D. Irwin, 1965.

Maslow, A. H. "A Theory of Human Motivation," in Philip L. Harriman, ed., *Twentieth Century Psychology*. New York: The Philosophical Library, 1946, pp. 22-48.

Mills, C. Wright. *The Sociological Imagination*. New York: Oxford University Press, 1959.

Pranger, Robert. *The Eclipse of Citizenship*. New York: Holt, Rinehart and Winston, 1968.

Riesman, David, with Nathan Glazer and Reuel Denney. *The Lonely Crowd: A Study of the Changing American Character*. Abridged by the authors. New York: Doubleday Anchor Books, 1953.

Rokeach, Milton. "Political and Religious Dogmatism: An Alternative to the Authoritarian Personality," *Psychological Monographs: General and Applied,* 70 (1956) 18, whole no. 425, 1-43.

Rokeach, Milton. *The Open and Closed Mind*. New York: Basic Books, 1960.

Rokeach, Milton. *Beliefs, Attitudes and Values: A Theory of Organization and Change*. San Francisco: Jossey-Bass, 1969.

Rokeach, Milton. *Value, Attitude and Behavioral Change* (tentative title). Forthcoming.

Sartre, Jean Paul (1965).

Smith, M. Brewster, with Jerome S. Bruner and Robert W. White. *Opinions and Personality*. New York: Wiley, 1956.

Stevenson, Charles L. *Ethics and Language*. New Haven: Yale University Press, 1944.

Arnold A. Rogow

Some Psychiatric Aspects of Political Science and Political Life

Professor Rogow is on the faculty of the Department of Political Science at the City University of New York. Portions of this paper have been published previously as part of "Psychiatry, History, and Political Science: Notes on an Emergent Synthesis" by Arnold A. Rogow, in *Modern Psychoanalysis: New Directions and Perspectives,* edited by Judd Marmor (New York: Basic Books, 1968).

I SUPPOSE THERE IS NO DISPUTING THE FACT THAT A PSYCHIATRIC approach to politics has yet to make a dramatic breakthrough in the political science universe or in the world at large. When I tell people "I am in the 'field' of psychiatry and politics," they react as if I had said that I was a student of the sex life of the elephant. Their first reaction is surprise, sometimes disbelief; and their second is curiosity. "What does psychiatry have to do with politics?" they ask—and, if we have met at a cocktail party, they are apt to take a generous swig of whatever it is they're drinking, as if to brace themselves for what is coming.

Within the political science profession, there is also surprise and curiosity, but, above all, skepticism. Most political scientists of my generation—there are about 15,000 young and old political scientists in the United States, many more than in the rest of the world combined —have grave doubts about the relevance of psychiatry to politics. They are aware, as I am, that the pioneering figure in what might be called political psychiatry, Harold D. Lasswell, published his most important books in that area almost forty years ago. Moreover, it has been more than twenty years since he wrote a book that specifically focuses on the relationship between personality and politics.

Furthermore, no more than a dozen—to be generous, let's say two dozen—political scientists have published anything in the area of political psychiatry. There are so few, in fact, that one tends to know all of the names: Lane, George, Leites, Wolfenstein, Edinger, Roazen, Greenstein, and a few more. (Of course, there are historians, sociologists, and psychologists who have contributed to the study of political psychiatry; here I am dealing only with political scientists.)

Finally, one looks in vain into the most respected books in political science for any recognition that psychology, much less psychiatry, has much to contribute: there is very little psychology or psychiatry in *The Civil Culture* (Almond and Verba, 1963), *Modern Political Analysis* (Dahl, 1963), or *Who Governs?* (Dahl, 1961), and even less in most of the voting studies and the writings on legislative behavior. We are forced to conclude that, if psychodynamics is an important dimension in the study of political behavior, it is a missing dimension—but if it is missing, how can it be important?

My thesis is that it is missing *and* important—missing for a number of reasons. Some of these reasons I have dealt with elsewhere: (1) Lasswell has never founded a "school" or cultivated disciples; (2) political science has been dominated by rational models of behavior; (3) there is the still-lingering suspicion that psychiatry is mainly about sex and mental illness, and what does this have to do with politics (especially sex!)? (For a long time it was believed that Freud was a dirty old man; now we know that Rousseau, Hobbes, and even Marx were dirty old men, too, and perhaps that fact has already begun to make a difference.)

Psychiatry and Scientific Politics

Certainly the "hard" behavioralists—by which I mean those who favor quantification and the application of rigorous scientific methods—are suspicious of the psychiatric approach because of a number of methodological difficulties. Against it they argue that such an approach is necessarily qualitative rather than quantitative. It focuses much more on the individual "case" or patient or political actor than on the group, collectively, or any political institution as such. Its findings are difficult to extrapolate or apply to political behavior, or when applied, are sometimes applied in a sensationalist and irresponsible fashion, as in the Goldwater campaign of 1964. Certainly some psychiatrists—but only some—are quick to (mis)apply their knowledge to all sorts of political situations, ranging from Soviet behavior to student demonstrations. Much of the psychiatric literature about politics *is* naive, simplistic, romantic, and, above all, given to argument-by-analogy.

But having said this, it seems to me that the case against applying psychiatry to political science is becoming much weaker. In a sense, the political psychiatrists are in a position similar to that of the group process students like Bentley (Bentley, 1908) and the quantifiers like Rice (Rice, 1928) of several generations ago. Bentley and Rice were well ahead of their time, and I think the same could be said of Lasswell's work in the 1930's (Lasswell, 1935). If it is true that nothing is as strong as an idea whose time has come, perhaps nothing is as feeble and unappreciated as an idea whose time is not yet.

The times, however, as the modern balladeers remind us, are a-changin', and not only in political science but in psychiatry, too. There, too, the methodology is moving toward quantification, rigorous testing of theories and hypotheses, controlled observation and experimentation, even computerization. It is both sign and portent that the third volume of the *American Handbook of Psychiatry* (Arieti, 1959-1966) contains articles on general systems theory and "computational linguistics." In other words, psychiatry like political science has been affected by the "hard" sciences and their methodologies.

It also is too little appreciated that political psychiatry is not *just* personality theory, or the generation of hypotheses about power drives. In some political science commentary on psychiatry and politics it is almost as if Lord Acton had been crossbred with Sigmund Freud to produce Harold Lasswell. Let me give two examples.

In his *Modern Political Analysis* Robert Dahl sums up the work of Lasswell and others as the attempt to develop theories about the search for power. According to Dahl, Lasswell sees the power-seeker as someone who "pursues power as a means of compensating for psychological deprivations suffered during childhood." But, says Dahl, Lasswell himself has noted that the compulsive power-seeker may not be effective in achieving power since he is likely to arouse dislike and distrust, thus losing support. And Dahl cites Lane's summary of some research to the effect that the desire to gain power over others is not correlated with political activity, mainly because the power-seeker lacks certain skills essential for a political career. Both Dahl and Lane are saying, in so many words, that there is something faulty about the psychology of power thesis as applied to American politics. Because this power-seeking guy doesn't get very far, they are suggesting, the thesis itself is not very important in understanding political behavior (although it may be important in understanding why someone's political career wasn't successful) (Dahl, 1963).

For another student of political behavior, Heinz Eulau, personality theory in political analysis is limited by its neglect of role functions. To illustrate his criticism, Eulau cites the example of the man who votes Republican not because he hated his father who was a Democrat, but because all of his friends vote Republican and he sees his interests as better served by the Republican Party. The point Eulau is making is that as long as a man's political behavior is in congruence with his role perception, status, income, class, social environment, etc., the question of how he feels about his father, or any other personality variable, is not important. As Eulau puts it, "In short, analysis of political behavior in terms of personality seems advantageous if we are confronted with deviant behavior, deviant in a statistical sense, not a pathological sense." Otherwise, Eulau in effect argues, forget it (Eulau, 1963).

Of course, Dahl and Eulau are correct in drawing our attention to some limitations of personality theory as applied to politics. The difficulty is this: I know of no one whose application of this theory, much less whose application of psychiatric findings, is as simplistic as their examples suggest. Who argues today that every politician is nothing more than a power-seeker? Who is insisting that the voting decision in any significant number of cases can be traced back to childhood and unresolved Oedipus complexes?

Political psychiatry is not merely or even mainly personality theory, and perhaps studies of voting decisions, or a particular candidate for office, or a successful politician—a president, for example—are of diminishing importance. As I have suggested on other occasions, the psychological study of a political actor—the psychobiography—is and should be the exception rather than the rule in the study of politics. Most political leaders neither require nor merit such treatment, which is not to say that any biography isn't aided or given depth by the author's psychological insight into his subject's motivations and the conditions that shaped his life and career. But a full-scale psychiatric study of a political figure is appropriate only when a particular career departs sharply from conventional political beliefs and behaviors, as in the case of revolutionists and extremists, or when it appears that decisions have been shaped by physical or mental illness, or when the career ends in suicide. Those who are compulsive in politics, to the point that they consistently take actions that insure their defeat—the "born losers" in politics—and those who almost always succeed in winning against great odds—perhaps these political types merit psychological treatment. Finally, interest always attaches to those who go back and forth on the spectrum of political ideologies and parties—the political figures who start as radicals and end as extreme conservatives, and vice versa. I am sure we can all think of names to go with these examples.

But even the psychological aproach where it is deserved or essential hardly begins to give us the measure, much less the promise, of what psychiatry can contribute to our knowledge of political behavior. Nor is it enough, I think, to suggest that more research needs to be done on the relevance of personality factors to opinion formation—how personality relates to the open and closed mind, for instance. As important as these areas may be, what is more important, I believe, is the development of what I want to call here preventive politics, or the politics of health, rationality, and creativity. By preventive politics I refer to the merger of psychiatry and the social sciences in a common effort to establish a society dedicated to human dignity and welfare. It seems to me that, in the absence of such a collaboration, the most that political science as a policy science can offer are quantitative changes that may leave the qualitative side of life unchanged or even diminished. And the most that psychiatry can offer are techniques and methods of treating the mentally ill that have nothing to do with increasing the number of those who are mentally healthy. Thus, to take an example, in political science we all are in favor of abolishing poverty or at least improving the lot of the poor by such means as the negative income tax. But when the poor become better off, will there also be roads for the cars they can buy, space for the housing they can afford, airports for the planes they will fly, doctors for the medical care they will demand, colleges for the education they will want, and so forth? If—and this is a hideous paradox, to be sure—the quantitative improvement is not accompanied by all sorts of other changes, there will be a qualitative falling off as a result of more congestion, more pollution, and more demand for services which already are in short supply. On the psychiatric side, psychiatrists are better able to care for at least some of the mentally ill, but the number of those ill is probably increasing much faster than the population, especially in certain age groups and sections of the population.

And here we come to a situation which should interest political scientists very much, and yet few of us have shown much concern. Despite the vast increase in the national wealth, despite the impressive rise in living standards, despite the growth and expansion of measures promoting welfare and social justice, there are many indications that basic unhappiness, maladjustments of all sorts, varieties of alienation and asocial behavior, and nihilistic and destructive tendencies have reached almost epidemic proportions. Thus

—an estimated 50,000 Americans commit suicide each year, and the rate is increasing;

—suicide is the second leading cause of death in the 19-24 age group, and the third leading cause in the 15-19 age group;

—about one million Americans are in mental hospitals or the psychiatric wards of general hospitals, and another million visit psychiatrists each year;

—the number of patients under age 15 in public mental hospitals was 325 percent higher in 1963 than in 1950, and NIMH predicts that during the next decade the rate at which young people are hospitalized will double;

—the proportion of students consulting the psychiatric services of university health clinics has more than doubled during the last decade;

—and all of the following are increasing relative to population: use of drugs, alcoholism, divorce, illegitimacy, crime, and violence.

Now, of course, the causes of these problems are multi-faceted and complex. Perhaps once it was easy to attribute social evils to a single causation: God's will, or human nature, or capitalism. Nowadays we know that both the problems and their solutions are more difficult than we imagined. But I want to throw out one possible explanation for our troubles, not the only one, but one that perhaps should be included among the others. What is it? I want to suggest that the recent political history of the United States, with its assassinations, its confused themes and moods, its failures of leadership, its seeming hopelessness and impotence in the face of many problems, its crisis of morals, ethics, and morale—that all of this has contributed greatly to the present malaise.

To the extent that we as political scientists have been indifferent to the relationship between politics and the present discontents, to that extent we, too, have contributed to the crisis.

What can political science offer psychiatry? Where are the interdisciplinary frontiers and "cutting-edge" areas, and the richest possibilities for innovative developments?

Psychiatric Orientation to
Political Issues

The research contributions of psychiatry to political science and history can be roughly classified under the headings of methods, emphasis, and insight. In terms of methodology, Freud's most significant achievement was undoubtedly the unstructured, free-association interview. Depending as it does on observational techniques that require special interpretational skills on the part of the investigator, the free-association interview has not been fully exploited by political scientists interested in contemporary affairs and the recent past. Yet it would appear that the psychoanalytic-type interview is an indispensable tool for intensively exploring and theoretically charting areas of political behavior that are not amenable to other methods of inquiry.

For example, much research by political scientists into the etiology of right-wing extremism suggests that members of organizations like the John Birch Society are plagued by high levels of anxiety, low self-esteem, strong needs for inviolacy, and hostile and misanthropic orientations toward the social order. Many of them belong to the discontinued classes of society—that is, they are the older residents of burgeoning towns and cities, the proprietors of neighborhood stores and small business threatened by the huge chains and shopping centers, the elderly retired who are made apprehensive by small children, nonwhites, noise, traffic, and tax increases—and these drop-out citizens are attracted to subcultures of despair such as the Birch Society. Unfortunately, they are much less likely to cooperate with social investigators using survey research and other "hard" instruments of research than individuals who are more sanguine in both personality and outlook. Hence, studies positing a relationship between, say, alienation and extremism are characterized by a high refusal rate for requested interviews and questionnaire returns, and consequent failure to demonstrate that the relationship holds at levels of statistical significance. In fact, we know very little altogether about those who consistently refuse to participate in survey studies whatever their nature. Surely, here is a collaborative area that would benefit from a merger of the "soft" technique of the clinician with the "hard" techniques currently used in political science.

Even less developed than the free-association interview is the application of free-association to the analysis of documents, letters, diaries, and written records of all sorts. Although the historian frequently deals with handwritten accounts, almost no effort has been made to analyze changes of handwriting, including sudden changes in the way one signs letters, that are known to occur under conditions of great internal as well as external stress. Hence we are uninformed about the relationship of such changes to life and career experiences. While handwriting, to a great and growing extent, has been replaced by the telephone, the typewriter, and the tape recorder, it is by no means impossible to search typewritten and spoken messages for clues to traumatic events. Much could be learned, for example, by approaching taped political interviews, speeches, press conferences, and so forth, in a fashion similar to that employed in the analysis of taped psychiatric interviews and group therapy sessions.

Related to the free-association interview is Freud's emphasis on the "latent, unconscious, irrational, and archaic aspect" of behavior, and the stress he placed "on the formatic influence of early childhood, of dreams and of phantasies," (Frenkel-Brunswik, 1952). Little of this emphasis has penetrated research in political science, although efforts are now under way, in political science, to study the processes by which children become interested, involved, and partisan in politics (Greenstein, 1960, 1965; Easton and Hess, 1960, 1962). So far as is known, no attempt has been made to collect and interpret the dreams and phantasies of political figures. No doubt this is due to the fact that what we know of living individuals is by and large what they want us to know, and what we know of the dead is by and large what their families and their posterity permit us to discover. But it is also true that special skills are required for the analysis of inferred motivations as opposed to those that are manifest; lacking such skills, political scientists tend to confine themselves to that which is conscious, declared, and easily observable. Thus the latent, underlying motivations of both individuals and institutions, in the concealment or disguise of which all advanced societies excel, may be totally overlooked by the political behavioralist.

The third or insight component of Freud's contribution to political science is that large body of psychoanalytic and psychiatric literature that deals with politics and history. The term insight is used because such literature is designed to provide an analysis in depth, based on psychoanalytic and psychiatric theory, of phenomena that are only partly explored or understood by political scientists and historians. Most of this literature, for reasons already discussed, has originated with psychiatrists themselves, but an increasing amount is being published by psychoanalytically-inclined social scientists.

Broadly speaking, the history of insight literature is, like other histories, a history of changing times, interests, and intellectual styles. Someone once remarked, in an effort to explain a Supreme Court decision, that the "Supreme Court reads the headlines." In a similar vein it may be observed that psychiatrists read the headlines and are affected by them, at least insofar as their insight writings are concerned. Thus, during the "long twilight" that glowed over Europe between the Franco-Prussian War and 1914, Freud and his colleagues wrote very little outside the area of primary concern, that is, the origins, symptoms, and treatment of neuroses and psychoses. While Freud early demonstrated an interest in literary and artistic themes—his essays "The Theme of the Three Caskets" and "The Moses of Michaelangelo" appeared in 1913 and 1914 respectively—he did not turn his attention to problems of war and peace until 1915 when he published "Thoughts for the Times on War and Death." His preface "Psycho-analysis and War Neuroses," appeared in 1919. During the relatively peaceful Nineteen Twenties he wrote little on the subject, but in 1930 his *Civilization and Its Discontents* was perhaps more prophetic than anything else that year of the approaching end of tranquility or, in Harding's coined phrase, "normalcy." The Freud-Einstein exchange of letters, "Why War?" was published in 1933 (although the letters were written late in 1932), on the eve of the Nazi long march.

The psychiatric interest in the conditions of war and peace, it need hardly be said had no cause to diminish since Freud observed in his letters to Einstein "that owing to the perfection of instruments of destruction a future war might involve the extermination of one or perhaps both of the antagonists. All this is true, and so incontestably true that one can only feel astonished that the waging of war has not yet been unanimously repudiated," (F. Vol. V. 285).

During and immediately after World War II the writings of Alexander (1941, 1942, 1943), G. Brook Chisholm (1946), Trigant Burrow (1941), and others argued that war is not inevitable from a psychiatric point of view, although it does serve as a release for frustrations and conflicts of all sorts. Much of the literature of this period built less on Freud's conception of the place of Thanatos in human affairs than on the sequential "frustration and aggression" theme developed by John Dollard and his associates in 1939 (Dollard, 1939).

With the founding of the Group for the Advancement of Psychiatry in 1946, usually referred to as GAP, the attention of psychiatrists was specifically drawn to the problem of war and related problems that beset the national and world communities. Since 1960 the writings of Jerome D. Frank (1960) and Judd Marmor (1964), some of which are addressed to lay audiences, have been influential, and in 1964 GAP itself published a widely read report titled *Psychiatric Aspects of the Prevention of Nuclear War*. Citing as difficulties in the way of nonviolent solutions such factors as psychological defense mechanisms, "primitivising effects of extreme fear or panic," increasing dehumanization, ethnocentric perceptual distortion, and other factors that contribute to the psychological escalation of aggression, the GAP study nevertheless insisted that other ways could be found "of conducting conflict between groups of people or between nations, that can serve these psychological needs more adaptively in our modern world." War, concluded the report, "is a social institution; it is not inevitably rooted in the nature of man."

A second area of interest between the two world wars and for some years after 1945, although perhaps an area rather more developed by psychoanalysts than psychiatrists, was the concept of dimensions of national character, especially the character of Germany. That Germany received focal attention is understandable in view of the fact that the disruptions attributable to German-provoked wars and, above all, to Nationalist Socialism, included the persecution and forced migration of a large number of psychoanalysts including, in addition to Freud himself, Rank, Adler, Stekel, Fromm, Fromm-Reichman, Alexander, Horney, and Reich, Erikson, and Reik. Almost all of these prominent exiles from Nazi-occupied territory were of Jewish extraction, and paralleling the interest in the psychopathology of German national character was a deep concern, personal as well as professional, about the possible spread of virulent anti-Semitism. To be sure, the Germans were not the only ones to receive attention. A survey of the relevant literature reveals numerous articles and a few books dealing with the Americans, British, Russians, Chinese, Japanese, and even Norwegian so-called national character. But in books such as Richard M. Brickner's *Is Germany Incurable?* (1943) and Wilhelm Reich's *The Mass Psychology of Fascism* (1946), in articles such as Erik H. Erikson's "Hitler's Imagery and German Youth" (1942) and Fritz Moellenhoff's "The Price of Individuality: Speculations about German National Characteristics" (1947), German national character and Naziism, its most virulent expression, were subjected to a psychoanalysis more searching than that accorded any topic or theme in the social sciences. Much of this analysis was devoted to an explication of paranoid tendencies in German history and thought and the means by which these tendencies could be abolished or at least reduced after the war, but there were also efforts, as in the writings of Erich Fromm, to gaze at Germany and the general problem of authoritarianism through spectacles, the right lens of which had been contributed by Freud, and the left donated by Marx (Fromm, 1941). Since 1950 interest in Nazi Germany has very largely been confined to historians, some of whom have attempted to apply psychoanalytic categories, while the study of national character as such is not now a central interest in either psychiatry or the social sciences.

Ethnic group prejudice, on the other hand, is a continuing concern. There have been shifts of emphasis, however, reflecting changing problems and research needs. A vast literature dealing with anti-Semitism, to which psychoanalysts and psychiatrists have made influential contributions, has succeeded in exposing the roots of anti-Semitism, although precise boundaries are not fixed as between religious, historical, social, economic, and psychopathological causal explanations. Since publication of *The Authoritarian Personality* in 1950, the most significant effort made to link anti-Semitism to a variety of individual and social disorders, most work on anti-Semitism has been in the form of surveys that attempt to measure the distribution of opinions in a given population.

After 1954, the year of the momentous school desegregation decision of the Supreme Court, interest conspicuously shifted to problems in white-Negro relations and related civil rights activities. Prior to the *Brown* vs. *Board of Education* decision of a unanimous Court in 1954, American psychiatry, like American society itself, did not demonstrate much concern for Negroes apart from an occasional article dealing with race riots or with the high incidence of mental illness in predominantly Negro communities. Perhaps this neglect owed something to the relatively small position that Negroes occupy in psychiatry either as doctors or as private patients. Whatever the explanation, not much was known about the psychiatric aspects of either segregation or desegregation prior to a 1956 roundtable on the subject sponsored by the American Orthopsychiatric Society. In 1957 a GAP publication *Psychiatric Aspects of School Desegregation* was an important contribution to the small body of literature on the subject, and since then race relations themes have been dealt with in a number of articles published by psychiatrists. It remains broadly true, however, that psychiatry, much less psychoanalysis, has not given to the civil rights area the attention it has given to other problems in the social psychiatry field, or the attention that civil rights problems deserve. Partly for this reason, there is as yet no published work as substantial as *The Authoritarian Personality*; indeed, the most significant book on race relations is still Gunnar Myrdal's *An American Dilemma* of 1944, and Myrdal was neither an American nor a psychiatrist, nor yet a political scientist or historian, but a combined economist-sociologist of Swedish nationality.

A fourth dimension of psychiatric insight literature, and one closely related to research on ethnic group relations, has been concerned with democratic and non-democratic model personality types. Most psychiatrists who have written on social issues have had something to say about contrasting authoritarian and non-authoritarian character structures, although it is fair to comment that their work, like that of political scientists with similar interests, is given more to implication than explication, especially with regard to non-authoritarian character structure. Much of what has been published is also vulnerable to a criticism similar to that leveled at *The Authoritarian Personality*, namely, that the nuclear concept excludes left wing behavior. While efforts have been made to study individual communists, the personality type occasionally referred to as the authoritarian liberal remains elusive, at least in research terms.

Insofar as authoritarian and non-authoritarian model types can be extrapolated from the diverse body of literature specifying certain essentials of democracy and dictatorship, it would appear that the authoritarian type, from a psychiatric point of view, is a coercive, anxious, suspicious and id-rejecting individual who is oriented toward power and extremely limited in his capacity to give and receive affection. Demanding from others either dominance or submission, the authoritarian type tends to be the total leader one kind of situation, and the total rebel in another. "Intolerant of ambiguity," in Frenkel-Brunswik's phrase, his problem-solving methods are rigid, quick, and direct, and his preferred solution is always simplistic. He prefers his wife passive, his children submissive, his home life undemanding, his friends deferential, and his employees docile. He is frequently skilled in masking his basic hostility behind a façade of spurious warmth and friendliness, and he is often a master in the art of dissimulation. Enjoying the delusion of rectitudinous grandeur, he may see himself as an honest man who has not been discovered by Diogenes, or as an appreciated Nehru who has every right to burn since Rome does nothing by fiddle. If he is conservative as well as authoritarian, phrases and words such as communist, socialist, Stevenson, one world, medicare, and beatnik may engender spontaneous combustion. If he is liberal as well as authoritarian, the inflammable terms are capitalism, Wall Street, Hoover (both Herbert and J. Edgar), CIA, military-industrial complex, and Catholic hierarchy.

The democratic type, by contrast, is a persuasive, secure, trustful, and id-accepting individual for whom power is only one of a number of values. Able to give and receive affection, his relations with others are characterized, in Erikson's working, by "mutuality." Lacking the desire to be either the absolute leader or absolute follower, the democrat as husband, father, and employer does not demand that others strip their own egos in order to clothe his own; his role may require that he be *primus inter pares* in decision-making situations, but he is supportive in such a role and he takes others into account. He can accept criticism, understand frailty in others as well as himself, and limit his hostile and aggressive impulses or discharge them harmlessly. Politically he may lean to either side, but whether a conservative or liberal he rejects devil theories of politics and controls his emotional reaction to manipulations of symbols irrespective of their plus or minus value in his belief system.

Clearly these characterological types should be of immense importance in the study of political behavior, and yet very little use has been made of them by political scientists. Some reasons for this have already been noted—the "hard" approach infatuation of many political scientists, for example—but in addition, many students of political behavior feel that the authoritarian and democratic personality models are more imaginative than descriptive, arguing that the key concepts are not dichotomized terminals between which a given population distributes itself, but points on a personality continuum within individuals. The same person, they maintain, will be authoritarian in one situation, and democratic in another, in accordance with his role perceptions. They also express doubts that the authoritarian subculture, assuming one exists, plays a significant role in American life, or that it is increasing in size and importance.

The reservations and criticisms may or may not be legitimate; what is certain is that they will not be resolved unless "hard" and "soft" methods are joined in a collaboration between psychiatrists and political scientists. From psychiatry, for example, we need much more specifically with regard to the interpersonal (family, school, workplace) environments that nourish democratic and authoritarian personalities, and recommended measures for strengthening democratic as opposed to authoritarian tendencies in society. From history we need more information about economic, social, and political conditions which have given rise to authoritarian subcultures and paranoid pseudo-communities in democratic societies. From political science we need to know more about the extent to which authoritarian tendencies in political life can be modified by role settings and expectations, by interaction between authoritarians and democrats, by enlightenment, and, finally, by restriction and confinement in the larger social environment. These demands made upon the several disciplines hardly exhaust the research needs and opportunities with reference to possible linkage between personality types and political behavior.

Indeed, it is difficult to think of any insight area in social psychiatry, or any research in political and historical behavior, that would not benefit from collaboration between the three disciplines. The study of voting behavior, for example, a "hard" research field in social science if ever there was one, would become more exciting and significant if voting motivation and intention underwent psychological scrutiny in depth; adaptations of the psychiatric interview would add an important dimension to research into the behavior of bureaucrats, congressmen, state legislators, city councilmen, and the like. While psychiatrists have gradually become aware of correlations between socio-economic variables and mental illness (and the treatment thereof), more research is needed on the national cultural aspects of mental health and illness. If biographies are to serve as the rich tapestries of entire lives and not merely pale sketches of names, dates, and places, biographers will have to acquire some skills from psychoanalysis in making inferences, reconstructions, and interpretations.

The frontier areas of these disciplines, however, require less an exchange of methods and insights than their merger into a comprehensive science of social behavior. In this development the psychiatrist is likely to find himself working in tandem not with medical specialists but with social scientists who share with him a common interest in man's fate. The merger of methods and insights in the future may even extend to practices, treatments, and therapies. It requires little imagination to foresee the time when there are psychiatric members of Political Science Departments, and when political scientists are attached to hospital and clinic staffs.

The interdisciplinary relationships I have in mind can only be explored by drawing on the resources of psychiatry and especially psychoanalysis in ways that go beyond any research that has so far been undertaken. The best I can do at present is state some hypotheses about the relationship between political life and what is sick in our society— but I do so in the hope that these hypotheses can be tested and refined. In that sense, they are not intended to be merely speculative; they are intended to guide certain research collaborations between political scientists and psychiatrists. If I state them in strong and perhaps exaggerated terms, it is because I also hope to shake us out of our complacency and smugness, our feelings that the American political system is, after all, in pretty good shape, requiring only minor incremental and limited changes. For it is a fact that political science books are still being written in which there is no mention of the Black revolution, the war on poverty, the unrest on campus, and the destruction of the physical environment. In fact, it was a political scientist some years back who published a book on the "silent generation" of college students even as the first symptoms of trouble were beginning to appear at Berkeley and elsewhere.

Alienation, Nihilism, and American Political Life

My central hypothesis about the relationship of political life to the moods of alienation and nihilism found almost everywhere is that there has been a general weakening of superego controls and a general breakdown of the institutions in society that have traditionally served to support those value systems upon which civilized life depends. In psychiatric terms, "acting out" has taken the place of inner restraints and controls over behavior; and "doing your thing" has replaced the older conviction that no community can survive unless its members have a guiding sense of the things that are not done, no matter what the occasion, situation, or provocation.

I think that these changes have come about because the authoritative institutions and elites have ceased to believe in themselves and, more important, they inspire disbelief in others. Is there a single authoritative institution that has not lost stature in recent years, to the point that it can no longer lay claim to obedience and allegiance? Consider the church and religion in general, for example. Who any more believes in papal infallibility, or even that the Pope is ever right about anything? Or in Billy Graham with his blend of religious fundamentalism and sharp business methods? Or Norman Vincent Peale who prepares his sermons, we are told by his wife, either in his 12-room cooperative apartment on Fifth Avenue "overlooking the Metropolitan Museum of Art" or in his 16-room house on 225 acres in Pawling, New York, "complete with sauna, covered swimming pool and Norwegian antique furniture. . . ."[1] Perhaps it is not so much that God is dead as that he is so embarrassed he wishes he were dead!

Who continues to venerate the Supreme Court as a model of integrity when it is revealed that a prospective Chief Justice is not aware of any conflict between his Court responsibilities and his continued politicking for the President and acceptance of very substantial fees for lecturing law students (although the combined annual income of his wife and himself is roughly $200,000 above the poverty level)? Who, especially among the youth, supports his local police and favors "law and order"? It is an irony of the times that when we see a bumper sticker saying "Remember the Pueblo" or the decal of an American flag on a car window we know that these are the signs and symbols not of a healthy Americanism but of a right-wing chauvinism that, if it had its way, would very soon rid the country of black militants, student rioters, hippies, Yippies, the SDS, the New York Review of Books, and much else. As some of the car bumper slogans say—and the drivers mean it— "America: Love It or Leave It."

Add to this the more than twenty-year procession of Presidents who could not capture either our admiration or respect because they seemed weak and pusillanimous at crucial moments: Truman with his bantam-cock image becoming more chicken-like through his capitulation to the beginnings of McCarthyism (the loyalty investigations begun in 1947-48; the harassment of Charley Chaplin; the trials of the Communist Party leaders); Eisenhower with his benevolent but increasingly irrelevant posturing about being "above politics," and he, too, morally disabled by the failure to take on McCarthy, despite the latter's treatment of General Marshall, prior to McCarthy's assault upon the Army; both followed by the brief moment of Camelot, a moment terminated by assassination, and leading into a six-year period during which many, perhaps most, Americans believed that the President of the United States was a habitual liar, was incredibly crude and vulgar, was a bungler in the international area, was, in fact, incompetent to serve in the highest office.

In the case of LBJ, I suspect that some part of the intense dislike for him among the youth may derive from their unconscious suspicion that he *was*, in some part, responsible for the death of John F. Kennedy. For many of the young people, I suspect that at the unconscious level the death of Kennedy at the hands of persons unknown but including LBJ was experienced as the murder of a younger, more virile son by an older, impotent father, a father jealous of the son's very youth and vigor and greater success—for until November, 1963, Kennedy had never failed in anything he had attempted.[2] If this was the case, certainly it was easy to imagine, to want to believe, that LBJ was somehow implicated and, believing this, easy to hate him, to mock him, to hold him in the deepest contempt. Certainly the popularity of *Macbird!*, the anti-Johnson jingles and buttons, the posters mocking his masculinity, and the obscene slogans, support such interpretations.

Without question LBJ was hurt by the war in Viet Nam, one of the most unpopular, costly, and lengthy wars in our history. But in many circles, especially in the universities, it is coming to be believed that *none* of the wars since 1945 has been necessary, that they have been waged not for freedom but in behalf of a new American imperialism, one-half composed of economic interest, the other half made up of a new-style manifest destiny or sense of mission. The Cold War, for example, is coming under great suspicion as not having been necessary, and historians and political scientists are beginning to turn their attention to the origins and conduct of the Korean War as well as Viet Nam. Whatever their conclusions, it cannot be doubted that the hot and cold wars since 1945 have diverted the nation and its resources from the urgent domestic problems of poverty, race, and urban deterioration, thus producing millions of blacks and other citizens—and most intellectuals, it should be remembered, live in cities—who have no special reason to think well of their country, least of all the reason that all of the wars since 1945 have been fought not against people like ourselves, but against people who were non-white, poor, badly armed, frequently hungry and sick, and above all expendable in accordance with our so-called kill ratio under which at least ten of them must die for each one of us. Is it simply fortuitous that we have not yet been goaded into war in Europe, no matter what the provocation—and there have been many —whereas we go to war in the Far East without hesitation when a patrol boat is alleged to have fired a few harmless torpedoes at our destroyers? A Congress quick to take action with the Tonkin Gulf resolution is seemingly helpless in the face of corruption, senility, pettiness, and irresponsibility in its own ranks; hence the unending and unedifying spectacle of the Dodds, Dirksens, Eastlands, and Thurmonds as examples to the nation.

And who are the heroes—the ego ideals, psychoanalysts might say —to serve the nation, the young people especially, as models for behavior and deportment? Not the political leaders since the death of the two Kennedys and the metamorphosis of McCarthy from Hero to anti-Hero. Not any moral figure since the death of Martin Luther King. The dominant images for the young are not those whose lives reflect the traditional values of courage, integrity, and uprightness, but the swingers, such as Hefner, Namath, and Sinatra; the nihilists, such as the earlier Bob Dylan and more recent Beatles; the existentialists, such as Timothy Leary, Alan Ginsburg, Norman Mailer, and what might be termed the Hippie Establishment; and the apostles of violence for good causes, on a range from Cleaver to Guevara.[3] In this context we might also note, as paralleling the death and rebirth of the hero, the death and rebirth of the villain that owes so much to the talents of certain actors and celebrities, among whom Marlon Brando is the most prominent. In his movie roles Brando has gotten us to invest libido in leather-jacketed motor cyclists ("The Wild Ones") and Nazi officers ("The Young Lions"), and more recently, through the skilled performances of Warren Beatty, we can identify with bank robbers and tough guys in general. Perhaps one day Brando or Beatty will play the part of Joseph Stalin, and then Stalin will not only be believable, but admirable and lovable as well.

But a society can probably survive failures of political leadership and the death of its heroes *if* the older generation is certain of its role and can inculcate its standards in the generation that follows it. Far from this being the case, the parents of today's youth are almost as confused as their children. Indeed, for the first time in history, an older generation is taking its cues in how to behave, how to dress, how to enjoy life, how to *live*, not from its own parents and the past, but from its children. Hence the vogue of hair pieces, miniskirts, mod clothes, even peace jewelry and hippie paraphernalia, among middle-aged people.[4] Children who look to their parents for guidance and example and see only mirror images of themselves, albeit slightly older selves, are hardly likely to respect and emulate what they see. And for both generations there is the daily parade of the Beautiful People, the Jet Set, for whom life is all fun and games—and, above all, fornication. Ann Landers and Abigail Van Buren may still recommend chastity before marriage and fidelity thereafter, but we all know better, having been truly instructed on these points by John Lennon and his girl friend, or Marianne Faithful and her boy friend, not to mention Roger Vadim, Anthony Quinn, and all those who are enjoying themselves too much to get married and have legitimate children. When Jacqueline Kennedy married Onassis she demonstrated conclusively that *noblesse oblige* does not apply to a President's widow, and perhaps with that demonstration we have ceased to believe there are any major differences between the lower depths of Las Vegas and Hollywood and the higher reaches of politics and business. In a way, this aspect of our contemporary malaise was well expressed during a week-long party at Hugh Hefner's temple to Eve in Chicago during the Democratic convention. One would expect to find there Hollywood celebrities and pop singers, but in addition— and while the kids were being beaten by the cops—there were Mayor Carl B. Stokes of Cleveland, Mayor Kevin White of Boston, Borden

Stevenson, Jack Valenti, Edward Day, Max Lerner, etc., etc. (*New York Times,* August 29, 1968).

In short, I suspect that the American Establishment, in a variety of ways, some avoidable, some not, has succeeded in disestablishing itself—in the home, in the schools and universities, in business and politics, in the unconscious itself (because it is there that the superego takes root and shape, or it does not). And with that disestablishment has come a variety of forms and expressions of alienation and discontent, as well as acts of violence and destruction.

Broadened Horizons for
Political Science

How all this will end I do not know. Even less do I know what the solution is, or even whether there is one. But I do know that we can't begin to find any solution unless we broaden our horizons as political scientists to include psychiatry and psychoanalysis and other behavioral sciences as well. It simply is not enough to study Congress or the Supreme Court or the electoral process, because many of our political institutions are contributing to the problems I have mentioned. What is needed, in my view, is an effort to determine how politics can serve to reduce tension, anxiety, and frustrations of all sorts, and thereby transform prevailing moods of alienation and nihilism. To be sure, such an effort will not be easy, requiring as it does understanding and skills that go far beyond the usual equipment of political scientists. But, assuming that in the near future we will be able to identify at least some of the causes and cures of the present malaise, what are some of the relationships we might find between social conditions and the discontents of both young and old?

We might discover, for example, that the repeated alarms about missile gaps, submarine shortages, or whatever serve less to enhance our preparedness than to sharply increase tension levels beyond the tolerance point for many individuals—in short, to put the nation's nerves on edge. If this is the case, it would follow that politicians should carefully avoid loose talk about defense inadequacies for fear of vastly increasing anxiety both here and abroad. Of course, if there is a proven and demonstrable need for more weapons of some type, that is a different matter, but in recent years it has been rare for such a need to be established beyond any doubt, as witness the current controversy about the ABM system.

Perhaps we should hear less about crime in the street—most Americans, when they hear crime, hear Black crime—and stress instead that the streets of many cities are safer than they were 100 years ago and even 50 years ago in some cases. Let the crime be dealt with quietly—by more police, better lighting, and above all by reducing provocations to crime. (In Switzerland, suicides are not reported in any detail because it is known that these often occur in waves, and there is also a tendency for the methods to be somewhat contagious. Is it possible that crimes beget crimes, in similar fashion?)

Perhaps we should put the housing in the cities and the office buildings in the suburbs, thus restoring the core of the inner city for what it was intended: culture, entertainment, social life, ambiance in general. By reversing commuting patterns, we might succeed in reversing rising curves of mental illness and alcoholism in cities, not to mention the consumption of tranquilizers. The very least result would be less boredom in the suburbs, and less resort to what is euphemistically termed social drinking, wife-swapping, and other sports that help suburbanites survive from Friday to Monday.

In view of what we know about the relationship between lung cancer and smoking, perhaps our celebrities and those much admired by young people should not be photographed smoking cigarettes. How can we expect the youth to forswear pot and LSD when they read that this actor or actress, not to mention John Lennon and Henry Luce, have also tried LSD. The point is *not* to prohibit any private activity whatever its nature, but to reduce the exhibitionism that is often connected with it. It is futile to expect the rich and the beautiful not to make the most of their opportunities for indulgence, but we have a right to expect that they not show off about it.

For example, it takes no special imagination to visualize the effect on a Black ghetto youth reading that Nieman-Marcus of Dallas has purchased 40 mink skins of the "Kojah" variety at a cost of $2,700 each, to be made into a coat that will cost $150,000 (*New York Times,* February 27, 1969). Nor is this an isolated or exceptional news story. Not long ago tax-deductible money estimated at more than $250,000 was used to fly 600 guests to what the *New York Times* described as a "three-day extravaganza" in Los Angeles, occasioned by the premiere of "Sweet Charity" in movie version; held at a time of severe budget cutbacks in welfare spending, education, and museum and library services, the celebration of anything titled "Sweet Charity" at the taxpayers' expense had ironic overtones, although not for the celebrants.[5] In the United States in 1969, there was widespread malnutrition in parts of the Deep South and elsewhere while Park Avenue poodles, wearing gold collars and, in appropriate weather, mink coats, were consuming daily "two medium rare lamb chops," steaks, caviar, fresh strawberries, and other varieties of dog food.[6] More than two million Americans opened stock market accounts during 1968 and no doubt many of these were among the voters who defeated an unprecedented number of school bond issues that year. One result of these defeats is that a large but undetermined number of public schools will close weeks or even a month earlier this year than is usually the case, and others will go without books, hot lunches, and recreational and athletic equipment. Most of these schools, it need hardly be said, are in ghetto areas, and it is becoming clearer each day that the inhabitants of the ghetto, especially the youth, are getting the message.[7]

The message is also getting through to a section of the college students. No one, least of all a professor, can find a justification for such extreme behavior on campuses as arson, destruction of files and books, physical attacks on teaching and administrative staff, stockpiling of rifles and shotguns, and the like. Nor do I intend to make light of these actions and treat them as if they were essentially students' fun-and-games, no more serious than the panty raids and goldfish-swallowing of another generation. But it is difficult not to conclude that the radical students are responding, at least in part, to their discovery that a good part of the educational elite, like the elites in government, business, and the military, does not merit their respect, much less their support. What does an intelligent, sensitive student think when he reads that the president of a state college in Texas, and a friend of former President Johnson, has been charged with plagiarism in connection with his Ph.D. dissertation? Instead of resigning immediately and demanding that the charges be investigated, the state college president, accusing some of his own faculty of a "conspiracy" against him and an attempt "to frame him on a narcotics charge," held his office for another nine months, during which he refused to answer questions or meet the press (*New York Times*, March 10 and April 20, 1969). As James Reston has commented with reference to high government officials, "the art of resigning on principle from positions close to the top . . . has almost disappeared. Nobody quits now. . . ."[8] It is just possible that had the Viet Nam doves in the Johnson administration resigned "on principle" and organized an effort to change our war policy, there would be fewer young people on the barricades. It also would be salutary for youthful morale if college counsellors did not enter on student records the real or alleged religious, sexual, and political inclinations of the students; for one thing, the counsellors can no longer be assured that their admittedly "unacceptable" and "unfortunate" notes will not find their way to the *New York Times*.[9] We forget too easily that the student sit-ins and occupations have had and continue to have some good results.

Perhaps the Establishment's disestablishment of itself has gone too far to be reversed, in which event we can anticipate a new order and a new leadership that is tough, single-minded, segregationist, and authoritarian. The backlash will not want to settle for less. But it may not be too late to restore and broaden the principles of *noblesse oblige*, reminding presidential widows that they are not supposed to marry aging international playboys, reminding politicians, corporate executives, and college presidents that they are not to remain in office if they cheat and steal, reminding celebrities that their celebrity carries with it a social responsibility *not* to be exhibitionist in flaunting the rules and customs, and, above all, not to popularize styles of behavior to which adolescents are extremely susceptible in imitative terms. Again, I want to emphasize that such behavior should be entirely free of restraint; the point is, let this behavior be strictly private. In short, as much or even more *in delicto,* but much less *flagrante* on the part of the Beautiful People.

In these reflections, of course, I am assuming certain cause-and-effect relationships that may or may not hold once research has been undertaken. My intention is to present hypotheses relating to the sources of some present discontents, hypotheses that should become central rather than remain peripheral to the interests of political scientists. As I suggested earlier, to the extent that political scientists refrain from studying disturbed aspects of our society and its culture, including its psychopathology, they are contributing to the problems that make the United States more and more difficult and dangerous to live and work in. Continuing neglect of such problems insures our continuing to become a society less of citizens and political men, as these terms have been traditionally understood, than a society of severely disturbed inpatients and out-patients who, one day, will surely combine forces. Then it will be the patients, not the doctors, who make the key decisions. Perhaps we can call that society the inmate society, where everything is possible. Normal people, David Rousset reminds us in *The Other Kingdom,* don't know that everything is possible. Only the inmates know.

The implications for political science training of this shift of research emphasis are many. Surely one of them is that political scientists embarking upon such research should receive some training in psychiatry and psychoanalysis, in addition to the conventional education already provided (courses and seminars in American, comparative, and international politics, political theory, etc.). They will also need to know a good deal about some of the other behavioral sciences, especially sociology and psychology, and training in statistics and, in certain cases, computer programming, would be desirable. If this sounds like too much, a possible compensation would be the removal of language requirements (few political scientists use German or French or Spanish after receiving their degrees) and reducing the number of required examination fields. Money would have to be found for the psychiatric and psychoanalytic training programs, but it is not beyond possibility that a determined thrust from the American Political Science Association or a few political science departments would be welcomed by one of the foundations or NIMH. In short, there are many difficulties, but they are not insurmountable, in my view. And it is encouraging to know that, according to a recent study of first-choice fields of specialization in political science, "Political Psychology" led all other fields in the age group born in or after 1930, that is, was the first choice with those who were 37 years old or younger in 1967 (Eulau, 1969).

Let me end, therefore, on an optimistic note. By now many of these younger political scientists are approaching their forties, full professorships, chairmanships of departments, and other positions of influence. They are strategically placed to make that thrust referred to above, and thereby to demonstrate that political science is not and does not have to be irrelevant to the troubles and torments of our time. *Allons-y!*

Notes

[1] *New York Times,* April 6, 1969. According to Mrs. Peale, who should know, "Norman just loves the [Pauling] house . . . he gets more sermons there . . . and inspiration!"

[2] Isaac Asimov has cited numerous instances of "hostility between royal father and heir-apparent son" leading to the death of the latter. Examples in Greek mythology include Cronos who, having castrated his father and replaced him, swallowed his sons to insure that he would not suffer a similar fate at their hands. Neither Zeus nor his brother Poseidon would marry Thetis with whom they were in love because it had been decreed that she would bear a son mightier than his father. Daedalus killed his nephew and pupil Perdix out of "overwhelming jealousy, when that young man showed signs of becoming superior to his teacher." Isaac Asimov in *Psychology Today,* April 1969, p. 39. Even if these examples do not overturn the Oedipus complex and its status in psychoanalysis, they raise the possibility that there never has been much love lost between generations!

[3] The new hero must not only "swing" which, in effect, means engage in tireless and endless fornication, he must do so in defiance of the usual moral standards and, if he is an athlete, training rules. Thus Joe Namath: ". . . The

night before the Oakland game I grabbed a girl and a bottle and went to the Summit Hotel and stayed in bed all night. . . . Same thing before the Super Bowl. It's good for you. . . ." Jimmy Breslin, "Namath All Night Long," *New York,* April 7, 1969, pp 24-27.

4 *The New Yorker* of March 1, 1969, advertised a gold-plated sterling silver pendant with the familiar peace symbol suspended from a "gold-filled, intertwining chain." The price was $14.50.

5 *New York Times,* March 30, 1969. The *Times,* in a rare editorial—the usual tendency is to look the other way when the leisure class is playing the role written for it by Thorstein Veblen—referred to the party as "Grossness in Los Angeles."

6 *New York Times,* April 13, 1969. Two weeks later another lengthy article dealt with the services of La Banque, a branch of the Franklin National Bank where a minimum of $25,000 is required to open a checking account. Among the accompanying pictures was one showing a female customer driving up in one of her three chauffeur-driven Rolls-Royces. The chauffeur was Black.

7 In view of this message, perhaps the miracle is not that the crime rate, especially mugging, is so high, but that it is as low as it is. In midtown New York, on a bitterly cold day, it is not unusual to see at a red light a chauffeured Cadillac along side one of those garment racks on wheels being propelled by a Black or Puerto Rican youth. These are the American rickshaw boys, and while this type of coolie labor exists elsewhere in the world, it is not to be seen anywhere in Europe, and it has been abolished in China.

8 In the *New York Times,* March 9, 1959. In this context perhaps the resignations of General de Gaulle and Northern Ireland's Prime Minister Terence O'Neill will have a salutary effect.

9 *New York Times,* March 16, 1969. The Oberlin College counsellor has included such comments as "he and his father remind me of the 'typical Jews' cliche. Pusher, aggressive, talker, high goals," and "this kid certainly won't help the male image on campus. It's too late even for hormones."

References

Adorno, T. W., *et al. The Authoritarian Personality.* New York: Harper & Brothers, 1950.

Alexander, Franz. "Aggressiveness—Individual and Collective," in *The March of Medicine.* New York: Columbia University Press, 1943, 83-89.

Alexander, Franz. *Our Age of Unreason.* Philadelphia: Lippincott, 1942.

Almond, Gabriel A. and Sidney Verba. *The Civil Culture.* Princeton: Princeton University Press, 1963.

Arieti, Silvano, ed. *American Handbook of Psychiatry,* 3 vols. New York: Basic Books, 1959-1966.

Bentley, Arthur F. *The Process of Government.* Chicago: University of Chicago Press, 1908.

Brickner, Richard M. *Is Germany Incurable?* Philadelphia: Lippincott, 1943.

Burrow, Trignat. "Neurosis and War: A Problem of Human Behavior," *Journal of Psychology,* 12 (1941), 235-249.

Chisholm, G. Brock. "The Psychiatry of Enduring Peace and Social Progress," *Psychiatry,* 9 (1946).

Colby, Kenneth M. *An Introduction to Psychoanalytic Research.* New York: Basic Books, 1960.

Dahl, Robert A. *Modern Political Analysis.* Englewood Cliffs: Prentice-Hall, 1963.

Dahl, Robert A. *Who Governs?* New Haven: Yale University Press, 1961.

Dollard, John *et al. Frustration and Aggression.* New Haven: Yale University Press, 1939.

Easton, David and Robert D. Hess. "The Child's Changing Image of the President," *Public Opinion Quarterly,* 24 (1960), 632-644.

Easton, David and Robert D. Hess. "The Child's Political World," *Midwest Journal of Political Science,* 6 (1962), 236-247.

Erikson, Erik, "Hitler's Imagery and German Youth," *Psychiatry,* 5 (1942), 475-493.

Erikson, Erik. "Wholeness and Totality," in C. J. Friedrich, ed., *Totalitarianism.* Cambridge: Harvard University Press, 1954.

Eulau, Heinz. *The Behavioral Persuasion in Politics.* New York: Random House, 1963, p. 103.

Eulau, Heinz, "Quo Vadimus?" *P.S.* (Newsletter of the American Political Science Association), II (Winter, 1969), 1.

Frank, Jerome D. "Breaking the Thought Barrier: Psychological Challenges of the Nuclear Age," *Psychiatry,* 23 (1960), 245-266.

Frenkel-Brunswik, Else. "Interaction of Psychological and Sociological Factors in Political Behavior," *American Political Science Review,* 46 (1952), 44-65.

Freud, Sigmund. *Civilization and its Discontents.* London: Hogarth Press, 1930.

Freud, Sigmund. "Thoughts for the Times on War and Death," (1915) in *Collected Papers,* IV. London: Hogarth Press, 1949, pp. 288-317.

Freud, Sigmund. "Why War?" (1932) in *Collected Papers,* V. London: Hogarth Press, 1950.

Fromm, Erich. *Escape From Freedom.* New York: Rinehart, 1941.

Greenstein, Fred. *Children and Politics.* New Haven: Yale University Press, 1965.

Greenstein, Fred. "The Benevolent Leader: Children's Images of Political Authority," *American Political Science Review,* 54 (1960), 934-943.

Group for the Advancement of Psychiatry. *Psychiatric Aspects of the Prevention of Nuclear War.* Report No. 57, September, 1964.

Group for the Advancement of Psychiatry. *Psychiatric Aspects of School Desegregation.* Report No. 37, May, 1957.

Jones, Ernest. *The Life and World of Sigmund Freud,* Vol. 2. New York: Basic Books, 1955, p. 57.

Kardiner, Abram. *The Psychological Frontiers of Society.* New York: Columbia University Press, 1945, p. 23.

Lasswell, Harold D. *Psychopathology and Politics.* Chicago: University of Chicago Press, 1930.

Lasswell, Harold D. *World Politics and Personal Insecurity.* New York: McGraw-Hill, 1935.

L'Etang, Hugh. "The Health of Statesmen," *The Practitioner,* (January, 1958).

Marmor, Judd. "War, Violence, and Human Nature," *Bulletin of Atomic Scientists* (March, 1964), pp. 19-22.

Moellenhoff, "The Price of Individuality: Speculations About German National Characteristics," *American Image,* 41 (1947), 33-60.

Myrdal, Gunnar. *An American Dilemma.* New York: Harper and Brothers, 1944.

New York Times, August 29, 1968; February 27, 1969; March 10, 1969; April 20, 1969.

Reich, William. *The Mass Psychology of Fascism.* New York: Orgone Institute Press, 1946.

Rice, Stuart A. *Quantitative Methods in Politics.* New York: Alfred A. Knopf, 1928.

Rogow, Arnold A. "Disability in High Office," *Medical Opinion and Review,* I (April, 1966), 16-19.